D1530957

**Environmental
Policy
Implementation**

Environmental Policy Implementation

**Planning and Management
Options and Their
Consequences**

Edited by
Dean E. Mann
University of California,
Santa Barbara

LexingtonBooks
D.C. Heath and Company
Lexington, Massachusetts
Toronto

HC
110
.E5
E49875
1952

Fairleigh Dickinson
University Library

Teaneck, New Jersey

To Helen, our children, and their children.
May the quality of their environment
be protected and enhanced.

Library of Congress Cataloging in Publication Data
Main entry under title:

Environmental policy implementation.

Includes indexes.
1. Environmental policy–United States–Addresses, essays, lectures.
I. Mann, Dean E.
HC110.E5E49875   333.7'0973   79-3829
ISBN 0–669–03516–5   AACR2

Copyright © 1982 by D.C. Heath and Company

All rights reserved. No part of this publication may be reproduced or transmitted in any form or by any means, electronic or mechanical, including
photocopy, recording, or any information storage or retrieval system,
without permission in writing from the publisher.

Published simultaneously in Canada

Printed in the United States of America

International Standard Book Number: 0–669–03516–5

Library of Congress Catalog Card Number: 79-3829

10/15/82 - 28.95

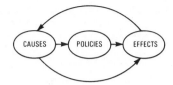

Policy Studies Organization Series

General Approaches to Policy Studies

Policy Studies in America and Elsewhere
  edited by Stuart S. Nagel
Policy Studies and the Social Studies
  edited by Stuart S. Nagel
Methodology for Analyzing Public Policies
  edited by Frank P. Scioli, Jr., and Thomas J. Cook
Urban Problems and Public Policy
  edited by Robert L. Lineberry and Louis H. Masoti
Problems of Theory in Policy Analysis
  edited by Philip M. Gregg
Using Social Research for Public Policy-Making
  edited by Carol H. Weiss
Public Administration and Public Policy
  edited by H. George Frederickson and Charles Wise
Policy Analysis and Deductive Reasoning
  edited by Gordon Tullock and Richard Wagner
Legislative Reform
  edited by Leroy N. Rieselbach
Teaching Policy Studies
  edited by William D. Coplin
Paths to Political Reform
  edited by William J. Crotty
Determinants of Public Policy
  edited by Thomas Dye and Virginia Gray
Effective Policy Implementation
  edited by Daniel Mazmanian and Paul Sabatier
Taxing and Spending Policy
  edited by Warren J. Samuels and Larry L. Wade
The Politics of Urban Public Services
  edited by Richard C. Rich
Analyzing Urban-Service Distributions
  edited by Richard C. Rich
The Analysis of Policy Impact
  edited by John Grumm and Stephen Washby
Public Policies for Distressed Communities
  edited by F. Stevens Redburn and Terry F. Buss
Implementing Public Policy
  edited by Dennis J. Palumbo and Marvin A. Harder
Evaluating and Optimizing Public Policy
  edited by Dennis J. Palumbo, Stephen B. Fawcett, and Paula Wright
Representation and Redistricting Issues
  edited by Bernard Grofman, Arend Lijphart, Robert McKay, and
  Howard Scarrow
Strategies for Administrative Reform
  edited by Gerald E. Caiden and Heinrich Siedentopf

Specific Policy Problems

Analyzing Poverty Policy
  edited by Dorothy Buckton James
Crime and Criminal Justice
  edited by John A. Gardiner and Michael Mulkey
Civil Liberties
  edited by Stephen L. Wasby
Foreign Policy Analysis
  edited by Richard L. Merritt
Economic Regulatory Policies
  edited by James E. Anderson
Political Science and School Politics
  edited by Samuel K. Gove and Frederick M. Wirt
Science and Technology Policy
  edited by Joseph Haberer
Population Policy Analysis
  edited by Michael E. Kraft and Mark Schneider
The New Politics of Food
  edited by Don F. Hadwiger and William P. Browne
New Dimensions to Energy Policy
  edited by Robert Lawrence
Race, Sex, and Policy Problems
  edited by Marian Lief Palley and Michael Preston
American Security Policy and Policy-Making
  edited by Robert Harkavy and Edward Kolodziej
Current Issues in Transportation Policy
  edited by Alan Altshuler
Security Policies of Developing Countries
  edited by Edward Kolodziej and Robert Harkavy
Determinants of Law-Enforcement Policies
  edited by Fred A. Meyer, Jr., and Ralph Baker
Evaluating Alternative Law-Enforcement Policies
  edited by Ralph Baker and Fred A. Meyer, Jr.
International Energy Policy
  edited by Robert M. Lawrence and Martin O. Heisler
Employment and Labor-Relations Policy
  edited by Charles Bulmer and John L. Carmichael, Jr.
Housing Policy for the 1980s
  edited by Roger Montgomery and Dale Rogers Marshall
Environmental Policy Formation
  edited by Dean E. Mann
Environmental Policy Implementation
  edited by Dean E. Mann
The Analysis of Judicial Reform
  edited by Philip L. Dubois
The Politics of Judicial Reform
  edited by Philip L. Dubois
Critical Issues in Health Policy
  edited by Ralph Straetz, Marvin Lieberman, and Alice Sardell

Contents

Acknowledgments   ix

Chapter 1   Introduction   *Dean E. Mann*   1

Chapter 2   Confronting Complexity and Uncertainty:
                 Implementation of Hazardous-Waste-Management
                 Policy   *Sam A. Carnes*   35

Chapter 3   Perilous Waste   *Malcolm Getz* and *Benjamin Walter*   51

Chapter 4   Equity Issues and Wilderness Preservation: Policy
                 Implications for the Energy-Environment Tangle
                 James L. Regens   65

Chapter 5   Technology, Domestic Structures, and Ocean-Pollution
                 Regulation   *James P. Lester*   79

Chapter 6   Interorganizational Coordination in Environmental
                 Management: Process, Strategy, and Objective
                 Joseph J. Molnar and *David L. Rogers*   95

Chapter 7   Congress, EPA, the States, and the Fight to
                 Decentralize Water-Pollution-Grant Policy
                 Richard T. Sylves   109

Chapter 8   Central Policies and Local Environmental Decisions
                 Robert Eyestone   127

Chapter 9   Incentive Systems in Environmental Regulation
                 Barry M. Mitnick   139

Chapter 10   Charges to Control Aircraft Noise   *Donald C. Cell*   157

Chapter 11   Converting Thought to Action: The Use of Economic
                 Incentives to Reduce Pollution   *Alfred A. Marcus*   173

Chapter 12   Response Options for Evaluating the Consequences of
                 Pollution Charges   *Jack A. Goldstone*   185

Chapter 13   An Examination of Population-Growth-Managing
                  Communities   *David E. Dowall*   193

Chapter 14   The Politics of Local Growth Control   *Robert A.
                  Johnston*   207

Chapter 15   Equity Implications of Local Growth Management
                  Seymour I. Schwartz   223

                  Indexes   249

                  About the Contributors   259

                  About the Editor   262

Acknowledgments

I wish to reiterate my appreciation, as expressed in *Environmental Policy Formation,* to the many people who contributed to the realization of this collective effort: to Stuart Nagel for his efforts to get this project off the ground and see it through to completion; to Gary Toenniessen of the Natural and Environmental Sciences Program at the Rockefeller Foundation, whose financial assistance, while modest in amount, made the enterprise feasible; to the contributors to this volume, whose insights on both intellectual and stylistic matters were both stimulating to me and contributory to a finer product. As in the first volume, the contributors represent diverse disciplines: political science, economics, sociology, planning, and environmental policy analysis. Their multiple and varied assumptions, methodologies, approaches, value judgments and perspectives make us aware of the contributions that each discipline can make to the understanding of environmental policy formation and implementation. I also express my gratitude to my colleagues in the Department of Political Science, University of California, Santa Barbara, for their continuing intellectual stimulation and support for projects such as these; and finally, to the staff of the department, especially my editorial assistant, Gail Clark, for efficiently processing mounds of material and keeping track of it all.

1 Introduction

Dean E. Mann

Implementation of Environmental Policy

Perhaps the most distinctive feature of political science in the decade of the 1970s has been the growth of interest in and sophistication of policy analysis; perhaps the most distinctive feature of policy analysis has been the great increase in concern for policy implementation. These developments are, of course, natural outgrowths of systems analysis, that reached a point of significant influence in the early writings of David Easton,[1] Once the system concept gained a foothold in the discipline, it was no longer possible to restrict analysis to the input side of politics, to the institutions that converted demands into policy, or even to the formal structure of government that had the responsibility for execution of policy. The political system clearly included products or outputs, and these products or outputs had outcomes that were fed back into the political system through alterations of the political environment.

The growth of interest in outputs and outcomes coincided with the rapid burgeoning of government. In the post–World War II period, particularly the 1960s, there was rapid expansion of existing programs and agencies and the creation of new programs and agencies to meet newly perceived needs. The new programs tended to have too little foundation for the asserted cause-and-effect relationship between proffered solution and identified problem; too much controversy about the programs and therefore inevitable resistance to their operations; too much dependence on technology that might or might not prove efficacious; and too little realization that policy space was being so densely occupied that the success of any one policy inevitably depended to some extent—and often to a crucial extent—on the performance of some needed service or function by some other agency.[2] The result was often failure or at least limited success and disillusionment with the public policy as an instrument of social problem solving.

Another important intellectual and practical development was the revival of political economy as a mode of policy analysis. Economists renewed their interest in the public sector and applied their analytical powers to the assessment of government programs both in terms of national costs and benefits and in terms of distributional consequences. They developed the conceptual tools to evaluate public programs and occasionally devised innovative schemes such as pollution charges as alternative approaches to the achievement of public goals. They argued that traditional modes of government administration, either direct regulation or provision of services, might lead to failure as unfortunate as market failure. Alternative approaches combining market incentives under public authority might prove efficacious. Their purpose was to reduce social costs while creating market-like incentives for changing the behaviors of those who would otherwise despoil the environment. They did not necessarily challenge the ends of public policy but they emphasized costs and alternative means of achieving goals.

The post-World War II period was one of great improvements in the material well-being of most Americans, derived largely from economic growth. But by the 1970s, rapid growth had been replaced by serious shortages of some commodities, escalating prices reflecting these shortages, and much reduced rates of growth and investment. Moreover, there was increasing recognition that growth often brought with it "bads" as well as goods, that is, environmental pollution, dangers to human health, loss of scarce and unique resources and natural treasures, and risks to both humankind and ecological systems. Although few were willing to entirely eschew growth as the appropriate stance for public policy-makers, larger numbers demanded that greater attention be paid to the consequences of growth and urged techniques for improved analysis and measures to mitigate the harmful effects. This attention to consequences inevitably led to increased attention to implementation.

Recognition of shortages emphasized even more strongly the linkages between circumstances and decisions made within the United States and those circumstances and decisions outside, both of individual nations and of international groupings such as the Organization of Petroleum Exporting Countries (OPEC). The United States was dependent on foreign sources for numerous minerals, not the least of which was petroleum. Environmental conditions in less developed areas often led to poverty, and these conditions had immediate impacts on U.S. policy. The United States—or at least domestic enterprises—was tempted to solve pollution problems by exporting them, first by setting up plants in countries with less stringent controls and second by actually exporting wastes to countries that were so poor that they were prepared to accept even the most noxious wastes for an appropriate price.

The demand by affected parties for enlarged and effective opportunities for participation in administrative decision making is further evidence of a concern for implementation. Discretionary authority granted administrative agencies under the statutes that defined their missions provided agency officials with the capacity to bestow great benefits and inflict great harm on individuals and groups and the natural environment. Affected parties demanded opportunities not only to be heard but also to participate in the planning and decision making with respect to specific projects. Moreover, Congress expanded the opportunities for public participation, both by calling for the creation of participative mechanisms and by creating the bases for possible legal challenges through such requirements as the preparation of environmental-impact statements.

Couching the discussion of implementation with reference to a generalized category of *decision makers* suggests that implementation as a concept or process is not something of relevance to only the administrative or judicial branches of government. Implementation strategies are decided, whether designedly or by inadvertence, by those who create the program, decide on the structure, prescribe the methods of funding, establish the constraints on procedure, impose requirements for reporting and coordination, or invite public participation. Thus, at the outset the distinction between policymaking and policy implementation is ultimately false. It is particularly false in the U.S. system of government in which legislative and judicial intrusions into administrative behavior are commonplace. The web of relationships among interest and constituent groups, members of Congress, and administrators makes the policy-making and implementation processes a variable and multidirectional flow of communication, influence, decisions, and evaluations that are part of the continuing process of administration.

On the other hand, for analytical purposes, it may be useful to concentrate one's attention on the administration of programs to ascertain the factors that make for program or project success once the initial ground rules have been laid down by the Congress and the president. By the very nature of their responsibilities, members of Congress, the White House, and the judiciary can pay only intermittent attention to the daily routines of administration. Their interest may be sparked by agitation from private groups, but unless they have continuing concern for a given program or project, Congress and the courts must direct their attention elsewhere. The implementation process is, therefore, a highly permeable process with actors passing over the boundaries of the administrative system with relative ease but with some required stimulation and effort.

Implementation Analysis

The problems of implementation have been formalized in an analysis by Daniel Mazmanian and Paul Sabatier. They conclude that implementation depends on factors that can be placed in three categories: (1) the tractability of the problem; (2) the ability of the statute to favorably structure the implementation process; and (3) the effect of various political variables on the support for statutory objectives.[3] The tractability question revolves around the seriousness of the problem, the availability of technology, difficulties in measuring the required changes, the diversity of the behavior subject to regulation, the number of people who must change their behavior, and the extent of behavior change required. The extent to which the statute structures the implementation process depends on the validity of the causal theory assumed by the legislation, the precision with which the priorities are determined, the financial resources of the implementing agency, the extent of hierarchical or horizontal relationships among agencies involved, the appropriateness of the decision rules governing agency behavior, the commitment of individuals and agencies toward goal achievement, and the degree to which outside interests favorable to policy objectives are allowed to influence the program. The nonstatutory variables include the social, economic, and technological conditions prevailing among government jurisdictions, level of media attention, public support, support by specific groups within constituencies, and levels of support among other related institutions—the legislatures, courts, chief executives.

The limitaions on the achievement of environmental goals lead to a conclusion that all parties, particularly environmentalists themselves, must have realistic notions of the timetables and the completeness with which environmental objectives may be achieved. The record of accomplishment also suggests the need for a strategy for achieving goals: a recognition that obstales must be overcome, competing groups must be challenged or dealt with through negotiation and bargaining, and uncertainties must be removed. This is especially true in periods of contracting budgets and political administrations that emphasize reducing the scope of governmental authority.

Effective strategy must reflect the substantive issue dealt with and the political circumstances surrounding the debate over a given implementation issue. In some cases the emphasis must be on science: the development of a technical base that will withstand attack from commercial interests. This is clearly the case with toxic chemicals: without additional scientific evidence, it will be difficult to establish the toxicity of various new chemicals and the host of old chemicals that already pervade modern industrial society. But the strategy may also involve the adoption of certain procedures or standards to simplify the tasks. In the field of chemicals, the Environmental Protection Agency (EPA) opted for classifying chemicals by their properties rather than relying on tests of each individual chemical. Nevertheless, the General Accounting Office, with agreement by EPA, concluded four years after passage of the Toxic Substances Control Act in 1956 that "neither the public nor the environment are (sic) much better protected."[4]

In legislating policy, members of Congress and executive officials are in effect designing a strategy for the achievement of public goals. Selection of an appropriate strategy in terms of situational variables is one of the principal tasks for which they are elected and appointed. Paul Berman groups the strategies into two classes: adaptive and programmed. The adaptive strategy is appropriate in a context in which the goals and perhaps even the means of policy are yet unclear. Implementation then takes on the character of problem solving in which the principal actors take important roles in fashioning policy: supplying information, granting consent, responding to change, and contributing to an evolving policy. A programmed strategy calls for clarity of goals, clear lines of administration, and specification of incentives in such a fashion that the principal actors will likely contribute to the achievement of a predetermined solution.[5]

Berman evaluates the settings in which such strategies may be appropriate and finds the following situational characteristics important in the determination of an appropriate strategy: (1) the scope of change, with the paradoxical conclusion that small changes are not necessarily less difficult nor large changes necessarily more difficult; (2) uncertainty of technology or theory—a point adverted to at the outset and clearly related to the question of whether the implementation system is relatively open or closed; (3) agreement over goals; (4) the institutional setting, that is, the extent to which the institutional units are loosely coupled or tightly coupled—exhibiting either distant, conflictual, ad hoc, and changing relationships or close, stable, and well-understood patterns of interactions; and (5) the stability of the environment—the occurrence of lack of unforeseen events and endogenous variables that may play havoc with a program.

The implementation of environmental policy is an especially thorny task because of the inevitable implications of some policies for other sectors of society and the economy. Limitations on discharge of pollutants into the atmosphere and watercourses of the nation have broad implications for all kinds of industry, the well-being of entire communities, and the behavior of large numbers of diverse groups. Coordination of policies that constrain economic activity and that facilitate economic activity is an especially difficult task. On the other hand, some policies, such as those dealing with the environmental quality of the workplace, would appear to be no different—in the direct sense but not necessarily the long-term-mortality sense—from other policies directed toward the health and well-being of workers in terms of implementation.

Another complication is the reliance on intergovernmental structures for achieving environmental goals. The usual pattern is for federal agencies to certify state agencies as those authorized to carry out the programs authorized by federal statutes. Authorization is granted those agencies that demonstrate the capacity to implement programs and that have adopted standards meeting federal minimum requirements. The relationships between state and federal agencies are always delicate, owing to the local sensitivities over federal domination and preferences for the protection of unique local interests. Moreover, whatever federal law may provide, local interests have powerful political support from their elected and bureaucrat officials, both in their own states and in Washington, D.C.

Finally, implementation is a different task, although it is not necessarily easier when the targets are few rather than many. The few may be powerful economically and politically and frustrate the efforts of the administrative agency through technical objections, judicial obstruction, and appeals to the public and elected politicians. On the other hand, when the targets are numerous and diverse, as in the enforcement of the 55-mile-per-hour speed limit, massive voluntary compliance or resistance may spell the difference in satisfactory achievement of programmatic goals. There is no doubt that in most cases enforcement steps could be taken, but budget limitations, personnel shortages, and prudence make such a rigid posture impractical.[6]

The Conditions Affecting Implementation

Implementation of environmental policy, like implementation of policies generally, depends on an array of historical, intellectual, socioeconomic and political, bureaucratic, technological, and interpersonal factors. The following provides a brief discussion of these factors as derived from recent literature and applied to environmental policy.[7]

History

Policies seldom drop out of the sky, like a new baby delivered by the stork. Rather, they reflect an evolutionary process or a process of accommodation in which various interested parties play roles in shaping those policies. In effect, they reflect a process of learning, often by trial and error, in which adjustments are made to meet the economic, moral, and technological demands of those concerned. Innovations in policy that fail to build on that which has gone before run the danger of significant opposition, technical breakdowns, and unintended consequences. As stated by Aaron Wildavsky. "if history is abolished, nothing is settled. Old quarrels become new conflicts. Both calculation and conflict increase exponentially, the former worsening detection and the latter impeding correction of errors. . . . Doing without history is a little like abolishing memory—momentarily convenient, perhaps—but ultimately embarrassing."[8]

The distinction between evolution and radical change is itself debatable. Some find evolution where others see abrupt disjunctures with the past. Pollution policy may provide an illustration. Some find the Clean Air Act of 1970 and the Clean Water Act of 1972 to be relatively radical departures in pollution-control policy, and in some senses they were. They were, however, in another sense, not a new departure at all.[9] They reflected a gradual evolution of policy that emphasized first a federal role in funding research and education, subsequently a broader role in negotiating pollution-control agreements, and finally a full regulatory role for the federal government built on technology-based standards. The technology-based standards were a new departure, but direct regulation on the basis of standards was, and is, a traditional mode of social control. It was the technology base that was the most controversial and, for some, the most wasteful element in the new regulatory regime. It is also notable that a still more controversial mode of achieving pollution control—effluent charges—has hardly gained a foothold in environmental policy because it is in fact a radical departure from the traditional regulatory approach. As some critics point out, only experience can provide the basis for determining that such charges are superior to direct regulation.[10]

This sense of history provides an awareness of what is settled and what is subject to reversal, modification, or redirection. As Helen Ingram and Dean Mann have pointed out, much policy is settled because there is virtually no possibility of significant alteration of its basic character.[11] Current discussions of social security focus not on fundamental change but on how much the present employed generation can pay, in what form, and how much the retired generation of today and the near future can expect to receive. In the management of the nation's natural resources, despite the preferences of Secretary of the Interior James Watt and the "Sagebrush Rebellion," is there a serious possibility that the public lands would be given to the states for their management? Is the dispute not over fundamental policy but over how the public lands will be managed and for whose benefit?

Agreement on Goals

Virtually all policy analysts concur that agreement on the goals is a necessary element in the successful implementation of legislation. Unfortunately, that agreement is seldom achieved even among the legislators who fashion goals. The political coalition that legitimized a given statute may have had multiple goals in mind, the emphasis on any one of which might undercut the possibility of achieving the others. Legislators clearly have diverse goals in mind, even within the context of some overarching social goal. One legislator wants to create a symbol that will satisfy a constituency clamoring for recognition. Another legislator wants economy and therefore emphasizes the granting of minimal and perhaps inadequate resources to achieve the stated goal. Some are more concerned about ensuring that the states have an important role in policy implementation. Still others may be concerned principally with ensuring adequate participation of the various parties interested in the policy issue.

These more limited concerns overlap with substantive issues for which they in fact may be the stalking horses. A concern for states' rights on environmental policy may really be a reflection of resistance to major elements of policy itself. Guarantees of participation may reflect a concern that traditional methods of achieving policy goals have not paid off and a belief that participation at the administrative level will strengthen the possibility of achieving substantive goals.[12] Because of the interplay of environmental and economic issues, the achievement of an environmental goal may have a direct and detrimental effect on specific economic activities and may even provide inappropriate incentives to achieving the environmental goals at least cost.

The Economic Development Administration (EDA) experience in Oakland, as recounted by Jeffrey Pressman and Aaron Wildavsky, suggested the difficulty of keeping the city from experiencing riots, putting otherwise unemployables to work, providing job training, supporting economic development, and making sound loans.[13] The National Environmental Policy Act similarly had multiple goals: to broaden environmentally sensitive options, provide a greater evidentiary base for environmental decision making, enhance research on the environment, provide opportunity for broader participation in decision making, and to impose on all agencies an obligation to make choices with environmental consequences as a primary consideration. The emphasis has clearly been placed on improving the evidentiary base and providing the basis for broader participation with the other goals falling behind.

Intellectual Factors

Effective implementation depends on understanding the causes of problems and correctly predicting, within reason, the consequences of the measures designed to resolve the problems. Achievement of a high level of certainty in either respect is a prodigious task and simply is not possible in the time frame within most decision makers must operate. Action frequently occurs with statements of probability providing the foundation for the proposed solutions. These statements of probabilities are often controversial, especially when the economic stakes are high. As well established as is the linkage between smoking and lung cancer and heart disease, the tobacco companies persist in their claims that clinical proof that such linkages exist is lacking.

Perhaps the most dramatic illustration of this kind of problem is the controversy surrounding the so-called Rasmussen Report on nuclear safety. This authoritative report on the likelihood of accidents at commercial nuclear plants was subsequently criticized as excessively optimistic, perhaps underestimating the likelihood of such accidents by a factor of 500.[14] Such estimates are clearly based on assumptions and definitions, on estimates of future consequences. Singly, any one of these factors can spell results wide of the mark, but together they can mean the creation of new, rather than the reduction of old, problems.

Reference has already been made to the frequent recommendations for adoption of effluent charges as alternatives to standard setting, regulation, and enforcement procedures. Not only the newness but also the underlying assumptions of this approach have been subjected to serious criticism, suggesting that even without the benefit of experience, there may be serious pitfalls in the adoption of this policy, either from the standpoint of its policy consequences or expectations of the results that may be obtained.[15]

Socioeconomic and Political Factors

General socioeconomic and political conditions can have an important bearing on the implementation of public policy generally and certainly of environmental policy. At this writing, for example, the Reagan administration has begun a number of initiatives with respect to environmental policy. The specifics may be classified in other categories but the overall impulse is derived from a change in the political regime. The secretary of the Interior has decided to eliminate many of the rules and regulations that had been prescribed with respect to the protection of the land surface once strip mining had been undertaken. The administrator of the EPA has reorganized the agency, dismantling the enforcement division and decentralizing its functions among the various divisions that focus on substantive environmental problems. The staff of the Council of Environmental Quality has been drastically reduced. The administration has indicated its preference for further decentralization to the states of the air-pollution-control program. These initiatives, if consumated, would constitute a significant reversal of environmental policy that has been building since the 1960s. It is not clear the extent to which any of or all these measures or policy changes reflect changes in public preferences in the realm of environmental policy. They clearly reflect a general preference for less obtrusive government in the lives of most people.

The economic variables have powerful effects on environmental policy, although they are constrained by the persistent public support for environmental quality.[16] The dismal financial condition of the automobile industry, especially the Crysler Corporation, has made the postponement of the imposition of more stringent controls on automobile emissions almost inevitable. The shortages of gasoline in the 1970s made the adoption of emission-control equipment that might reduce gas mileage less feasible. Chemical companies complain that stringent controls over the marketing of new chemicals may place their firms and the United States at a competitive disadvantage with firms in other nations where such stringent controls are not in effect.

Social factors may also play a role. These concern special classes of citizens with specific values and modes of behavior. Efforts to reduce rates of population growth have encountered opposition from specific religious groups but also from ethnic groups that interpret such efforts as genocidal in character.

Structural Variables

The scope and expansiveness of environmental policy virtually precludes the effective implementation of any environmental policy by single agencies. Agencies that have given missions inevitably must rely on other agencies for information, research, cooperation, political leverage, financing, facilities, or personnel in achieving their goals. Often the reliance on multiple agencies in mission accomplishment is written into the statute: the Bureau of Reclamation shall consult with the U.S. Fish and Wildlife Service on matters affecting fish and wildlife in the construction of a storage reservoir. The EPA must endeavor to work through the states in the implementation of water-pollution-control policy. The Federal Aviation Agency in the Department of Transportation and the EPA are both involved in the setting of standards for airport noise.

This is not a tidy way of doing business, and there is an incessant urge among policymakers and implementers to restructure and reorganize to facilitate the performance of their complementary functions. In the decade of the 1970s, presidents Nixon and Carter strove to create a Department of Natural Resources, both of them unsuccessfully.[17] The centrifugal forces of bureaucrats and private actors in the policymaking system militate against successful accomplishment of these reorganizations, but the logical justifications for functions remaining where

they are because of settled policy and bureaucratic relationships are important
keys to the lack of excitement over major restructuring.

Reorganizations usually suggest concentration of decision making and implementation around a function that has been singled out for attention, but the
logic is not always clear or overwhelmingly persuasive. In the Reagan administration, for example, a reorganization in the EPA eliminated the division concerned
with enforcement of laws and regulations and placed all enforcement functions
in the divisions concerned with each form of pollution: air, water, toxic wastes.
The function of enforcement was focused on the media rather than on the function itself. Environmentalists looked on this change as a weakening of the resolve
of EPA to enforce the law.

Concentration of authority is a controversial subject. Alfred Marcus lists the
advantages and disadvantages of concentrated and divided authority. In general,
he finds the advantages of divided authority to lie in the satisfaction of a broader
array of interests and values and the tendency to maintain flexibility and permit
the correction of errors.[18] Helen Ingram and Scott Ullery find that pluralistic
decision-making arrangements lead to possible innovations in policy because of
the multipilicity of sources of ideas and influence, quite the reverse of the thinking of those who favor comprehensive, concentrated planning and decision
making.[19]

Resources

At the outset of the Reagan administration, the staff of the Council on Environmental Quality was replaced and its numbers drastically reduced from around
fifty to approximately ten people. Budgetary support for the Water Resources
Council was eliminated. Budgetary support for virtually the entire social-science
section of the National Science Foundation (NSF) was proscribed by the Office
of Management and Budget. These actions and attempted efforts suggest the
importance of resources in the implementation of legislation. The Reagon administration made it clear that it no longer desired independent review of environmental-impact analysis or overall evaluations of environmental progress;
it no longer wanted the kinds of studies and coordinative efforts that took place
through the Water Resources Council; it considered social-science research as
sponsored by NSF as relatively superfluous in terms of desirable public programs.

Ultimately, public resources may be measured in money, but in practice
they are measured in numbers of staff, skills of employees, physical facilities,
opportunities to travel and monitor how programs are being carried out, equipment to conduct research, engage in communication, or undertake computer-
ized analysis. No agency, by definition, has enough resources to carry out its
mission as effectively as it would like. NASA has more experiments it would like
to carry out with its satellites than it has resources or rockets to support. The

National Park Service could expand its public information and education program immeasurably at its scenic sites and thus improve its value to the public but for the lack of financial resources. EPA could improve its toxic-substances enforcement program if only it could find trained toxicologists. The list is endless.

What is not endless or bottomless is the public treasury. And this clearly is a good thing. Public servants, although unable to evaluate a profit-and-loss ledger to measure efficiency, must allocate scarce resources according to some set of priorities or some calculation of costs and benefits. More may almost always be considered superior to less, but in some cases, the inadequacy of resources may suggest that some program or project is not worth doing at all. Enforcement is expensive, and, as Roland McKean points out, it would be a good idea to estimate enforcement costs before embarking on regulatory programs.[20]

Behavioral Assumptions

The achievement of the goals of environmental protection and enhancement depend on sound assumptions about the behavior of individuals, groups—including firms, and public institutions. Like public policy in general, environmental policy may fall far short of its goals if the premises about motivations, incentives, and constraints are improperly structured into the decision-making system.

Individuals are likely to behave generally to maximize their own benefits and reduce costs. Private individuals, in dealing with environmental conditions, usually find the costs—information and transaction costs—exceed any benefits they might hope to receive by active involvement in the decision-making system. As individuals, few are prepared to invest much time or money in reducing air and water pollution. Clearly, it is a question of intensity of concern and impact. Those living next to the Love Canal and under the flight path of jet planes have an intense interest and therefore heightened levels of activity. Their very real costs in terms of health and annoyance may be much greater than others who are farther removed.

The actors whose behavior affects the successful implementation of environmental policy include the public generally, and, often, special interest groups such as private corporations, environmental groups, narrow sectors of the public, and government bureaucrats. Correct assumptions about their behavior in specific situations are necessary components of any environmental-implementation strategy.

Individual and group activity also depends very much on the access provided by public institutions. The courts are always available, but barring major threats to individual welfare, citizens are unlikely to use the judicial process because of its expense. When public institutions provide access through hearings, advisory boards, open planning, and various other devices for public participation, public involvement and influence may increase substantially.

Individuals are not likely to have much incentive for supporting the implementation of environmental policy, especially of the common-property sort. Their individual benefits are too slight compared to the cost of the effort and resources they might expend. They may respond to exhortation under conditions of emergency or crisis, but it is not clear that moralizing or exhortation provides a permanent basis for eliciting responsible environmental behavior.

For most analysts, price is considered the principal motivating factor in changed behavior. Conservation is most likely to occur when the price of gasoline, water, lumber, or use of waste sinks increases. Individuals are allowed to make the appropriate adjustments in demand in accordance with their tastes and needs, but the general trend is toward lowered demand, the development of substitutes, and more careful use of that which one does buy. The equity of price as a device for dampening demand for environmental amenities remains controversial.

The high cost of individual effort in dealing with environmental problems may be alleviated in part by participation in interest groups that are committed to oversight of public and private behavior in this policy sector. Expectations about what interest groups can accomplish must be realistic, however. In contrast to producer organizations with their clear-cut economic base, environmental organizations are membership organizations, which must struggle to maintain membership while developing a strategy that maximizes their impact. They must husband their resources, choose their targets carefully, and engage in strategies that are cost effective and likely to assure membership support. In some cases tactics involve mass-advertising campaigns, and in others representatives of environmental organizations may find it to their advantage to work quietly with public and private officials in reaching satisfactory solutions.

Private firms exist to make profit and therefore are cost minimizers, especially in a competitive market. They have traditionally avoided certain social costs—their external effects on the environment—by treating them as "commons" for which payment was never charged. With the passage of environmental-control legislation, these private firms face paying the cost of these side-effects in a variety of forms: installation of new technology to control emissions; payment of charges for treatment of their effluent through waste-treatment systems; payment for transportation and disposal of solid wastes; taxes in the form of effluent charges for discharges of wastes into streams and atmosphere; higher costs for land owing to the elimination of certain lands for development because of environmental sensitivity.

As a class of actors in the environmental-policy arena, private profit-making firms inevitably resist government regulation because of its direct costs and the interference that it constitutes in management. With respect to nearly all policy proposals, they are to be found on the side of less effective action for protecting the natural environment. Polluters of air and rivers point to the cost of installing pollution-control equipment. They are found on the side of doubters about the effectiveness of a given control approach. They point to the cost of rehabilitating land that has been strip mined. They object to "locking up" of public lands because of their value as natural habitat for wildlife, as scenic wonders, as geologic spectacles, as wilderness.

On the other hand, actors from the private sector may be environmental protectionists under the appropriate incentives. It may be argued that private forestry-management companies have a vital stake in renewing their resource because of its potential for producing profits on a cyclical basis. Similarly, oil and mining companies are likely to respond to price increases by enhanced levels of recovery of minerals from ores of low concentration. New firms enter the market to recycle materials that formerly were discarded—for example, recovery of methane gas from waste deposits becomes a profitable enterprise.

The final actors in environmental policymaking are government agencies and bureaucrats. Their historical role has been a mixed one. On the one hand, bureaucratic agencies have been in the forefront of economic development, and this has placed them in the vanguard of those who would disturb fragile and unique environments. On the other hand, other public agencies have taken responsibility for husbanding of resources: reservation of the public lands, especially those valued for their timber, water production, recreation, and wildlife, and regulation of private activities to ensure compliance with environmental standards with respect to air and water pollution, radiation, pesticides, and other hazardous substances.

Like other individuals and private firms, however, bureaucrats and their agencies tend to respond to incentives that lead to growth of their roles, their budgets, and their numbers. Lacking standards of efficiency supplied by a private market and depending on appropriations that reflect political considerations, government agencies seek to expand budgets and authority. Stimulated by congressmen who live by the same political laws, bureaucrats respond with more and bigger projects, often without economic justification.

Moreover, bureaucrats may fall victim to ideology—a commitment to values that may not reflect current knowledge or societal values. The ideology leads to doctrinaire norms that govern individual behavior. Being monopolists, their decisions may be less susceptible to attack, because the consumers have few means of challenging them. The Army Corps of Engineers was long considered the best example of an agency impervious to new ideas and values and political influence derived from them. Its recent record, however, suggests a far greater capacity to make adjustments than was previously recognized.[21]

Bureaucracies often suffer, however, from burdens that far outstrip their capacities. They seldom are provided the money, talent, or time to accomplish their tasks in a satisfactory manner. Too few inspectors, scientists, and enforcement officials; too little talent, because society has failed to produce qualified individuals or they have been siphoned off into the private sector because of higher salaries; too little time because Congress makes assumptions about deadlines that cannot possibly be kept. The results are loss of credibility among its clientele and loss of stature with the general public.

The varying and often conflicting impulses that propel government agencies toward their policy goals impose a premium on coordination of their manifold efforts. Such coordination is difficult to achieve because there are few in the hierarchical chain of command who are willing to make hard decisions and still fewer who are willing to accept them when they contravene their views on policy. The result is likely to be patchwork policy, with each agency moving haltingly in its chosen direction, negotiating differences where conflicts are severe and progress toward their goals is impeded by the stances of other agencies.

Implementation of Environmental Laws

As indicated previously, laws affecting the environment are no less subject to the influences of those forces constraining the implementation process than other laws. Indeed, those exogenous influences may be more powerful because of the bold, sweeping, and controversial forms that environmental controls are likely to take. The following studies are designed to illustrate or describe these forces as they impinge on the implementation of environmental laws and programs. In general form, they follow the classification established by Mazmanian and Sabatier, with an additional section dealing with the policymaking and implementation in the area of local growth management.

The Tractability of the Problem

The tractability of the problem, according to Mazmanian and Sabatier, concerns the inherent nature of the problem involved. Tractability varies to the extent that human ingenuity may be capable of devising a reasonable solution within a reasonable period of time. It is not necessarily limited to the technical character of the problem but may also concern the extent to which the target population is susceptible to changed behavior, the diversity of behavior involved, and the size of the population whose behavior must be changed. It may involve the question of whether there exists a causal theory, either technical or social, that provides the basis for confidence that given policies will produce the desired result.

Problems are particularly intractable when they first arrive on the policy horizon, when they create strongly held but divergent opinions about the equities associated with various policy options, and when the consequences of the behavior sought to be controlled are likely to be felt years, decades, and perhaps even centuries hence. The control of toxic substances is perhaps the best example of at least some of these conditions. This control effort arrived on the policy scene only in the late 1970s; the chemical industry has vigorously opposed control; the consequences of misuse or abuse of these chemical substances or the inadequate storage of them may not be felt for generations to come; and control has certain equity consequences for various participants in the chemical industry (producers, consumers).

Major legislation to deal with toxic substances are the Toxic Substances Control Act (TSCA), and the Resource Conservation and Recovery Act (RCRA), both passed by Congress in 1976. TSCA is designed to regulate chemical substances during their entire life cycle—from prior to their manufacture until their disposal. EPA must inventory existing chemicals, require premanufacture notice of testing, and elicit reporting by industry of the relative risks of all new chemicals. The administration of this act has been fraught with conflict and uncertainty and charges that EPA has been both too slow and conservative and too fast and too radical. By mid-1980, only five chemicals—polychlorinated biphenyls (PCBs), chlorofluorocarbons, phthalate esters, chlorinated benzene, and chloromethane—had been subject to any regulations at all. EPA encountered numerous problems, especially the recuitment and training of new personnel, resistance from industry, and development of appropriate test procedures and standards. EPA has had difficulty deciding on the character of the tests, the basis on which tests should be conducted—on individual substances (which are staggering in number) or on entire categories of substances sharing similar chemical characteristics, and whether to concentrate on a few chemicals known to have dangerous properties or on the large number of chemicals whose effects are yet unknown. Moreover there have been serious issues raised with respect to the revelation of trade secrets by firms that are required to submit information on new chemicals they intend to manufacture and purvey.

The Resource Conservation and Recovery Act was designed to deal with hazardous wastes by a system that regulated them "from the cradle to the grave." The act imposes on generators, transporters, and disposers of hazardous wastes an obligation to handle and dispose of them in a way that does not endanger human health or the environment. EPA is obligated to set standards and enforce them through requirements of reports and permits. The key element in the regulatory structure is the manifest system, through which generators must identify hazardous wastes and label and package them appropriately, transporters must deliver the wastes to designated disposal sites, and disposers must dispose of the wastes in an acceptable manner.

As with toxic substances, the task imposed on EPA is staggering. EPA has estimated that 77 billion pounds of hazardous waste are generated each year but only 10 percent is disposed of in an environmentally sound way. Moreover, there are major legacies of unsound practices in the past: Love Canal, the Valley of the Drums, Pine Barrens in Southern New Jersey, Sullee landfill in Arkansas, and Pine River, Michigan, are all sites of waste dumpings that have caused serious threats to life, both present and future. Injured parties, EPA, and Congress have moved in several ways to deal with these past actions. In 1979 EPA sued several companies for $125 million to compensate for cleanup of the various sites in the Love Canal area. Individuals who contracted asbestosis have sued asbestos companies and the federal government. Congress in 1980 passed a superfund program establishing a $1.6 billion fund to pay for cleanup of spills of hazardous substances and inactive waste-disposal sites.

Two chapters in this book deal with the RCRA but from quite different perspectives. The first, by Sam Carnes, deals with the problems of rulemaking by EPA. EPA entered a policy-implementing thicket in which its efforts were confounded by the problems of relating waste control with other environmental statutes, by the requirements of public participation, by the obligations to cooperate with the states, by legislative oversight activities by Congress, by the course of events, and by the active opposition by industry. Although Carnes finds that EPA did about as well as it could under the circumstances, the story is nevertheless instructive. Congress has filled up policy space and has taken on staggeringly complex tasks that are likely to incur the wrath of numerous parties; Congress needs to make realistic judgments about what may be accomplished and in what time frame.

In their chapter Malcolm Getz and Benjamin Walter deal with the distribution of equities associated with the hazardous-waste legislation. Equity considerations basically deal with the distribution of benefits and costs to various groups in society. A competitive market system distributes these benefits and costs in a way that presumably maximizes efficiency in the utilization of the resources of society while doing nothing about the capacity of various sectors of society to command the use of those resources. Purchasing power reflects other forces, notably the competitive power of the labor force in dealing with management and changes in technology.

Leaving aside the equitable or ethical considerations associated with a perfect market economy—an area of great controversy in itself—serious equity considerations are raised when government intervenes in the economy as it clearly does in dealing with toxic substances. What groups are likely to benefit or pay additional costs, and what is the justification of providing additional benefits to those groups? A. Myrick Freeman et al. point out the equity considerations that must be carefully delineated in evaluating pollution-control policy.[22] Air-quality improvements may help the urban poor, but much depends on whether land-value increases raise rents for the poor and how the air pollution control is paid for. Similarly, water-pollution control may benefit most those who are attracted to water-based recreation—notably the relatively well-to-do—but its location near urban centers may make such recreation more available to the poor. Various forms of charges, taxation, and subsidies may pay for the environmental enhancement, but these may have two effects: to redistribute income toward those least needing it and to increase unnecessarily the costs to society in general because of the incentives they create.

Getz and Walter are concerned precisely with the impact of governmental intervention in what basically is a private market and how the costs and benefits will be distributed. Their ultimate concern is that by the increase in the costs associated with the controlled and environmentally safe disposal of waste, there will be a direct impact on both the firms generating waste and other firms disposing of wastes. Their concern is that higher costs will impose additional burdens on the entry of new firms in producing and waste-disposal sectors, thus significantly altering the character of both markets. They conclude that this legislation might distribute income to the less rather than the more needy through the reduction in competition. They examine the incentives of the various parties and find some of them perverse in light of the environmental goals of waste management. Finally, they conclude that the general public may suffer because the incentives created by an overly ambitious system of waste management may actually cause the public to be more rather than less exposed to hazardous wastes.

The question of equity becomes even more complex when dealing with actions that threaten irreversible consequences, the loss of option values and intergenerational equities. In part the complexity comes from lack of information: information about the consequences and the values of those not currently affected by the resource decision. For some it is basically a philosophical and ethical question involving the moral obligations of present generations to future humankind.[23] Except for extreme rationalists and those concerned only for economic efficiency, the affirmative obligation to future humankind is obvious.

Option values are those held by individuals who are not current resource or amenity users who would like to preserve the option of utilizing that resource in the future. An irreversible action obviously would preclude exercising such an option: a Grand Canyon flooded by a dam would no longer be the extraordinary geological and aesthetic wonder that many hope and long to see. Economists argue that such aversion to the risk of losing such option values should be taken into account in environmental decision making, making the actors more cautious in the face of such risks.[24]

But the most important questions may be the means of achieving these equitable solutions. For some, the equity questions, even those associated with intergenerational equity, can be left to the marketplace. J.E. Stiglitz, for example, argues that government may play a role in "indicative planning," that is, helping to forecast future demand, but it should not allocate resources. He contends that future generations may be better, not worse, off and that monetary policy aimed at changing the rate of interest should be the principal instrument of achieving intergenerational equity.[25] On the other hand, Herman Daly contends that "intertemporal distribution is a question of ethics, not a function of the interest rate."[26] Daly does not eschew the market but instead proposes new institutions within which the market might operate: transferrable-birth options, depletion-quota auctions, and guarantees of minimum incomes.

Unfortunately, markets often do not operate effectively with respect to common-property resources, and thus the policy of "internalizing externalities," bringing all important side effects into the decision-making process through taxes, subsidies, interest rates, and so on are irrelevant; government must play a direct role.[27] Consideration of the various values associated with the national forests and the competing values associated with wilderness are precisely those that nonmarket decision-making processes must deal with.[28]

James Regens addresses the procedures followed in the Roadless Area Review and Evaluation (RARE II), the effort to achieve substantive equity in the conflict over wilderness and other values, particularly those associated with energy development on the forested lands. Despite studious concern for preserving procedural equities and for arriving at a conclusion of the process with the participants perceiving substantive equity, the results were enhanced conflict and severe disagreement about both the process and the substantive results. Expanded participation, for example, far from reducing conflict, provided increased opportunity for conflict. Examining all tracts at one point in time—a rationally comprehensive approach—merely exacerbated the sense of disenchantment among the interested parties. The intensity of the feelings was no doubt sharpened by the fact that the environmentalists felt that this was their one chance: once the land was designated open for energy development, that designation precluded possible inclusion in the wilderness system in the future; on the other hand, inclusion of tracts as wilderness did not preclude development at some time in the future. Although Regens does not see the lesson simply in terms of alternatives to rational-comprehensive planning, he does suggest that more cautious, piecemeal consideration of specific tracts for wilderness designation would have avoided some of the conflict and perhaps achieved the goals of perceived equity, both procedural and substantive.

Coherence of the Implementation Process

The second set of variables that affect policy implementation are those that concern the extent to which the statute coherently structures the implementation process. These variables include the validity of the causal theory on which the policy is based; the precision and clarity with which objectives are ranked; the financial resources available to the implementing agency; the extent of hierarchical integration within and among implementing institutions; the extent to which decision rules of implementing agencies are supportive of statutory objectives; the assignment of responsibility to officials and agencies committed to the statutory objectives; and the extent to which opportunities for participation by actors external to the implementing agencies are biased toward supporters of statutory objectives.

Although many of these issues are relevant and related to the questions addressed in several of the chapters in this book, the principal focus of this book is the structural variables: the hierarchical and geographical allocations of authority, responsibility, and power among the many units of government in the

United States. In effect, the authors ask how such structures of decision making are arrived at, how the complexities associated with various distributions of power and authority are dealt with, and what differences such structures make in the implementation of environmental policy.

Generally speaking, the government of the United States would be considered among the more fragmented, decentralized, loosely coupled (to use Berman's phrase) institutional structures among the modern industrialized nations and even among those nations that may be classified as democratic. Indeed, with the trend toward political parties that are less able to mobilize and aggregate interests, with the growth of single-issue politics, with the decline of centralized controls in Congress, and with the limitations of the powers of the president, the United States may be moving in the direction of further fragmentation. This may have significant consequences for the capacity of the political system generally to respond to serious demands. There are those who doubt that the United States is capable of governance or at least wise governance given the fractionalization of power in this country.[29]

Even those with a bias in favor of pluralism, that is, who perceive and favor a broad distribution of economic, social, and political power, ultimately must come to grips with the need for political mechanisms that are capable of making timely and effective decisions. There are limits to which matters of concern to the nation as a whole, which therefore must be treated as functional unities, can be decentralized to the states. There are limits to the fragmentation of functional responsibilities for the performance of given tasks within the national government. These limits may be tested during the Reagan administration, and it is yet uncertain the extent to which environmental issues—so often perceived as ecological unities—can be dealt with effectively in a decentralized and fragmented political structure.

The international system is by its very nature fragmented and individualistic. The nation-state reigns supreme, despite the interdependencies that exist economically and environmentally. Indeed, these very same interdependencies have enhanced the role of the nation-state in that governments have had to increase their authority and their political power within their boundaries to accomplish environmentally necessary purposes. It has been written that "the nation-state may all too seldom speak the voice or reason. But it remains the only serious alternative to chaos."[30] In the absence of international regimes capable of effecting environmentally sound policy, the nation-state may provide the only vehicle by which even an approach to sound policy may be achieved. Intelligent fisheries management, for example, is today largely the handiwork of individual nations which administer fisheries within their 200-mile economic-interest limit and who cooperate for limited purposes in other areas.

There is general agreement that any assumed disassociation between domestic and foreign policy is no longer tenable.[31] The OPEC oil embargo of 1973 etched this fact indelibly on the minds of all Americans and decision makers who strove to deal with oil restrictions. Their efforts to establish oil independence by costly schemes to develop rapidly alternative sources of domestic energy or to create regional international organizations and programs to meet potential future curtailments of oil were manifestations of this internal-politics–external-politics linkage. This linkage of policy may be extended further: that is, it may be argued that structures through which policy are made are often dictated by considerations of domestic politics and that these structural arrangements then have an impact on substantive foreign-policy decisions.

This is precisely the argument made by James Lester in his analysis of the stance of nation-states with respect to the issue of ocean pollution. With reference to the United States in particular, the structure for policymaking is highly fragmented, reflecting the political values that far transcend considerations of foreign policymaking. The divided authority, the permeability of bureaucratic structures to the influence of private groups, and the differential priorities found in the process for making ocean-pollution policy are deeply characteristic of policymaking in the United States. The presidency, nominally a unitary element in the American political system and designedly so for matters of foreign policy, seems a weak structure indeed in the face of these pluralist forces, both because the presidency (when defined as an institution rather than a person) is hardly a single entity and because the presidency must deal on both the domestic and foreign-policy fronts with these same forces.

Lester concludes with an appeal for clinical and intensive examinations of the process of policymaking with respect to oceans in other nations to validate his conclusion. In effect, this kind of investigation is currently taking place involving studies of Japan. This NSF-sponsored research at the University of Southern California is examining Japanese policymaking with respect to a number of issues under consideration at the Law of the Sea negotiations. One of their principal investigators, Haruhiro Fukui, raises important questions regarding Lester's conclusions. In a forthcoming study, Fukui will argue that despite the usual assumption that Japan's political structure for policymaking, especially for foreign policymaking, is highly centralized, it is in fact segmented and compartmentalized to a considerable degree. Moreover, despite the vaunted benefits that accrue to polities with more centralized structures, he finds hidden benefits in compartmentalization: benefits in the form of consensus building and flexibility in responding to new circumstances.[32]

The solution to fragmentation, as everyone hopes, is coordination. Because division of labor is necessary, especially when dealing with highly technical matters concerning management of the environment, and because a coherent, uni-organizational approach to the environment as a whole is an intellectual and managerial impossibility, coordination is the magic wand that will bring about concerted, integrated, timely, and effective actions. Unfortunately, the hope is seldom borne out. Moreover, it is probably true that those who write statutes requiring coordination among various agencies know just how difficult it is to obtain such concerted action. But where else can they turn when the political forces, the logic of bureaucracy, and the technical character of the policy issue all lead in the direction of fragmentation?

In a sense, the injunction to coordinate is often an overt admission that politicians have failed to establish the ground for concerted action. They recognize the diverse missions, mandates, and priorities under which agencies in related fields operate. They cannot sort out and integrate these mandates and priorities by statute through lack of time, ignorance, or because of the composite and often internally contradictory nature of policy in a country with diverse interests and values. Thus, the bureaucrats are often left holding the bag.

Surely it is futile to argue either that coordination can be achieved effortlessly by statutory requirements, by the exercise of good will, or by some structural device or that coordination is a useless concept, designed merely to frustrate bureaucrats who are earnestly trying to accomplish their missions. Statutory requirements and exhortations may have some effect, particularly if they are backed up by enforcement actions when the principal actors fail to observe even the niceties of communication, joint planning, and participative decision making. When the courts say to a construction agency that it has not adequately considered the impacts of a project on fish and wildlife, one may assume that it is effectively saying to the agency "coordinate" or, at least, do it better.

Moreover, it is fair to say that much of the literature on implementation fails to recognize the coordination that does exist. Within agencies, programs are developed that do suggest a coordinated and coherent strategy for achieving management goals. When the Bureau of Land Management develops a management plan for a given area of public land, it reflects the contributions from individuals representing various orientations and skills: recreationists, range management and minerals experts, perhaps even economists. The plan may not pass muster by some idealized standard of coordination and coherence, but it reflects a commonly accepted approach to the management of that piece of land within a given level of resources.

It is when one leaves this working level of coordination that one encounters its lack. What does one do about the excessive number of wild horses on a given range? Will the emissions from a power plant impair the scenic values of a national park? What are the reclamation requirements appropriate for land to be strip mined? All the issues involve the need for coordination, but they involve political conflicts that transcend the agencies' poor powers to do so.

Joseph Molnar and David Rogers make the argument that coordination essentially is a strategy that is based on objectives and on a careful assessment of the structures of power with which one is having to deal. Moreover, they point out that coordination has numerous faces: in one case it may be merely exhortation to communicate among hierarchically equal units; in another case a coordinating mechanism may be established with nominal authority to bring actors together on matters of common interest. They explore the conditions leading to the need for coordination, the strategies that may be followed in its achievement, and the costs that may be associated with either the effort or the achievement.

Perhaps the most important aspect of coordination is what it does to the structure of interests and their representation in a decision-making process. An illustration may be helpful. The Upper Mississippi River Basin Commission was established at the request of the governors of the five states in the region "to encourage the conservation, development and utilization of water and related land resources on a comprehensive and coordinated basis by the Federal Government, states, localities, and private enterprise with the cooperation of all affected federal agencies, states, local governments, individuals, corporations, business enterprises, and others concerned."[33] The Upper Mississippi traditionally had been the preserve of the Army Corps of Engineers because of its responsibility for inland waterways and the Federal Fish and Wildlife Service. The commission was designed to provide coordination, but this term can be read more realistically as greater access to and influence over the Corps of Engineers. The commission has no statutory authority to make decisions to which the federal agencies or the states must adhere, but it is fair to say that the structure of influence has been altered by this coordinative device. As river-basin commissions were about to go out of existence in 1981 because of lack of support from the Reagan administration, the basin states strove to find some mechanism equivalent to the commission to sustain the influence they have now achieved.[34]

A special case of coordination is the relationship between central governments and subunits of government, whether regional, state, or local. At least superficially, one expects the problems of coordination to be especially severe in federal systems, where the subunits have distinctive constitutional authority and where the people within those subunits may be described as distinctive political communities.[35] The divisions of policy authority, various sets of elected and appointed officials at the different levels of government, the unique value systems adhered to by publics defined by political boundaries, and the interest groups that find the legalisms and the various forums to their liking all make smooth coordination a difficult if not impossible condition to achieve. Americans are familiar with these conflicts, but such conflicts are also found in other federal systems such as in Canada. The provinces have demonstrated a strong penchant for having their own way with respect to the development and disposition of their natural resources.

In environmental policy, like public policy generally, it is probably nearer the truth to describe federal-state-local relationships in terms of cooperation rather than conflict. For decades the growth of federal responsibility has meant the development of cooperative relationships with the states in policy areas where they traditionally operated or the creation of incentives for the states to embark in a policy area that they traditionally have avoided. In the environmental area, federal involvement in air and water pollution stimulated action at the state and local levels in traditional areas of their responsibilities with respect to public health, but it also created incentives for the states to go beyond the public-health issue to issues of environmental quality. For decades, the Forest Service has been engaged in a cooperative program with state forestry agencies. The stimulation from the federal government through housing and water-quality legislation and through the Coastal Zone Management Act have stimulated activity in state and local planning beyond anything anyone could have imagined before those acts were passed.[36] Failure to produce general land-use legislation at the national level simply bespeaks a strong preference for state and local controls.[37] With respect to energy development and regulation, Joan Aron finds a major role for the states remaining, even with heavy federal involvement.[38]

The role the states play in the implementation of environmental legislation reflects both public sentiment and the stakes of interest groups in substantive decisions with respect to the treatment of the environment. States'-rights doctrines still have political appeal and can be relied on to rally political support by those who have more substantive matters in mind. Major actors, especially those who only reluctantly submit to environmental regulations, are usually confident they can persuade state officials regarding the justice of their causes. Even when the standards are prescribed by federal statute and regulation and when the implementation plan of each state must be approved by a federal agency such as the EPA with respect to air and water quality, there is enough latitude in the eyes of the interested parties to warrant state administration.

Richard Sylves argues that considerations of this sort were involved in the congressional decision to enact the Cleveland-Wright Amendment as part of the 1977 revision of the Clean Water Act of 1972. States, supported by the developmental interests, argued for a change in the relationship between EPA and state agencies with respect to grants for sewage-treatment-plant construction. The change nominally was to eliminate delays, duplication, and excessive numbers of reviews, but the real stake was the locus of decision making with respect to the disposition of the federal money. It was true that money would be spent faster but also in ways that might be less effective in environmental impacts. EPA would be denied authority to review individual plans and projects and would be restricted to certifying that the states had a program that met federal standards. Moreover, EPA would lose some of its leverage over states in getting them to comply with less attractive features of the Clean Water Act, namely, those that required compliance but brought no money. At this date there is little evidence regarding the impact of the Cleveland-Wright Amendment, but Sylves does provide suggestive hints that states have found advantages in the arrangements made pursuant to the amendment's enactment.

We assume, as indicated before, that the federal system enhances or exacerbates the natural conflicts that arise when national, regional, and local interests differently perceive goals and means. Yet it must be recognized that these strains exist in any polity larger than the city-states of Monaco and Luxembourg. State political structures may be unitary in character, but the society may be highly pluralistic, even to the extent of incipient nationalist expressions of separatism or at least special treatment. Thus, the implementation of nationally approved legislation requires the design of procedures, the coordination of priorities and schedules, and minimum agreement on the values that will be achieved through a given program.

England is usually classified as one of the prime examples of the unitary state. Yet Robert Eyestone clearly demonstrates that the structure of decision making there is hardly unitary. The Scottish Office, hardly comparable to a state in a federal system, has both formal powers and informal influence that are vital to the relationship between local planning authorities and the central government. Dislocations that are inherently possible in any rapid-development situation occurred and were resolved, to the extent they were satisfactorily, by a process of mutual communication and accommodation with the Scottish Office playing a critical role in the process. In environmental terms, providing a lesson for American energy planners, the process of negotiation with the intermediation of the Scottish Office provided more rational environmental solutions, that is, protection for scarce land resources, than the headlong pursuit of energy goals by national authorities.

Regulation versus Charges

Protection for and enhancement of the environment are achieved by a variety of approaches, depending in considerable part on the character of the resource or the amenity but also on public preferences regarding those approaches and the structure of the sector of the private economy with which one is dealing. Resources that are subject to individual capture and ownership may be treated differently from resources that are common property goods. The public, and important segments of that public, may be more comfortable with one approach because it fits its image of what government can and should do to those who despoil the environment. The approach to be used on a concentrated industry may be different than the approach to be used on a highly dispersed, competitive industry made up of many small units or the general public.

The range of options to achieve environmental protection and enhancement extends as far as the range of options for all public-policy purposes: from government ownership and management to completely voluntary activity on the part of private environmental managers. In between are joint public-private enterprises; regulation by government agencies according to publicly dictated standards; licensing and permits of various kinds, in some cases to use public resources and other cases to use private resources; economic incentives such as taxation, subsidies, and charges; and voluntary cooperation among private interests. Indeed, one can find examples of virtually all these forms of management with respect to the environment—government ownership and management of land and water resources but also private ownership as in those areas controlled by Nature Conservancy. Regulatory programs abound dealing with air, water, wastes, and pesticides. And some of these regulatory programs have adopted features of the economic-incentives approach through fines and charges for failure to adhere to standards imposed by a regulatory agency.

The question and form of public control are both analytical and empirical questions. There are those who argue that both empirically and analytically, government management of resources tends toward failure. John Baden and Rodney Fort cite examples of mismanagement of timber and public-land resources by the Forest Service and the Bureau of Land Management and argue that bureaucrats are "natural predators" who will inevitably make decisions contrary to the public interest.[39] Baden argues that wilderness is better protected when the land is in private hands. Others would dispute this, arguing from the evidence of history. They would content that public management may not be ideal but is clearly preferable to private management, with its preference for short-term economic gain. But not all private managers are the same; some find the Weyerhauser Company, the largest private owner of timber land in the United States, appropriately environmentally sensitive, or at least the "Best of the S.O.B.s."[40]

In large part, the question is one of incentives. Given an appropriate set of incentives, one may expect human beings both individually and aggregated into institutions to behave in reasonably predictable ways. At the most general level, they will function in ways to serve their self-interest, however that is defined. Business people will seek profits; bureaucrats will seek to maximize budgets and enlarge and improve programs; politicians will seek to increase their vote-getting power. The task of the institutional designer is to create institutional arrangements that will at least point those who influence the character of the environment in the right direction and to do so at least possible cost to society. In common-property-resource situations, the problem of incentives is clearly crucial: the individual has an incentive to exploit the resource to its fullest because there is no common agreement on appropriate levels of exploitation and fair shares. Similarly, polluters have an no incentive to reduce their effluent when there is no mechanism to impose the costs of their pollution borne by others on its producers. In a very real sense, bureaucrats are in a common-property situation with respect to the budget: it is a public domain from which they hope to extract the maximum advantage because they in no way pay the costs borne by others for doing so.

Barry Mitnick undertakes an assessment of the incentives structures that operate in environmental regulation, at first at an abstract level by exploring a range of institutional options, focusing chiefly on direct regulation and economic incentives. He then relates these options to regulatory target levels, including individuals, facilities and organizations, and entire regions. He notes also that incentive systems may perform differently with respect to top officials than with line officials, who are charged with the direct task of exacting the required behavior from regulated interests. Empirically testing these propositions about incentives, he investigates the perceptions of state mining inspectors. He finds a dual incentive system functioning, one in relation to the regulated interests and another in relation to a federal regulatory agency. The character of these relationships, he argues, is likely to sway the agency in terms of the policy position it adopts.[41]

One of the current intellectual and policy issues is the appropriateness of direct regulation as against charges of various kinds in the achievement of standards of environmental quality. Direct regulation has been the principal approach through the establishment of ambient standards and the imposition of direct controls or requirements for adoption of certain technologies to achieve those standards. Economists have argued strongly in favor of effluent charges as a more efficient and more effective means of achieving the environmental goals, especially with respect to air and water quality.[42] Although posed as virtual polar opposites, they in fact partake of some similar characteristics. Both involve the hierarchical imposition of pollution-control standards. These are fixed by statute and regulation. Both must satisfy standards of fairness, certainty, and procedural justice as enforced by the courts. Both require administration and monitoring, although their characteristics may be considerably different.

The advertised advantages of the charges approach over direct regulation are numerous: they permit flexibility in the response of those regulated rather than impose similar technological requirements on all firms; they elicit immediate compliance through the payment of the charges and thus avoid the delaying tactics used by recalcitrant subjects; they reduce the need for information that firms are unlikely to offer willingly if at all; they minimize the coercive aspects of most regulatory arrangements; finally, and perhaps most importantly, they hold out the possibility of reducing the costs of environmental regulation, both because of an expected deemphasis on standardized technology as the means of meeting environmental goals and because of the opportunity for firms imaginatively to tailor their response to the charges to their unique production situation.

Donald Cell undertakes an analysis of the problem of achieving reductions of noise in the aircraft industry, comparing the advantages of charges with the existing system of technology-based regulation. He finds significant advantages in economic efficiency and administrative effectiveness in the charges approach. He makes a persuasive case, but it is tempered with caution. The conditions that make the charges approach distinctly advantageous may be inherent in the industry itself: the character of the harmful emissions is standardized and relatively simple to measure; the social harm caused by noise can be measured (but not completely) in some fairly precise terms; there is an existing administrative structure to administer the charges; the costs are concentrated on people residing around the airport; the industry is relatively concentrated; and the character of the process that produces the emissions is reasonably standardized. Where such conditions do not prevail, he advises, a regulatory approach may be clearly advisable.

Despite the vaunted advantages, the charge approach has not met with much favor in the United States. The reasons for their limited success are probably mixed and numerous and include the following considerations: (1) Environmentalists often oppose charges because they consider them "licenses to pollute"; they tend to believe that polluters should not be able to "buy" their way out, not appreciating that the marginal-cost notion is explicitly part of the charges approach. (2) Polluters tend to prefer the regulatory approach because they can bargain and delay, achieving modifications in the requirements and through negotiation with the regulatory agency, Congress, or the courts or at least avoiding the costs of changes in their productive process as long as possible. (3) Familiarity with the regulatory approach on the part of both the regulators and the regulated is a factor: like most human beings, they are reluctant to embark on a relatively uncharted course. (4) Technical problems exist.[43]

Alfred Marcus examines the regulation-versus-charges issue from the standpoint of members of the major environmental regulatory agency of the federal government, the Environmental Protection Agency. He finds them generally hostile to charges, although he finds compatability in some areas. The agency members cite uncertainty, interference in the achievement of statutory goals, and successes under the regulatory arrangement. In addition, they found technical reasons for opposing the charges approach, opposition that has found an echo in the environmental-policy literature.

The technical problems are major in character and undoubtedly unsettle those who are searching for a more efficient way of meeting environmental goals. Marcus, in chapter 11, relies on responses from EPA officials and the literature to detail the reservations with respect to the charges approach. These reservations concern: (1) the enormously difficult problem of calculating the level of charges with reference to societal benefits; (2) the difficulties of proceeding by trial and error to set charges for 60,000 sources of pollution; (3) the assumptions that static efficiency can be achieved with uniform charges is unwarranted; (4) changes in technology and society are likely to lead to inefficiencies unless the charges are adjusted; (5) information costs and monitoring needs are likely to remain extremely high; (6) the scope of political bargaining may remain as important in the charges approach as in the regulatory approach; (7) delays associated with regulation will remain because of the requirements of due process of law; and (8) the charges approach might lead to significant changes in the character of some industries, giving some firms competitive advantages tending toward monopoly.

Lettie Wenner points out that we have very little empirical evidence regarding the charges approach, and she gives some detail concerning the use of charges at the state and local levels in the United States. She finds that administrators encountered serious problems of an economic and legal sort. She suggests operationalizing on a small scale the sale of pollution rights or the use of effluent charges to make direct comparisons with the regulatory approach. Clifford Russell suggests grafting the charges approach on to the regulatory approach, in effect creating a hybrid system in which charges would remain on any effluent remaining after the regulatory goals had been met.[44]

One of the most important areas of inquiry concerning the charges approach is the response of those regulated to the charges. It is commonly assumed that economic rationality will dominate the decisions made by the management of regulated firms. But economic rationality is a less than pellucid term in explaining precisely how managers might react to the imposition of specific charges. Nor does it explain how the consumers of the product of a given polluting firm might react to increases in the cost of that product, particularly if it changes in character in response to increased costs of some factor of production.

Jack Goldstone provides an abstract but nevertheless instructive catalogue of the possible options for the manager as well as for the ultimate consumer. He finds several options available to the managers—passing the charges on to the consumer, absorbing them, or investing in pollution controls—and then traces the potential consequences of these options for the market structure and for the responses of consumer and the market distributional system. He concludes by observing that a market structure and such distributional and consumer responses must receive preliminary attention in the design of any charges system if they are to achieve their environmental and societal goals. Such analysis would obviously play an important part in any carefully designed experiment to test the validity of the claims for the charges approach.

Growth Controls and Their Consequences

The final section of the book deals with local growth controls and their consequences. The logic of their location in this book may seem strained, inasmuch as two of the chapters deal with the factors that influence policy formation and only the third deals with policy consequences. Nevertheless, it seemed preferable to group the three chapters dealing with growth in a single place, particularly since all three articles draw to a varying extent on experience in California, where growth controls have been implemented for a considerable period of time.

Local growth control is considered either a logical extension of the right of local communities to determine their own character and quality of life or a device to protect the stakes of those who were fortunate enough to locate early in desirable communities and subsequently want to deny those benefits to others. To some it is a legitimate exercise of the police power; to others it is virtually an unconstitutional intrusion on the right of individuals to move about and locate where their preference dictate. To some it is an environmental boon; to others, it is a "hustle."[45]

Growth controls are largely the instruments of incorporated cities that seek to avoid the environmental consequences that accompany growth that is itself largely a regional phenomenon. City councils pass ordinances that constrain population or housing densities, rates of new-residence construction, additional utility hookups or location of industrial or commercial facilities, as means of exempting the city and its population from the economic and demographic forces at work in an area. It is clearly local planning, but it is equally clearly a response to the almost universal lack of regional planning. Regional-planning instruments hardly exist in the United States, and local communities can hardly rely on such planning to protect their environment. And, if effective regional planning did exist, there is nothing to guarantee that a given community might not be assigned a role in the region that was wholly unacceptable to any given community.

Growth controls, nominally available to every community, are practical instruments only for certain classes of communities. Central cities, for example, can hardly engage in growth control inasmuch as they for the most part are losing population and economic activity, and their housing stock is deteriorating. Central cities must behave as supplicants, willing to accept schemes that generate jobs and housing despite their implications for environmental amenities. Ironically, environmental laws and regulations may impose some growth controls on central cities in that they proscribe additions to the effluent already entering their atmosphere. Thus, EPA has endeavored, admittedly with a signal lack of success, to impose restrictions on downtown parking, a move, if it were successful, that might further dampen enthusiasm on the part of both businesses and employees to enter the central city.

One might also expect a bias toward the use of growth controls among communities with middle- to upper-class populations because of the political skills required to undertake the political movement that leads to their successful imposition. Clearly, these groups have something at stake: property values, amenities, life-styles, small-town atmosphere. But to defend those stakes requires the assertiveness, the confidence, the experience, and the techniques of political mobilization that are far more likely to be found among the more affluent members of society.

What, then, are the correlates of growth-control communities? David Dowall provides an analysis of these relationships using cluster analysis to classify 228 communities that have undertaken growth controls. He concludes, not unexpectedly, that the growth-control communities strongly tend to be faster growing, whiter, wealthier, and of higher social status than the national average. Given these correlations, one assumes that the citizens are attempting to deal with the effects of growth: economic and fiscal, environmental and social.

As Dowall points out, however, this analysis is based only on correlations and not on detailed case-study investigations of what citizens actually want when they press for or approve growth-management plans. Robert Johnston provides some insight into this aspect of the problem. Contrary to the charges of some, particularly from the inner city, growth controls are not, in California at least, the result of efforts toward social-class exclusion (even though this may be the result). They are the result of several factors: the desire to maintain environmental quality, especially the environment of a small town; the desire to preserve agriculture as an important element in the local economy—a desire not unrelated to the environmental quality goal; and resistance to the increased costs of government that are attributed to growth.

Johnston makes the point, however, that one cannot only look at the original motivations of those supporting growth controls but that one must also look at the motivations of those who reside in the community once the controls have been imposed. Their self-interest in higher home values (their own) that are often the result of rationing of new-housing starts may dictate that they oppose any effort to relieve housing shortages by relaxation of growth control or measures that mitigate the housing shortage.

But motivations for and correlations of population characteristics with growth controls are only one side of the coin; the other side is the consequences, intended and unintended. If the studies of motivation are correct, what happens to housing prices is an important unintended consequence. As Seymour Schwartz demonstrates, there are important equity implications of these consequences, that is, differential impacts on various classes of citizens. Those entering the housing market for the first time, minorities, renters, and those owning land that cannot be developed, are all immediate losers. Over the longer haul, the equity effects are in the direction of a redistribution of wealth upward, with lessened social mobility and life opportunities for those who are unable to buy homes and rear their children in the kind of environment an individual home provides.

Both Dowall and Schwartz are concerned about the consequences, the political repercussions that might result, and the policy options available for dealing with them. Dowall notes, for example, that various control strategies or motivations may have different consequences or be subject to different policy solutions. If the members of the community are concerned principally about fiscal problems, then state action to relieve them of excessive property-tax burdens may be particularly effective in lessening their concern about growth. One can be certain that groups disadvantaged by growth-control policies will make efforts to reduce those impacts, and communities may feel an obligation and recognize a necessity to provide meliorative policies such as affordable housing, higher densities for some areas and lower for others, or direct subsidies.

The widespread movement toward growth controls, whatever their motivation and specific character, unquestionably creates inequities for specific groups and for specific communities. These inequities are likely to invite intervention by the state in land-use planning that will provide a more rational and equitable allocation of benefits and costs in a region. Despite the attraction of such high-sounding planning efforts, one must at least question whether such land-use efforts are likely to bear beneficial fruit or only more thorns and thistles. The forces of the market are so powerful, the preferences of the public are so strong, and the investments in the existing resources and infrastructure so massive that one must wonder about the viability of laws and regulations as means of controlling regional land use. Unless laws and regulations are stringent and backed by greater resources and public support, they are likely to be as successful as King Canute holding back the tide.

Notes

1. David Easton, *A Framework for Political Analysis* (Englewood Cliffs, N.J.: Prentice-Hall, 1965), and David Easton, *The Political System* (New York: Alfred A. Knopf, 1953).

2. Aaron Wildavsky, *Speaking Truth to Power: The Art and Craft of Policy Analysis* (Boston, Toronto: Little, Brown, 1979).

3. Paul Sabatier and Daniel Mazmanian, "The Implementation of Public Policy: A Framework of Analysis," *Policy Studies Journal* 8, Special Issue No. 2 (1980):538–560.

4. U.S., Comptroller General, *EPA Is Slow to Carry Out Its Responsibilities to Control Harmful Chemicals,* General Accounting Office, CED 81-1, 28 October 1980, p. i.

5. Paul Berman, "Thinking about Programmed and Adaptive Implementation: Matching Strategies to Situations," in *Why Policies Succeed and Fail,* ed. Helen M. Ingram and Dean E. Mann (Beverly Hills, Calif.: Sage Publications, 1980), pp. 205–227.

6. Charles T. Clotfelter and John C. Hahn, "Assessment of the National 55 M.P.H. Speed Limit," in *The Practice of Policy Evaluation,* ed. David Nachmias (New York: St. Martin's Press, 1980), pp. 396–411.

7. Paul Sabatier and Daniel Mazmanian, "The Conditions of Effective Implementation: A Guide to Accomplishing Policy Objectives," *Policy Analysis* (Fall 1979):481–504; George C. Edwards, III, *Implementing Public Policy* (Washington, D.C.: Congressional Quarterly, Inc. 1980).

8. Wildavsky, *Speaking Truth to Power,* p. 38.

9. Helen M. Ingram and Dean E. Mann, "Environmental Policy: From Innovation to Implementation," in *Public Policies in America,* ed. Theodore J. Lowi and Alan Stone (Beverly Hills, Calif.: Sage Publications, 1979), pp. 131–162.

10. Lettie McSpadden Wenner, "Pollution Control; Implementation Alternatives," *Policy Analysis* 4 (Winter 1978):47–66.

11. Helen M. Ingram and Dean E. Mann, "Policy Failure: An Issue Deserving Analysis," in *Why Policies Succeed or Fail,* ed. Ingram and Mann, pp. 11–32.

12. John A. Haigh and John V. Krutilla, "Clarifying Policy Directives: The Case of National Forest Management," *Policy Analysis* 6 (Fall 1980):409–439.

13. Jeffrey L. Pressman and Aaron B. Wildavsky, *Implementation* (Berkeley, Los Angeles, London: University of California Press, 1973).

14. National Academy of Sciences, *Energy in Transition 1985–2020,* Final Report of the Committee on Nuclear Energy and Alternate Energy Systems, National Research Council (San Francisco: W.H. Freeman, 1980), pp. 53–55, 60–61.

15. Giandomenico Majone, "Choice among Policy Instruments for Pollution Control," *Policy Analysis* 4, no. 2 (Fall 1976):589–614; Clifford S. Russell, "What Can We Get from Effluent Charges?" *Policy Analysis* 5 (Spring 1979): 155–180.

16. Environmental Protection Agency, *Environmental Outlook,* 1980, Office of Research and Development (Washington, D.C., 1980).

17. Dean E. Mann and A. Theodore Anagnoson, "Federal Reorganization: Does It Matter? A Retrospective Look," in *Reorganization* (Durham, N.C.: Duke University, 1979); Douglas M. Fox, "The President's Proposals for Executive Reorganization: A Critique," *Public Administration Review* 33 (September 1973):401–406.

18. Alfred A. Marcus, *Promise and Performance: Choosing and Implementing Environmental Policy* (Westport, Conn.: Greenwood Press, 1980).

19. Helen M. Ingram and Scott Ullery, "Policy Innovation and Institutional Fragmentation," *Policy Studies Journal* 8 (Spring 1980):664–682.

20. Roland N. McKean, "Enforcement Costs in Environmental and Safety Regulation," *Policy Analysis* 6 (Summer 1980):269–289.

21. Daniel A. Mazmanian and Jeanne Nienaber, *Can Organizations Change?: Environmental Protection, Citizen Participation, and the Corps of Engineers* (Washington, D.C.: Brookings Institution, 1979).

22. A. Myrick Freeman, III, Robert H. Haveman, and Allen V. Kneese, *The Economics of Environmental Policy* (New York: John Wiley, 1973).

23. Edward Partridge, ed., *Responsibilities to Future Generations: Environmental Ethics* (Buffalo, N.Y.: Prometheius Books, 1981).

24. Anthony C. Fisher and John V. Krutilla, "Valuing Long Run Ecological Consequences and Irreversibilities," *Journal of Environmental Economics and Management* 1 (1974):96–108.

25. J.E. Stiglitz, "A Neoclassical Analysis of the Economics of Natural Resources," in *Scarcity and Growth Reconsidered,* ed. V. Kerry Smith (Baltimore: Johns Hopkins University Press, 1979), pp. 36–66.

26. Herman E. Daley, "Entropy, Growth and Political Economicy of Security," in *Scarcity and Growth Reconsidered,* ed. V. Kerry Smith (Baltimore: Johns Hopkins University Press, 1979), pp. 67–94.

27. Anthony C. Fisher and Frederick M. Peterson, "The Environment in Economics: A Survey," *The Journal of Economic Literature* 14 (March 1976): 1–33.

28. John Baden and Richard Stroup, "Externality, Property Rights and the Management of Our National Forests," *The Journal of Law and Economics* 16 (1973):303-312.

29. Theodore J. Lowi, *The End of Liberalism,* 2nd ed. (New York: W.W. Norton, 1979); Grant McConnell, *Private Power and American Democracy* (New York: Alfred A. Knopf, 1966).

30. David Calleo and Benjamin Rowland, *America and the World Political Economy* (Bloomington Indiana University Press, 1973), p. 191.

31. Wolfram F. Hanrieder, "Compatibility and Consensus: A Proposal for the Conceptual Linkage of External and Internal Dimension of Foreign Policy," *American Political Science Review* 61 (December 1967):972-982; Harold Sprout and Margaret Sprout, *Toward a Politics of the Planet Earth* (New York: Van Nostrand Reinhold, 1971).

32. Haruhiro Fukui, "Does Japan Have a National Ocean Policy?" December 1980 (mimeo).

33. Water Resources Planning Act, P.L. 89-80, 1965, 79 Stat. 245, 42 USCA 1962a (1971 Supp.).

34. Upper Mississippi River Basin Commission, *Preliminary Comprehensive Master Plan for the Management of the Upper Mississippi River System,* Minneapolis, 1 January 1981.

35. Daniel J. Elazar, *American Federalism: A View from the States,* 2d ed. (New York: Thomas Y. Crowell, 1972).

36. Zigurds L. Zile, "A Legislative-Political History of the Coastal Zone Management Act of 1972," *Coastal Zone Management Journal* 1 (1974):33.

37. Martin R. Healy, "National Land Use Proposal: Land Use Legislation of Landmark Environmental Significance," *Environmental Affairs* 3 (1974):355-396.

38. Joan B. Aron, "Intergovernmental Politics of Energy," *Policy Analysis* 5 (Fall 1979):451-471.

39. John Baden and Rodney D. Fort, "National Resources and Bureaucratic Predators," *Policy Review* 11 (Winter 1980):69-82.

40. Robert Cahn, *Footprints on the Planet* (New York: Universe Books, 1978), pp. 97-107.

41. Barry M. Mitnick, *The Political Economy of Regulation: Creating, Designing and Removing Regulatory Forms* (New York: Columbia University Press, 1980).

42. Allen V. Kneese and Charles L. Schultze, *Pollution, Prices and Public Policy* (Washington, D.C.: Brookings Institution, 1975).

43. Frederick R. Anderson et al., *Environmental Improvement through Economic Incentives* (Baltimore and London: Johns Hopkins University Press, 1977).

44. Wenner, "Pollution Control; Implementation Alternatives"; Russell, "What Can We Get"; Majone, "Choice among Policy Instruments."

45. Bernard J. Frieden, *The Environmental Protection Hustle* (Cambridge, Mass.: M.I.T. Press, 1979).

2

Confronting Complexity and Uncertainty: Implementation of Hazardous-Waste-Management Policy

Sam A. Carnes

The circle of environmental-protection policy that began with clean-air and clean-water legislation in the 1960s was closed in 1976 with the passage of the Resource Conservation and Recovery Act (P.L. 94-580). In subtitle C of that act Congress and the president declared that human health and the environment would be protected against future threats from improperly managed hazardous wastes. The Environmental Protection Agency (EPA) was given principal responsibility for promulgating regulations to guide the implementation of the Resource Conservation and Recovery Act (RCRA), and the states were expected to implement the law. Congress specified that the EPA's final regulations were to be promulgated by April 1978 and that they were to become effective by October of that same year.

Almost four years after RCRA's passage and two years after the congressionally mandated deadline for regulations, the law has yet to be implemented. Proposed regulations, interim final regulations, and some "final final" regulations have been issued by the EPA, but in no way can one characterize the implementation of RCRA as anywhere near complete. In fact, the Council on Environmental Quality (CEQ) now estimates that five to ten years will elapse before the law is fully implemented.[1]

Why is the EPA so late in performing its assigned tasks? What have the states been doing while waiting for federal regulations to be emplaced? Once the full set of federal regulations is in place, will the states be able to fulfill the requirements for EPA authorization and implement and enforce their hazardous-waste-management programs?

The Perils of Rulemaking

The difficulties and delays that have characterized hazardous-waste-management rulemaking, the first stage of RCRA's subtitle-C implementation, are a consequence of factors both within and beyond the control of the EPA. On one hand, it is quite clear that EPA's rulemaking strategy was to develop legally

defensible regulations through extensive consultation with diverse interests, even
if that strategy resulted in missing Congress's deadlines.[2] On the other hand,
EPA could only react to a wide variety of external events, decisions, and reali-
ties (which will be described later) that confounded and complicated rulemaking
and implementation.

Paul Sabatier and Daniel Mazmanian have recently proposed an analytical
framework for investigating the policy-implementation process. This framework
identifies three major factors—and numerous constituent variables—that affect
the success or failure of implementation: the tractability of the policy problem,
the ability of the statute to structure implementation; and a number of nonstatutory contextual variables.[3] Although each of these factors and many of
their component variables have been in evidence in the case of hazardous-waste-
management rulemaking by the EPA, this chapter describes in detail only a few
of the more dominant factors that have confounded the rulemaking process.
The argument is made that subsequent implementation of hazardous-waste-
management policy by the states will continue to be problematic. Continuing
uncertainty and debate on definitions of hazardous waste, new policy initiatives,
a complex and convoluted regulatory system, and inadequate fiscal and personnel resources will likely hinder efforts by the states to protect human health
and the environment from the dangers of hazardous wastes.

Statutory Provisions for Implementation

The RCRA is a complex law with eight subtitles and over fifty sections. Although it deals extensively with solid-waste management, research, and resource
and energy recovery from wastes, national attention has focused on its provisions for hazardous-waste management (subtitle C). Protection of human health
and the environment was to be achieved in RCRA through the promulgation of
"cradle-to-grave" regulations of hazardous-waste activities by the EPA (sections
3001–3005) with subsequent implementation and enforcement by the states
through EPA-authorized state hazardous-waste-management programs (section
3006). If states chose not to participate in RCRA's implementation, the EPA
was to assume responsibility for its implementation and enforcement. To accomplish these objectives, the act laid out a compliance calendar to be met by the
EPA and other agencies during implementation.

To qualify for EPA authorization, states were expected to engage in a number of initial and ongoing activities. Initially, a state must, through its governor,
designate a state implementation agency (for example, state EPA, pollution-
control agency, or so on) that, with full public participation, would designate
administrative areas and prepare a state implementation plan. The state legislature must pass hazardous-waste-management legislation that is "equivalent to"
and "consistent with" RCRA, and the state's implementing agency must promulgate guidelines, standards, and regulations at least as stringent as those of the
federal EPA.

The state legislature and implementing agency must also make initial budgetary decisions. Financial assistance for developing and implementing hazardous-waste programs was made available to the states with a grant format, with an initial authorization in RCRA of $25 million for each of the fiscal years 1978 and 1979 (section 3011). These funds were to be distributed to the states on the basis of regulations to be promulgated by the EPA, which were to take into account the level of hazardous-waste activity and the extent of exposure of human beings.

The state's ongoing activities include constant coordination with an intergovernmental budgetary process, with the RCRA compliance calendar and any calendar established within a state plan, with regional EPA activities, and with officials of state-designated areas. Once these administrative activities are established, states must inventory and monitor hazardous-waste-management practices and facilities and enforce the law.

Other measures of RCRA that are relevant include sections dealing with the law's integration with other environmental-protection statutes, citizen suits, imminent hazards, and public participation. Section 1006(b) provides that the administration and enforcement of RCRA must be integrated with appropriate provisions of the Clean Air Act, the Clean Water Act, and the Safe Drinking Water Act, among others, and EPA was to avoid duplication of the regulatory programs of the various environmental-protection programs. Section 7002 provides for citizen suits against any person for violation of any permit, standard, regulation, or other order pursuant to RCRA or against the EPA for failure to perform any nondiscretionary act or duty. Section 7003 authorizes the EPA to bring suit to immediately restrain any waste activity that presents imminent and substantial endangerment to health or the environment. Finally, section 7004 requires the EPA and the states to provide, encourage, and assist public participation in the development, revision, implementation, and enforcement of any regulation, guideline, or program pertaining to the statute.

Rulemaking Complexity and Uncertainty

Worobee has noted that EPA's hazardous-waste regulations are the most complex and voluminous ever promulgated by the federal government.[4] They have been proposed, reproposed, reorganized, and promulgated in bits and pieces between February 1978 and May 1980, and EPA has not yet finished. EPA's rulemaking strategy was based on the development of consensus among diverse interest groups through public participation and careful and comprehensive internal deliberations prior to the promulgation of final regulations. One of the results of this strategy has been a failure to comply with Congress's strict compliance calendar (table 2-1).

Rulemaking has been complicated by a variety of factors.[5] The most significant of these include: protracted lobbying and public participation; the intervention of events related to hazardous wastes (for example, discovery of the

Table 2–1
Rulemaking Schedule for RCRA, Subtitle C (Hazardous Wastes)

Section/Title	Statutory Deadline for Promulgation	Actually Proposed	Actually Promulgated	Anticipated Promulgation
3001: Identification and Listing of Hazardous Waste	April 1978	December 1978 August 1979	May 1980[a]	Fall 1980[b]
3002: Standards Applicable to Generators of Hazardous Waste	April 1978	December 1978	February 1980	
3003: Standards Applicable to Transporters of Hazardous Waste	April 1978	April 1978	February 1980 May 1980	
3004: Standards Applicable to Owners and Operators of Hazardous Waste Treatment, Storage and Disposal Facilities	April 1978	December 1978	May 1980[c]	
3004(b): Financial Requirements	April 1978	December 1978 May 1980		Uncertain
3005: Permits for Treatment, Storage, and Disposal of Hazardous Waste	April 1978 July 1978	June 1979	May 1980	
3006: Guidelines for Authorized State Hazardous Waste Management Programs	April 1978 July 1978 October 1978	February 1978 June 1979	May 1980	
3010: Preliminary Notification of Hazardous Waste Activity	July 1978	July 1978	February 1980	

[a]Final rule, interim final rule, and proposed rule

[b]On integration of regulation of polychlorinated biphenyls under RCRA and the Toxic Substance Control Act, on wages that are used, reused, reclaimed, or recovered, and a number of the listed wastes from the proposed regulation

[c]Final rule and interim final rule

abandoned-waste site at Love Canal) and the attendant impacts on public opinion and the rulemaking agenda; legislative oversight and executive redirection; and technical/scientific and other dimensions of uncertainty (for instances questions like: what is hazardous?).

Lobbying and Public Participation

Public participation can be an effective tool in developing support during the implementation process, but it also can be strategically costly.[6] In the case of subtitle-C rulemaking, an argument can be made that rather than leading to a consensually derived and legitimated regulatory system, public participation, as manifested by intense lobbying on technical/scientific and institutional issues, may have led to increased polarization and extended political conflict.

EPA proposed regulations for sections 3001, 3002, and 3004 in December 1978. The agency held five public hearings, heard testimony from several hundred persons, and received over one thousand sets of comments on its proposed regulations. The response was so great that additional public hearings were sponsored, and the comment period on the proposed rules was extended by two months. These protractions added substantially to the input EPA had to consider in its continuing rulemaking.

The numerous comments that EPA received during its rulemaking were incisive and critical and were indicative of serious lobbying by various affected interests. Comments from environmental groups on the various renditions of RCRA rules ranged from negative to neutral. Their chief concerns have been: (1) the tardiness of rulemaking and the adverse health and environmental impacts that such tardiness allowed to continue; (2) EPA's inclination to delay regulation of some hazardous wastes (that is, carcinogenic, teratogenic, mutagenic, and phytotoxic substances); and (3) the exemption from regulation by EPA of hazardous-waste generators and disposers that generate or dispose of relatively small quantities of hazardous wastes (now set at less than 1,000 kilograms per month).

The affected industries, particularly the chemical industry through the Chemical Manufacturers Association, the Soap and Detergent Association, and others, lobbied strenuously in Congress, as well as within the EPA, to effect the development of regulations that would be compatible with their interests. Specifically, they argued that: (1) rulemaking delay was necessary and proper, given the need for additional research; (2) regulations should reflect actual management conditions rather than a worst-case scenario; and (3) strict regulation would disproportionately harm small companies and stifle innovation. The waste-management industry's trade association, the National Solid Waste Management Association, lobbied in favor of a "degree-of-hazard" approach comparable to the one employed by California and argued that such an approach would allow for an exemption on the basis of quantity of hazardous waste generated or disposed without jeopardizing public health and the environment.

Federal agencies lobbied for their particular interests as well. For example, the Department of Energy requested in its comments on the December 1978 proposed rules that EPA add the waste from coal-conversion processes, industrial coal-burning facilities, and urban-waste energy systems to EPA's "special-waste" category, which already included coal-fired utility wastes and oil-drilling muds and brines, among others.[7] Other government groups, such as the National Conference of State Legislatures, the National Association of Counties, and the National Governors Conference, lobbied heavily in the formulation of RCRA as well as during EPA's rulemaking and were especially concerned about the potential roles and responsibilities of their respective jurisdictions. They have been and will continue to be active during congressional deliberations on proposed hazardous-waste-disposal–facility-siting legislation, since questions of federal and/or state preemption of state and/or local decisions are being considered seriously.

Intervention of Related Events

In August 1978 the New York Department of Health officially characterized the Love Canal area of Niagara Falls as "a grave and imminent peril" to the health of nearby residents, and President Carter declared Love Canel a disaster area eligible for federal disaster relief.[8] Shortly thereafter, other horror stories of abandoned and inactive hazardous-waste dumps and the adverse health effects associated with them were discovered and documented in Massachusetts, Maine, Louisiana, Kentucky, Michigan, and Tennessee. The media presented these and other stories (including the Three Mile Island accident) almost on a daily basis at times, to a public that was feeling increasingly besieged by tales of gloom, doom, and disaster. CBS ran a segment on hazardous wastes on *60 Minutes,* and ABC broadcast *The Killing Ground,* a news documentary on hazardous wastes and their detrimental health effects.

In contrast to the almost contemplative atmosphere in which RCRA was passed and during which EPA conducted its first two years of rulemaking, the after-Love-Canal period was characterized by frantic, almost frenetic, concern and activity. Congressional hearings were held, lawsuits were filed, reports were issued, and, in general, EPA was publicly indicted for its failure to anticipate and deal with the nation's newest environmental tragedy. Charges and counter-charges were filed within EPA as well as from outside, the agency was reorganized, proposed rules were issued in December 1978, and the public was still not satisfied.

Unfortunately, with the exception of section 7003—a relatively weak imminent-hazard enforcement provision—RCRA did not authorize the EPA to do anything at all about inactive and abandoned dumpsites. Congress had only empowered EPA to regulate future wastes through RCRA. Only in 1979 did Congress begin to consider liability and compensation legislation ("superfund") to finance the reclamation of past hazardous-waste abuses.[9] These measures have emerged from the multiple jurisdictions of congressional committees and their client interest groups, with the passage of the comprehensive Environmental Response, Compensation, and Liability Act in 1980 (P.L. 96–510).

Legislative Oversight and Executive Redirection

Sabatier and Mazmanian have noted that successful implementation depends on the continued support for statutory objectives from "sovereigns" of implementing agencies (for example, relevant legislative committees, the chief executive, and the courts) and that this support can come through oversight and changes in the agency's fiscal and legal resources. In the case of RCRA, the effects of legislative oversight and executive redirection on subtitle-C implementation have been mixed.

The conditions at Love Canal that intervened directly in EPA's rulemaking intervened indirectly through congressional oversight. It is likely that, since 1978, Administrator Costle and his deputies and their staffs have spent more time on Capital Hill testifying on Love Canal, EPA's hazardous-waste activities, RCRA regulations, and the lack of regulations, than on any other EPA mission. The Subcommittee on Oversight and Investigations of the House Committee on Interstate and Foreign Commerce held formal oversight hearings in 1977, 1978, and 1979. In 1980 congressional concerns with hazardous waste centered around the cleanup of and compensation for exposure to abandoned and inactive hazardous-waste-disposal facilities and the siting of future facilities.

Since the Love Canal announcement, the subcommittee's hearings on RCRA have dealt almost entirely with subtitle C. After compiling almost 2,000 pages of testimony during its 1979 hearings, the subcommittee criticized EPA, hazardous-waste generators, transporters, and disposers, and Congress itself.[10] It accused industry of carelessness to the point of occasional criminal negligence and blamed Congress for failing to provide EPA with additional legislative authority and appropriations. EPA was criticized for its failures to meet the statutory deadlines for its hazardous-waste regulations and to determine the location of all hazardous-waste sites, its laxity in enforcement actions, and the inadequacy of its listing and identification of hazardous wastes pursuant to section 3001. Members of the subcommittee also took this opportunity to identify and to inquire into the status of hazardous-waste dumpsites in their own districts.

Oversight was not limited to the legislative branch. Soon after RCRA's passage, the Office of Management and Budget (OMB) intervened in EPA's implementation of the act. In 1977, the OMB instructed EPA to integrate and consolidate the grant programs among its various substantive areas (that is, air, water, and land), which led to delay in implementation.[11] By far the most significant executive redirection of RCRA rulemaking occurred when EPA, on the basis of Congress's mandate in section 1006(b) to integrate RCRA with other environmental-protection statutes and a recommendation of the Regulatory Agency Review Group, decided to consolidate its permit programs under RCRA, the Clean Water Act, the Clear Air Act, and the Safe Drinking Water Act.[12] The overall objective of this decision—coordination and consolidation of permitting— was laudatory, but one of the consequences, at least in the short term, has been increased complexity and confusion for states and the regulated community in understanding and eventually complying with the law.

In addition to complexity and confusion created simply by reorganizing the structures of regulations pertaining to sections 3005 (Permits) and 3006 (State Guidelines), EPA compounded the complexity in its final regulation on section 3006 by creating a second phase of interim authorization of state hazardous-waste programs by the EPA. Initial proposed regulations related to section 3006 (February 1978) indicated that a state hazardous-waste program could receive partial, interim, or full authorization from the EPA. EPA deleted the partial authorization possibility in its June 1979 proposed regulations. EPA justified the creation of a second phase of interim authorization in its May 1980 rule-making on the grounds that the rest of the RCRA regulatory system was being phased in at separate times (table 2-1) and that EPA wanted the states to be able to begin their incorporation into the federal system and their assumption of formal RCRA responsibilities as early as possible.[13]

The extent to which state programs should be required to be substantive and procedural duplicates of the federal program before EPA grants its authorization has been operationally distinguished by the EPA for interim and final authorization. EPA has decided that the goal of nationally consistent state programs is essential for final authorization but that such a goal is unrealistic for interim authorization.[14] To this end, EPA has defined "substantial equivalance" in language that is equally vague: "to a large degree, or in the main, equal in effect," where *effect* refers to both protecting health and the environment and establishing requirements to be imposed on regulated industries and other affected interests. To achieve a nationally consistent program, EPA will not approve for final authorization any state program that includes a ban on interstate transportation of hazardous wastes, a prohibition of hazardous-waste treatment, storage, or disposal, or does not guarantee a sufficiently complete manifest system for tracing the movement of hazardous wastes.

The consolidation of permitting and state program requirements under RCRA, the Clean Water Act, the Clean Air Act, and the Safe Drinking Water Act follows a trend of one-stop licensing already well established in several states. Ultimately, it should reduce the reporting burden on the related community and, more importantly, allow EPA and state implementing agencies to consider at one time the total environmental impact of a proposed facility in all the environmental media.

Uncertainty

Rulemaking under RCRA was also complicated by substantial uncertainty on technical/scientific and other issues. As mentioned earlier, wastes that are hazardous due to their carcinogenic, teratogenic, mutagenic, or phytotoxic characteristics have proved particularly troublesome. As the regulations now stand, the public will be protected from these risks to the extent that particular wastes are specifically identified and listed by the EPA; tests for these characteristics have yet to be established with any consensus from the scientific community, and, thus, wastes that may be hazardous according to these characteristics but that are not listed are exempt from regulation. EPA's attempt to document chromosomal damage to residents of Love Canal has generated considerable debate among scientists and policymakers because of the methodological difficulties encountered in the study and the limits of scientific and technical validity of epidemiological studies per se in tort litigation.[15] Technical and scientific uncertainty also exists with respect to leachate migration, the effects of intermixing different kinds of hazardous wastes, and testing protocols for hazardous determinations, among others.[16]

The questions of what is hazardous and what is risk have traditionally been confined to epidemiology, health physics, economics, and product engineering among other technical disciplines. The debate between J.P. Holdren and Herbert Inhaber on the risks associated with alternative-energy-supply systems typifies the conventional approach to risk analysis.[17] Questions regarding voluntary versus involuntary risks, the cost and risk of a riskfree society, and multiple perspectives and perceptions of risk, which are now beginning to be addressed, did not enter substantially into RCRA rulemaking.[18]

Even though EPA and its contractors performed an economic analysis of the benefits and costs of implementing and complying with RCRA, its utility is marginal.[19] How the costs will vary with alternative definitions of hazardous was not seriously addressed. An additional uncertainty not incorporated into EPA's analysis and rulemaking relates to the different kinds of costs that should be included in the benefit-cost analysis. Although EPA did estimate the technical and, to some extent, the administrative costs of implementation and compliance, there was no attempt to take into account possible social and political costs of implementation and compliance, such as those that might be incurred during the siting and /or permitting process to ensure initial and ongoing local-community approval of hosting a hazardous-waste-disposal facility.[20]

Ethical, political, and legal uncertainties are also abundant and were not, for the most part, formally made a part of the rulemaking process. Determining an equitable distribution of benefits and risks associated with the production, at specific sites, of goods for nationwide consumption and benefit is an important consideration. When the distribution of hazardous-waste-generating activities is skewed, as in the United States with twenty states hosting 90 percent of all hazardous waste generated, the siting policies of states and the federal government need to address equity questions explicitly.[21] This is particularly true for hazardous wastes that do not decompose or decay and that, therefore, permanently affect the host area and its present and future operations.

Questions related to the siting of hazardous-waste-disposal facilities also illustrate political and legal uncertainties in RCRA and pending legislation: who decides, under what authority and with what finality, whether a facility will be sited in a particular area? In the event of damage once a facility is in operation, and once the cause of damage is established, who is liable for compensation? As originally passed, RCRA left open the possibility that hazardous-waste activities could be subject to EPA's regulations and to any regulations of states and local jurisdictions more stringent than their federal counterpart.[22] In the most recent rulemaking EPA has noted that this stipulation will remain in effect unless a state program or local regulation interferes with the consistency of RCRA's intended hazardous-waste-management objectives. For instance, in its quest for national consistency, EPA will not authorize a state program that prohibits interstate movement of hazardous waste or the treatment, storage, or disposal of such wastes, and, by implication, any state program allows its municipalities to interfere with such activities. This appears to weaken the powers of state and local governments as originally stated in RCRA. The question of liability is currently in litigation in the Love Canal comparable situations.

State Implementation of RCRA, Subtitle C, 1976–1980

Although many states have been frustrated by the complexity, uncertainty, and delay in EPA's rulemaking, they have not been idle. The responsible implementing agencies have been identified in every state, and most states have implemented public-participation programs and have held public hearings and meetings throughout their jurisdictions.

With respect to the other state activities that RCRA mandates, however, substantial variation exists among the states. Some states adopted a wait-and-see attitude regarding ultimate EPA regulations, others proceeded to enforce their existing hazardous-waste-management programs or passed new legislation, promulgated accompanying rules, and enforced their new laws and regulations (table 2-2). Significantly, six of the ten states generating the greatest quantities of hazardous wastes deferred initial and/or additional rulemaking on hazardous-waste management until after EPA promulgated its regulation.[23]

Not all states that have had long-standing waste-management authority and programs (for example, Texas, California, Pennsylvania, and New Jersey) have regulatory systems adequate to RCRA's charge. For instance, as of 1979 New Jersey's system did not provide for long-term care of hazardous-waste sites,

Table 2-2
Status of Hazardous-Waste Management in States Generating Greatest Quantities of Hazardous Wastes

	Estimated Wastes Generated in 1980 [a]	Hazardous-Waste Legislation prior to RCRA [b]	Hazardous-Waste Legislation Adopted 1977-1979	Legislation Pending [c]	State Legislative Impediment to Promulgating Hazardous-Waste Regulations	Awaiting EPA Regulations
New Jersey	4640	1974				
Ohio	3840		X	X	X[d]	
Illinois	3840	1975	X	X		
California	3760	1972	X	X		
Pennsylvania	3710	1974				X
Texas	3850	1969	X			X
New York	3500		X	X	X[e]	
Michigan	2640	1973	X			
Tennessee	2480		X			X
Indiana	2020	1975		X		X

Sources: U.S. Comptroller General, General Accounting Office, *Report to the Congress: Hazardous Waste Management Programs will not be Effective: Greater Efforts are Needed*, CED-79-14 (Washington, D.C.: U.S. Government Printing Office, Jan. 1979, p. 22-23. U.S. Congress, House, Hearings before the Subcommittee on Oversight and Investigations of the Committee on Interstate and Foreign Commerce, House of Representatives, *Hazardous Waste Disposal Part II*, 96th Congress, 1st Session, Serial #96-49 (Washington, D.C., U.S. Government Printing Office, 1979, pp. 1313-1315).

[a]Figures represent thousands of metric tons.

[b]Includes some with limited hazardous-waste authority

[c]Includes strengthening of previous legislation

[d]Ohio law provides that state regulations cannot be more stringent than EPA regulations; in the absence of EPA regulations Ohio cannot develop their regulations

[e]New York regulations tied by law to EPA's rulemaking calendar and thus delayed.

although efforts were under way to establish a revolving contingency fund for such care. Pennsylvania and Texas officials did not believe in 1979 that their states had viable waste-management systems and seriously doubted that their states would provide sufficient funds to develop adequate programs.[24]

State hazardous-waste-management programs are facing serious financial and staffing problems. A General Accounting Office report estimated, on the basis of interviews and contacts with officials in twenty-six states, that in fiscal year 1978 there was a shortfall of $9.3 million and 414 staff members, and these inadequacies affected programs in each of the twenty-six states.[25] An official of the Indiana Solid Waste Management Program complained that even when staff could be hired they were subsequently lured by more promising opportunities into the private sector.[26] In Ohio in 1978, only one permanent staff person was available to work on solid and hazardous waste in the headquarters Ohio EPA office, although that situation was improved later by the addition of two additional staff members.[27]

During RCRA rulemaking states have also been concerned about the problems of licensing existing hazardous-waste-disposal facilities and siting new facilities in their states, the transportation of hazardous materials on their roads and railroad tracks, the RCRA compliance calendar, financial responsibility and perpetual care of treatment, storage, and disposal facilities, and regulatory uncertainty.[28] In spite of these state problems and concerns, EPA remains hopeful about RCRA's implementation. Assistant Administrator Eckhardt Beck in 1980 stated that EPA believes that approximately forty states should be able to qualify for the first phase of interim authorization.[29] He was less optimistic about state enforcement resources and capabilities, but noted that the fiscal year 1981 federal budget increase of $12 million over the fiscal 1980 level for state grants (section 3011) should enable states to secure the necessary resources. It should be noted, however, that for fiscal years 1978 and 1979 Congress authorized $50 million for hazardous-waste state grants, but no funds were actually made available in fiscal 1978, and in fiscal 1979 only $15 million, 60 percent of the funds authorized for that year, were appropriated for that function.[30] State officials have recently complained that "slow and erratic federal funding," delays in EPA's adoption of RCRA rules, and the inflexibility of those rules have constrained the effectiveness of state programs.[31]

Conclusions

Administrator Costle, in a statement made in late 1979, said, "I have made every effort to assure myself that the agency has a management system and plan of action which, with a high degree of confidence, can achieve the promulgation of a high quality, legally defensible, operational hazardous waste regulatory program. . . ."[32] Given the limited control it has had, the diverse demands placed on it, and the technical and institutional complexity of its mandate, it may be that EPA has performed as well as could be expected during its rulemaking on subtitle C of RCRA. Certainly it had no control over the discovery of Love Canal and little control over what that discovery did to public opinion and the implementation agenda. EPA also had little control over the myriad dimensions of uncertainty that are integrally involved with the act and its objectives. How then, might EPA and others have done better? What can still be done to enable the states to protect society from the hazards of hazardous wastes?

EPA's decision to involve the public during rulemaking was not ill advised, but the manner in which interest groups and the public participated created substantial problems. The structure of EPA's public-participation program was altogether conventional. Individuals and groups reacted to the EPA and its preliminary rulemaking decisions through public meetings, public hearings, and comments on draft and proposed regulations; they did not directly interact with the EPA or, more importantly, with one another. This approach appears to have solidified positions within and differences among participating interests and resulted in directing all communications and disagreements at the EPA. The EPA put itself in a defensive position vis à vis all its clients. Innovative approaches, such as arbitration and negotiation, could have been modified to conform to whatever "mass" public-participation requirements were judged to be necessary and, at the same time, could have enabled the many publics to help EPA develop its regulations rather than merely react to them.[33]

Congress could have conducted its oversight activities in ways more compatible with EPA's immediate and limited mandate of developing regulations pursuant to subtitle C. Additional policy initiatives, particularly regarding the siting of new hazardous-waste facilities, are extremely important, but until EPA and the states have control over operating facilities under the existing law, public health and environment remain in jeopardy. Many states cannot or will not develop adequate regulatory systems of their own until subtitle C regulations are in place.

Finally, problems of financial and personnel resources must be resolved. Even when EPA has completed all its rulemaking, and even when states qualify for EPA authorization, if states cannot secure the resources necessary to design, implement, and enforce their programs, public health and the environment will be compromised. Federal revenues for states under section 3011 of RCRA are helpful only when appropriations are commensurate with authorizations and when those revenues are made available on a timely basis. Prescribed funding levels may be inadequate, even if appropriations are faithfully executed, given the broad range of activities for which states are responsible.[34] States must also face up to the reality of developing more of their own resources.

According to the EPA's most recent rulemaking, states will soon have the statutory responsibility of confronting the complexity and uncertainty associated with hazardous-waste management—they will need to apply sequentially to EPA for two stages of interim authorization and final authorization. They must demonstrate that they can protect human health and the environment from the threats of hazardous wastes, even in the face of insufficient funds, continuing complexity, and myriad uncertainties. Congress's mandate was overwhelming for the EPA. One can only hole that the states will find the resources and have the endurance to meet that same challenge.

Notes

1. Council on Environmental Quality, *Environmental Quality–1979* (Washington, D.C.: U.S. Government Printing Office, 1979), p. 183.

2. Testimony of Douglas Costle, administrator, Environmental Protection Agency, in U.S., Congress, House, *Hearings before the Subcommittee on Transportation and Commerce of the House Committee on Interstate and Foreign Commerce on Implementation of the Resource Conservation and Recovery Act,* 95th Cong., 1st Sess. (1977). Mary Worobee, "An Analysis of the Resource Conservation and Recovery Act," *Environment Reporter: Current Developments* 11:637 (22 August 1980); and Richard B. Stewart and James E. Krier, *Environmental Law and Policy,* 2d ed. (New York: Bobbs-Merrill, 1978), pp. 665–666.

3. Paul Sabatier and Daniel Mazmanian, "The Implementation of Public Policy: A Framework of Analysis," *Policy Studies Journal* 8:538–560 (1980). Other attempts to conceptualize the implementation process include Eugene Bardach, *The Implementation Game* (Cambridge, Mass.: MIT Press, 1977); Jeffrey Pressman and Aaron Wildavsky, *Implementation* (Los Angeles: University of California Press, 1973); Charles O. Jones, *Clean Air* (Pittsburgh: University of Pittsburgh Press, 1975); and Theodore Lowi et. al., *Poliscide* (Ithaca, N.Y.: Cornell University Press, 1975).

4. Worobee, "Analysis," p. 633.

5. S.A. Carnes, *Potential Institutional Conflicts in the Implementation of the Resource Conservation and Recovery Act and their Impacts on the Department of Energy: Background Information,* ORNL/OEPA-8 (Oak Ridge, Tenn.: Oak Ridge National Laboratory, 1979); and S.A. Carnes et. al., *Impacts of the Resource Conservation and Recovery Act on Energy Supply,* ORNL/OIAPA-15 (Oak Ridge, Tenn.: Oak Ridge National Laboratory, 1980).

6. Sabatier and Mazmanian, "Implementation of Public Policy," p. 547.

7. Carnes et. al., *Impacts on Energy Supply,* p. 18.

8. Council on Environmental Quality, *Environmental Quality–1979,* pp. 176–177.

9. H.R. 7020, H.R. 85 and S. 1480 are all currently under consideration in various congressional committees.

10. U.S., Congress, House, *Report of the Subcommittee on Oversight and Investigations of the House Committee on Interstate and Foreign Commerce on Hazardous Waste Disposal,* 96th Cong., 1st sess. (September 1979). p. iii.

11. Testimony of Edward F. Turek, acting assistant administrator for Air and Waste Management, Environmental Protection Agency, in U.S., Congress, House, *Hearings before the Subcommittee on Transportation and Commerce of the House Committee on Interstate and Foreign Commerce on Implementation of the Resource Conservation and Recovery Act,* 95th Cong., 1st sess. (1977).

12. *Federal Register* 44:34244-34344 (14 June 1979); and *Federal Register* 45:33287-33588 (19 May 1980).

13. *Federal Register* 45:33386. State implementation may be facilitated by the thirty-five interpretive memoranda, which EPA is in the process of preparing; alternatively, these clarifications may simply create additional misunderstanding. *Environment Reporter: Current Developments* 11:629-631 (22 August 1980).

14. *Federal Register* 45:33385.

15. Barbara Culliton, "Continuing Confusion over Love Canal," *Science* 209:1002-1003 (29 August 1980); and Daniel Bronstein, "Love Canal and Legal Precedent," *Science* 209:1470 (26 September 1980).

16. Carnes et. al., *Impacts on Energy Supply,* p. 14.

17. Herbert Inhaber, "Risks with Energy from Conventional and Nonconventional Sources," *Science* 203:718-723 (23 February 1979); and J.P. Holdren et. al. *Risk of Renewable Energy Sources: A Critique of the Inhaber Report,* ERG-79-3 (Berkeley: Energy and Resources Group, University of California, 1979).

18. William K. Lowrance, *Of Acceptable Risk* (Los Altos, Calif.: William Kaufman, 1976); Lennart Sjoberg, "Strength of Belief and Risk," *Policy Sciences* 11:39-57 (1979); Aaron Wildavsky, "No Risk Is the Highest Risk of All," *American Scientist* 63:32-37 (1979); and Peter W. House, "Politics and Risk" (Paper presented at the National Conference on the Management of Energy-Environment Conflict, Wye Plantation, Maryland, 20-23 May 1980).

19. U.S. Environmental Protection Agency, *Draft Economic Impact Analysis Subtitle C, Resource Conservation and Recovery Act of 1976* (Washington, D.C.: Office of Solid Waste, 1979).

20. As presently prepared in response to Executive Order No. 12044, economic-impact analyses and regulatory analyses do not seriously address social, political, ethical, and legal impacts and costs. They are similar in approach and format to the first generation of environmental-impact statements and typically do not evaluate impacts that are uncertain or potentially contentious.

21. Carnes et. al., *Impacts on Energy Supply,* p. 28.

22. Section 6001 of RCRA stipulated that solid- and hazardous-waste-management activities of any federal-government department or agency would be required to comply with all federal, state, interstage, and local requirements.

23. U.S. Congress, House, *Hearings before the Subcommittee on Oversight and Investigations,* Committee on Interstate and Foreign Commerce, *Hazardous Waste Disposal, Part II,* 96th Cong., 1st sess., Serials 96-49 (Washington, D.C.: United States Government Printing Office, 1979), pp. 1314-1315.

24. U.S. Comptroller General, General Accounting Office, *Report to the Congress: Hazardous Waste Management Programs Will Not Be Effective: Greater Efforts Are Needed,* CED-79-14 (January 1979), pp. 8–9.

25. Ibid., p. 16.

26. S.A. Carnes, *Potential Institutional Conflicts in the Implementation of the Resource Conservation and Recovery Act and Their Impacts on the Department of Energy: A Case Study,* ORNL/OEPA-9 (Oak Ridge, Tenn.: Oak Ridge National Laboratory, 1979), pp. 15–16.

27. Ibid., p. 18.

28. Ibid., p. 15–18; William DeVille, "State Initiatives in Hazardous Waste Management and Hazardous Materials Management" (Paper presented at the International Conference on Hazardous Materials Management, Detroit, 4–5 December 1979).

29. *National Solid Waste Management Association Reports* 15:1,9 (March 1980).

30. U.S. Comptroller General, *Report to Congress,* p. 15.

31. *Environment Reporter: Current Developments* 11:650–651 (29 August 1980).

32. Worobee, "Analysis," p. 637.

33. Nelkin and Pollak have identified numerous approaches to public participation and have differentiated them according to the particular needs and goals of the participation. Dorothy Nelkin and Michael Pollak, "Public Participation in Technological Decisions: Reality or Grand Illusion," *Technology Review* 81:55–64 (August/September 1979).

34. William Goldfarb, "The Hazards of Our Hazardous Waste Policy," *Natural Resources Journal* 19:259 (April 1979).

3

Perilous Waste

Malcolm Getz and
Benjamin Walter

The firms, farms, and households that make up the nation's economy regularly leave behind useless residues: pencil shavings, discarded draft copies of scholarly articles, smoke, sludge, empty tin cans, degraded chemical compounds. Because the costs of returning these wastes to productive use exceed their current economic value, they are not allocated in any market. Instead, they accumulate in the environment—a large but finite supply of remote forest clearings, sandy barrens, abandoned mine shafts, and river bottoms, which nature or society makes available. If no one has legally defensible property rights in these sinks, nature and society combine to supply them as free goods. Generators flush their wastes down these receptacles, without obligation to pay anyone for the privilege. Others are owned by private firms or governments, which demand fees from generators for getting rid of their wastes.

If there were no more to the matter than that, no problems or dislocations would arise. But the chain of significant relationships does not terminate when by-products are chucked down a sink or poured into a lagoon. Wastes haphazardly pumped today into a inconspicuous hole may perversely find their way back into the market in a decade's time and disrupt future consumption and production. Toxic industrial wastes may seep through subterranean fissures and collect in municipal or agricultural water supplies. Costs of drinking contaminated water can be totted up in many ways: dead or diseased livestock, reduced labor productivity, excess medical costs, premature deaths, diminished property values, fouled swimming holes. Previous actions may result in current catastrophes, and present actions may ripen into future calamities.

Governments may respond in two ways. The first is to mitigate evils that have already occurred. They may allocate tax revenues or earmark receipts to cover the costs of cleaning up polluted sinks or to compensate innocent victims of ecological mishaps. Or they may, as Sanford Weiner and Aaron Wildavsky have observed, act to forestall future calamity.[1] The Resource Conservation and Recovery Act of 1976 (RCRA) is an example of the "prophylactic planning" that Weiner and Wildavsky find alarming.

The regulatory strategy implied by RCRA could not be simpler nor its tone more predictable. The act grants the U.S. Environmental Protection Agency (EPA) two broad areas of discretionary authority. One is the prerogative to call certain waste streams hazardous (subtitle C, sections 1004 and 3001 a–b). Taken together, these portions of the law direct EPA to develop criteria for identifying and listing harmful residues, described in the legislation as "solid wastes which . . .

cause or significantly contribute to an increase in mortality or an increase in serious irreversible, or incapacitating reversible, illness; or . . . pose a substantial present or potential hazard to human health or the environment when improperly . . . managed."[2] The other discretionary authority concerns the design and enforcement of coordinated control mechanisms to be imposed on hazardous wastes in an unbroken stream from generation to their eventual disposal in specially designed incinerators, lagoons, or landfills, where wastes are to be impounded forever. Firms are required to identify the components and quantities of their hazardous wastes. Generators must file manifests that specify waste volume and composition as well as the facility the generator has designated to receive and package them. While in transit, shipments are to be governed by Department of Transportation (DOT) regulations covering the placarding and packaging of hazardous substances. At the end of the journey, wastes are to be buried or incinerated in EAP-licensed facilities operated by private firms or state agencies. Alternatively, generators may choose to bury or burn their wastes in facilities constructed on factory grounds. These installations also require licenses. Generators electing to internalize hazardous-waste disposal are legally able to escape the costly manifesting schemes mandated for off-site shipment. But, no matter which option the generator chooses, at no link in the chain are hazardous wastes to escape governmental surveillance.

RCRA divides responsibility for implementation between regional EPA offices and state governments. States are first given the opportunity to develop detailed routines for licensing facilities that will pass EPA muster, for developing their own versions of the manifest forms, and for tracking down and prosecuting violators. Residual authority remains with EPA; if any portion of a state plan fails to measure up to minimal agency criteria, it is authorized to step in and operate the program on its own.

RCRA draws at least four different classes of actors into its integrated regulatory system. The first is the EPA. Its role stems from its statutory obligation to identify wastes that are hazardous, establish location and design standards for disposal facilities, and formulate a manifest system for tracking wastes from generation to disposal. The second class of actors comprises all firms generating such wastes as unwanted by-products. Firms in the waste-disposal industry comprise the third group. Last are local communities whose concurrence must be obtained before any disposal facility can be situated in areas subject to their jurisdiction. Although unmentioned in legislation and regulation, their role is pivotal in shaping ultimate disposal options. Each set of actors responds to different incentives. It is still an open question whether their divergent and incompatible interests can be meshed through a series of continuous mutual adjustments into an effective regulatory scheme.

EPA: Error and Consequences

EPA has so far delineated eight general categories of potentially perilous residues thought to be present in waste streams. The agency currently plans to defer until

1982 the promulgation of regulations covering four of them: radioactivity, infectiousness, phytotoxicity (lethal to plant life), and teratogenicity-mutagenicity (capable of producing monsters or other genetic aberrations).[3] For three additional categories of hazardous wastes, EPA has proposed test protocols and standardized criteria. Flash-point coefficients define *ignitability*. *Corrosivity* is gauged by a pH level that is neither excessively acid nor excessively alkaline. *Reactivity,* the seventh characteristic, is not quantitatively defined. Instead, EPA has published lists of substances present in many industrial wastes that will trigger abrupt and dangerous reactions when commingled—acids and bases, for example.

Toxicity poses the eighth peril. Proposed routines for calling waste streams "toxic" proceed in two discrete stages. First, the *Federal Register* assumes that industrial wastes will eventually produce toxic concentrations in water supplies if they contain substances already proscribed by the Safe Water Drinking Act (arsenic, endrin, 2-4D, and other chlorinated hydrocarbons, for example) at one-hundred times the concentration permissible in drinking water.[4] Nearly all these toxic substances are either simple metals or stable hydrocarbon compounds, making it very expensive for generating firms to redesign their technologies so that the harmful components in waste streams will be decomposed or detoxified inside factory walls. Since they cannot be economically neutralized within the plant, they must be incinerated or impounded outside it.

Second, wastes thrown off by firms in such industries as chemicals, leather production, and metals fabrication are presumed to be toxic; it is up to generating firms to prove their wastes do not exceed allowable toxicity thresholds if they are to escape regulation under RCRA.[5] By reversing normal presumptions of innocence in declaring waste streams hazardous prima facie, the agency heaps both the burden of proof and the expense of testing on firms in regulated industries.

In justifying its proposed regulations, EPA asserts that unregulated hazardous-waste streams harbor intolerable health or environmental risks, but the insinuation is not substantiated. EPA does not provide (as does OSHA) a hazard index estimating tangible, measurable outcomes (animal and human fatalities, genetic aberrations, crop failure, burns, sterility, fish kills, and crop failures) that can be expected if waste streams do not receive special treatment. In short, EPA's standards are not empirically correlated with expected benefits that can be expressed in terms of reduced morbidity, fewer premature fatalities, or increased agricultural productivity.[6]

In fact, EPA deals not with risk (which is measurable) but with uncertainty. Like many other bureaucratic agencies faced by uncertainty, EPA employs a tacit decision rule that will enable it to avoid the worst conceivable outcome. Asked to render judgment about the peril posed by a particular waste stream, an EPA official may commit opposed errors. He can erroneously call an innocuous waste hazardous, a *false positive*. Or he can decide not to regulate a really noxious waste, an error symmetrically called a *false negative*. EPA is understandably averse to false negatives. It has much to lose. The agency will appear culpable if a waste stream it has certified as benign subsequently causes disastrous outcomes its regulations are supposed to prevent: sickness in human and plant life, explosions, chemical burns, biological sports, and genetic abnormalities. The agency will face an angry Congress, a distraught public, and a torrent of journalistic exposés. Agency jobs may be lost, appropriations sliced, and functions shifted to other agencies. All are outcomes agency officials wish to avoid; they want to make current decisions that will minimize future regret. The agency has, therefore, a powerful incentive to steer clear of false negatives.

Although the agency is understandably averse to false negatives, it has no corresponding incentive to be chary of the opposed error. Only rarely will a dubious or false positive stir up very much of a fuss. One such is saccharin. When the Federal Drug Administration (FDA) banned it, the effects of the proscription were both immediate and perceptible to many consumers. Deprived of all sugar substitutes, diabetics would be unable to consume sweetened food and confections. The FDA was able to ride out the storm by claiming that it was abiding by congressional intent as expressed in the Delaney Amendment. By contrast, any costs stemming from EPA false positives will be shunted around the economy rather than borne by the agency. Real resources will be expended in battling harmless residues a fearful agency has termed perilous. These costs will not explicitly appear in the EPA's budget nor will they be made visible in congressional appropriations. They will be transferred to consumers in the form of higher prices, to workers in the form of lower real wages, and to investors in lowered rates of return on their capital.

Because responsibility for adverse economic effects will be deflected away from the agency, EPA officials have no tangible inducements to be concerned with any remote economic effects flowing from false positives. For reasons of organizational maintenance, they are more sensitive to the need to minimize total agency costs, rather than to reduce total social costs. The real social costs flowing from agency false positives, the loss in social welfare that springs from consuming too many scarce resources to ward off imaginary or exaggerated evils, do not fall on the agency. The market disperses then on citizens who are compelled to buy more safety than they might individually prefer.[7] Total social welfare drops because of EPA's rational efforts to diminish its own culpability for future mishaps.

The primary impact of agency decisions on market relationships arises from its statutory authority to designate wastes as hazardous. To comply fully with the law, generators producing such wastes must steer them through the complicated and costly management routines elaborated under subtitle C. We have already mentioned that firms generating residues the agency has deemed dangerous will have to foot the bill for testing their own waste streams if they want to prove them innocuous. Firms will have to shoulder other costs as well. Although the agency does not directly fix prices for waste-disposal services, the impact of its regulations will nonetheless be reflected in prices charged by all firms in the waste-disposal industry, including firms that comprise the black market.

Wastemakers

To appreciate some probable outcomes, one must forecast the likely responses of waste generators facing alternative disposal options. Following the imposition of the regulations, generators will incur two additional types of production costs: extra waste-handling costs and extra administrative costs. Whether firms choose to dispose of their wastes on their own premises or truck them to a facility off-site, they will have to cover the expenses of the more elaborate methods of waste disposal mandated by EPA. Administration of required new manifesting and reporting schemes will also be expensive. Not all generators will bear these costs with equal ease. Some will find them cutting deeply into expected profits. In extreme cases, particularly vulnerable firms will have to switch to different product lines or face going out of business altogether. Depending on the combination of assumptions one chooses, generating firms will spend between $510 million and $2 billion annually. In addition, EPA forecasts that compliance costs will force more than eighty firms out of business altogether.[8] Other firms, paradoxically, stand to gain when they have below-average cost increments due to the regulations. Understanding the ramifications of the proposed regulations requires careful analysis, which is not made any easier because it is prospective rather than retrospective.

Any generator will face a menu of options for dealing with its hazardous wastes, and each bears a price tag. Analysis must assume that any firm will select the option it calculates will minimize overall disposal costs.[9] Land-filling or incinerating wastes on-site appears the most attractive option, possessing at least three tangible advantages. First, shipping and transportation costs are held to a minimum, a consideration certain to become even more decisive as fuel prices rise and as generating firms purchase insurance policies covering accidential spills en route. Second, generating firms can legally evade the expensive manifesting and reporting routines required for off-site disposal. Third, they will avoid the payment of economic rents to other firms for specialized services they provide in burning or ditching wastes. The appeal of on-site disposal will be further enhanced if EPA adheres to its provisional licensing schedule. The agency anticipates issuing over 30,000 licenses for hazardous-waste-disposal facilities in the first five years following the publication of final regulations. That figure comes to more than 500 a month. So clogged a docket will clearly strain the agency's capacity for detailed review and will at the same time reduce its ability to track down and inspect all on-site landfills, lagoons, and incinerators currently in use or likely to be put in operation. Many are sure to evade detection by an agency busy with other tasks.[10] These considerations lead us to conclude that on-site treatment will be the preferred mode of disposal for the foreseeable future.

However, "foreseeable" is not "indefinite." On-site disposal capacity is depletable. Once firms exhaust their stocks of suitable land, they will have to bid against many other generating firms for off-site disposal capacity, including new plant sites. It will not be easy to augment off-site capacity, for reasons that will be elaborated in the next section of this chapter. Hence, it is reasonable to expect that prices charged for legal off-site disposal will rise, and generators will be burdened additionally by the costs of agency-dictated manifesting schemes and of specialized transportation services to cart wastes away.

Suppose that the total quantity of noxious wastes produced in any time period exceeds the physical capacity of all licensed facilities, both off- and on-site. No matter what price they are charged, some generators will be unable to dispose legally of their residues. Generators squeezed out of the legal market are then likely to seek out illegal disposal services, an alternative they will find more attractive than operating at a loss or going out of business altogether. A generator stuck with small volumes of nondescript waste and irregular or infrequent disposal needs will find black-market outlets appealing. He knows it will be difficult for regulators to predict what night an illicit hauler-disposer will truck the stuff away. The probability of detecting clandestine dumping is inherently small.

Ironically, agency regulations are likely to discourage use of safer waste-disposal methods by making them much more expensive than alternative black-market arrangements. It is reasonable to predict a sharp rise in unit costs for legal methods as increasing volumes of hazardous wastes press against limited authorized-disposal capacity. It is also reasonable to predict that more generators will be tempted to divert their wastes into black-market channels as unit prices between legal and illegal markets diverge.[11] Ironically, dump-by-night haulers and disposers, the shadowy middlemen dominating the illegal market, may emerge as the unintended beneficiaries of agency regulations. Black-market operators will have a clear incentive to raise their fees as RCRA regulations inflate prices charged for legal disposal. So long as they retain some price advantage, they will be able to capture a sizeable share of the entire market.

Generators comprise an extremely variegated group of manufacturers, wholsesalers, and governmental agencies. All covered firms will encounter increased waste-handling costs as a result of RCRA regulations, but they will not all bear them to the same degree. Some established firms will be well situated to comply at relatively small additional cost. In particular, those already operating on-site disposal facilities may be able to secure a license with little additional investment, as will firms owning large tracts of land in remote areas that can be inexpensively converted into graveyards that meet agency standards. Firms with no land at all or with potential sites that will fail soil permeability and other hydrogeologic criteria are in a much worse position. They will be compelled to ship their wastes to off-site disposal facilities other firms will operate for profit. Thus, firms using off-site disposal now and in the future seem the most vulnerable.

RCRA will inevitably raise operating costs of regulated firms. As is conventional, these increased costs can be portrayed as decreases in supply levels for affected industries.[12] Figure 3-1 depicts three distinguishable cases. In case A, the supply curve is horizontal. The entire cost increase resulting from regulation will be registered in higher prices for final products. Higher prices also lead to

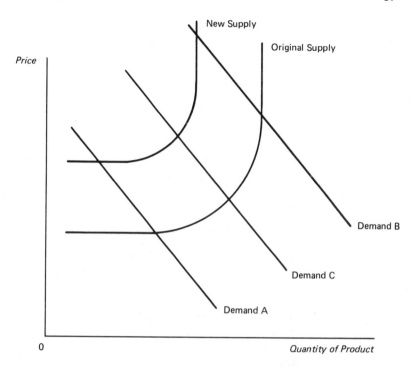

Figure 3-1. Regulatory Impact on Industry

diminution of output, the precise quantity lost depending on the demand elasticities governing consumers' willingness to pay. Thus, the effects of regulation will be divided among consumers who will pay higher prices, workers who will lose wages, and shareholders who will receive smaller dividend checks.

Case B presents another possibility. The full effect of the regulations is registered in diminished capacity. Once more the size of the price increase is determined by elasticity of demand. If demand is perfectly elastic (horizontal), there may be no price increase at all. This would be the likely outcome if purchasers of the affected product can shift to a close substitute unaffected by regulations. Price increases will occur if demand is imperfectly elastic. The more general case is described by case C. It involves a combination of supply and demand adjustments. Cost increases are passed partially along to consumers in the form of higher prices. Total capacity will also decrease.

The analysis so far presented is incomplete because it takes no account of the observable heterogeneity of individual firms in the affected industry. For a variety of reasons already presented, some firms may be better situated than others to cope effectively with the regulations, a possibility presented in figure 3-2. Firms

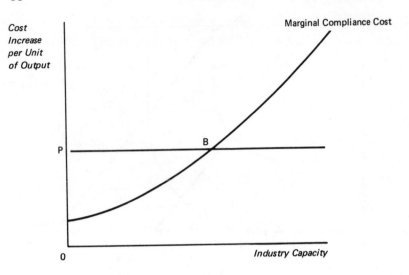

Figure 3-2. Differential Effects on Firms in Regulated Industry

within an industry are arrayed left to right along the horizontal axis from those who can meet regulations at lowest cost to those incurring the largest costs. The vertical axis indicates cost per output unit of meeting regulations. The upward-sloping line indicates the marginal costs of complying with the regulations for each firm in the industry. The slope of the line, then, portrays interfirm differences in compliance costs. (In the exceptional case where all firms bear exactly the same compliance costs per unit of output, the curve would be a horizontal line.) It is of course, not likely to be horizontal for the reasons given herein.

Now the final product market will exhibit a particular price increase as production costs of all firms in the industry increase in response to RCRA regulations. This new price appears as point P in figure 3-2. The firm located at point B will find that the price increase exactly covers increased compliance costs. Regulation will not alter its profit position. Firms located on the curve to the right of point B will encounter costs greater than the uniform price increase. Such firms will have decreased profits. (If they manage to stay in business, it is only because they have earned rents on such other dimensions as a favorable geographical location or brilliant managerial skills. Even so, rents earned by these assets will be reduced to offset the excess of cost over the price increase forced by regulation.) Firms located to the left of point B will experience cost increases that are smaller than the increase in price. Hence, they will enjoy increased profits that can be charged up to agency regulation. Such firms stand to benefit from agency regulatory efforts, at least in the short run. They will thus have very little incentive to oppose them strenuously.

Thus final product prices will increase over the long run by a margin sufficient to cover the full economic cost of the least profitable firm able to stay in business. All firms with lower cost increments stand to enjoy increased levels of profit. These could be substantial for firms that enjoy access to good sites. Of all crucial variables, sheer firm size is most likely to shape the differential impact of RCRA regulations. Small firms are likely to suffer the most. Many of the important administrative costs imposed by RCRA regulations are not scaled to firm size and can be considered as new fixed costs of doing business. In general, smaller firms will face higher relative costs of compliance with manifesting and reporting requirements and are less likely to have in-house capacity for testing and monitoring waste streams.[13] Unable to shoulder compliance costs and still turn a profit, some small firms will enter the black market or will be forced out of business entirely. In addition, prospects of having to comply with RCRA regulation may well discourage potential new entrants in covered industries. All these considerations would on balance appear to lead to greater market concentration and attenuated competition.

Increased concentration is likely to possess several undesirable consequences for society. First, less competitive firms charge higher markups in setting prices. Thus, regulations may increase final market prices more than proportionately to actual cost increases. Second, firms in less competitive industries may have less incentive to promote technological change. Innovations that imperil the market power of existing firms are likely to be throttled.[14]

Siting Facilities: Concentrated Costs, Dispersed Benefits

Broadly conceived, EPA's mission is to minimize future costs society stands to bear from the reckless disposal of hazardous wastes. The potential future harm posed by these dues will be nullified only if safe facilities with sufficient aggregate capacity can be constructed to accommodate them. EPA is alert to the special role it plays in creating demand for these facilities; in his preamble to the proposed regulations, a top agency administrator acknowledged, "In particular, the requirement that generators of waste must manage (it) . . . in an environmentally sound manner *will create large new demand* for adequate waste management capacity. . . ."[15]

How can this governmentally generated demand be satisfied? RCRA does not authorize EPA to build and operate hazardous-waste-management facilities, and the agency is not empowered to commandeer land for leasing to private firms. The act leaves open only one option: firms in the disposal industry must assemble property through normal market transactions. It has so far not been easy for firms to secure the necessary land, largely because of the interactions between land use and community attitudes.

Facilities for burying or burning noxious wastes possess certain troublesome characteristics.[16] First, people living near the site have to endure noise, fumes, and confront the possibility that drums will roll off trucks and burst open on the roadbed. In addition to these and other short-run discomforts, neighbors are also frightened about possible future events: geological subsidence, corrosion of the barrels used to impound hazardous wastes in their subterranean vaults, tremors, floods. Singly or in combination, such circumstances may cause toxic leachate to invade water supplies or seep into ponds used for fishing and swimming. Thus, prospective neighbors view these installations as unpleasant over the short haul and in the long run as potentially lethal. Almost any other conceivable use of the land will be preferred to a hazardous-waste dumpsite.

Balanced against current and future welfare losses the facility will concentrate in the immediate neighborhood are the streams of widespread benefits presumed to flow from it. Chief among these is the provision of a benign environment for the entire region, a collective good. Once provided for one, it is necessarily provided for all. It cannot be rationed or priced.

Hazardous-waste-disposal facilities thus produce a peculiar configuration of distributional effects. They disperse their benefits over wide regions for many to enjoy. But they perversely concentrate their costs within small areas, where they are felt intensely by much smaller numbers of worried people. Each community wants only benefits for itself. Whatever the predicted costs, each community has an incentive to shunt them off on others. Since all communities have the same desires and fears, the predictable result is that everyone wants these facilities as long as they can be sited somewhere else. If these strategic incentives can be translated into effective political power, there will be an insufficient supply of disposal sites.

Local Influence: Best-Laid Plans

There is many a slip 'twixt cup and lip. Hazardous-waste-disposal facilities cannot be imposed on local communities without their consent by administrators working in Washington or in any of EPA's regional offices. American political institutions and traditions allow aggrieved citizens opportunities and resources to stall or obstruct projects they either do not like at all or would like very well elsewhere.[17] Local zoning restrictions and other land-use controls can be manipulated to freeze them out entirely. Even if antagonistic local officials cannot change zoning codes quickly enough to exclude unwanted neighbors, they can refuse to extend utility lines or access roads to the proposed installation. Few sites can operate efficiently without these complementary resources, and local authorities possess the constitutional power to grant or withhold them.

In addition to surmounting the obstacles erected by local governing bodies, any site developer faces a series of discretionary reviews, both administrative and judicial. The agency has served notice it will require some mode of public participation before granting a permit for a new installation or when recertification for an existing facility is requested.[18] In particular, the prospective developer or existing site operator must demonstrate that the installation will not endanger "public health and the environment." Since protection of public health and the environment is a standard that is simultaneously indefinite and equivocal, the entrepreneur does not know what to say or how to say it. Preparing these studies consumes a great deal of time, and the public hearings where they are aired typically take place in an adversary setting charged with tension and acrimony. The function of such hearings is only incidentally to expose technical arguments to a searching the judicious review; they mainly serve to give "environmental advocates" opposed to the project an opportunity to enlarge the area of controversy and consolidate opposition to the project.[19]

Even if the proposed project nimbly hurdles initial local opposition, it is not yet in the clear. Entrepreneurs have to weigh the possibility that their facilities will be shut down by court decree. In Wilsonville, Illinois, a facility operated by the Earthline Corporation was compelled to cease operations by court action. During the legal proceedings, the Illinois EPA entered as *amicus curiae* in behalf of Earthline when the state's attorney general filed suit to shut down the facility.[20] Since strategic veto points pop up at various points in a complicated clearance process, such locally unpopular projects as hazardous-waste-disposal facilities can be cancelled, modified or delayed at any one.

Effective planning presupposes effective power. If planners have to share legal authority with actors pursuing incompatible or contradictory goals, they can see their efforts degenerate into pious resolutions chased by frustrated expectations. Firms in the disposal industry are understandably wary of committing large investments in installations with slender prospects of ever coming "on-line." Shortages of disposal facilities are certain to grow more severe. Voluntary action will not redress the imbalance because each prospective host community calculates it has more to lose than gain by accepting a site.

Overambitious Goals May Make Matters Worse

RCRA proposed laudable goals. Without cradle-to-grave regulation, how can we be assured some insidious sludge will not invade water supplies and poison us all? Even though governmental forces guarding the environment are stretched thin, can we afford to let any pass go undefended?

In fact, we can never be assured of perfect safety from chlorinated hydrocarbons and other dangerous substances that might be let loose on the environment, no matter what EPA proposes to do. Even spending the entire gross national product every year on the effort would not yield an ironclad guarantee. Moreover, if regulatory resources are too widely dispersed, real dangers will receive little substantial attention. If we are to be as safe as possible from actual perils presented by hazardous wastes, EPA must target its efforts. Regulatory efforts should be concentrated on substances presenting the greatest threat to health and controllable at modest costs. More people may fall ill or die because EPA squanders its limited resources trying to control mild wastes while devoting too little attention to things that really hurt.

EPA's efforts to put a thumb in every hole in the dike may actually make the public less safe than it would be with no regulation at all. This astonishing possibility follows from the interactions of all the contingencies we have identified. The envisaged regulatory strategy will boost charges for legal disposal, primarily because an insufficient number of sites exist. Shortfalls will arise for several reasons. First, EPA's understandable aversion to false negatives will lead to enormous quantities of administratively defined hazardous wastes. Second, few entrepreneurs will invest resources in developing installations until they know what design standards will pass EPA muster. "Retrofitting" is expensive. Third, many current sites are perched on five-hundred year flood plains or in other locales EPA views with suspicion. These are likely to be ineligible for certification, cutting further into aggregate capacity. Fourth, and perhaps most important of all, by generating the crisis atmosphere EPA needs to sustain general political support for its efforts, agency officials simultaneously intensify local opposition to siting facilities. Thus, regardless of EPA's public stance, its regulatory efforts have led and seem likely to lead to a chronic shortage of legal sites. Consequently, we expect a marked shift to the illicit sector of the waste-disposal industry. Not only will unlawful disposal be cheaper but it will also be hard to police, given the cessation of subsidies to state enforcement agencies. The illicit dumping that is likely to absorb larger shares of the total waste-disposal market may actually pose greater short- and long-term threats to public health than conventional practices in the absence of regulation.

Overall, efforts to regulate hazardous wastes seem to be failing, not because EPA is foolish, not because wastemakers are devious, and not because most communities perversely intend to inflict hardships on remote towns and villages. Rather, efforts are unsuccessful because none of the crucial actors seems especially concerned with maximizing a transcendant public interest at his own expense.

Notes

1. Sanford Weiner and Aaron Wildavsky, "The Prophylactic Presidency," *The Public Interest,* no. 52 (Summer 1978):3–19.

2. P.L. 94-580 (42 USC 6903), paras. 5A–5B.

3. The lag in publishing final regulations apparently stems from difficulties so far encountered in devising conclusive testing protocols for various substances contained within these four categories. A *testing protocol* is a detailed description of laboratory procedures to be used for detecting the presence and measuring the quantity in a waste stream of a particular substance known to be perilous

in chemically pure form. To be legally defensible, any protocol must be experimentally reproducible, so that all laboratories testing samples of the same waste stream will reach identical conclusions about composition and quantity. Only after a stable testing protocol has been formulated may the agency establish criteria for calling suspicious waste streams hazardous.

Since other legislation bestows on the Nuclear Regulatory Commission (NRC) authority to frame regulations ensuring safe disposition of radioactive wastes, it is not certain how EPA and NRC will settle the boundary dispute.

4. *Federal Register* Vol. 45 (19 May 1980):33111-33112. Regulations proposed earlier set more stringent limits at ten times the concentration allowed in drinking water. See *Federal Register* (18 December 1978):58956. The revised definition presumably will focus regulatory attention on more concentrated hazards. The facile manipulation of the definition illustrates the lack of a factual basis for setting the limits of the regulation.

5. *Federal Register* Vol. 43 (18 December 1978):58958-58960.

6. Some state regulatory codes are more discriminating than proposed EPA regulations. California and Louisiana differentiate among waste streams to concentrate regulatory effort on the most hazardous substances. "Hot" wastes such as some chlorinated hydrocarbons are diverted to extremely secure facilities with impermeable clay liners and other expensive engineering safeguards designed to eliminate any possibility of seepage; milder wastes are sent to other installations where they can be impounded at much lower cost. See Louisiana Department of Natural Resources, *Hazardous Waste Management Plan* (Baton Rouge: Louisiana Department of Natural Resources, 7 June 1979), appendix A and State of California, *Hazardous Waste Regulations,* Title 22, chap. 2, arts. 9 and 10.

7. Because costs are likely to be widely diffused, it will prove difficult for geographically and occupationally dispersed interests to coalesce and rally potent counterpressure against EPA. See Mancur Olson's lucid discussion of organizational difficulties faced by such "latent groups" in *The Logic of Collective Action* (New York: Schocken Books, 1971), especially pp. 48-52. Regulated firms able to blend compliance costs into final product price and having the market power to pass them along to their customers will also lack the incentive to protest strenuously EPA regulations.

8. *Federal Register* Vol. 45 (19 May 1980):33072. EPA's estimates of economic impact also heroically assume that there will be enough off-site disposal capacity to absorb all wastes generated during the conceivable future.

9. Technically, it is possible to "mine" waste streams to extract substances that can be recycled for further productive use. Currently, virgin feedstocks are much less expensive than chemically identical recycled inputs, a consideration precluding widespread factor substitutions of this sort.

10. RCRA lodges the responsibility of detecting substandard installations with state EPAs. "Seed" subsidies are to be made available to the states to help them get their enforcement programs under way. They are scheduled to terminate

in fiscal year 1981. Unless states voluntarily assume the burden and expense of enforcement, EPA will need additional congressional appropriations to pick up the slack.

11. Because black-market operators do not customarily publish their prices, comparative cost data for licit and illicit markets are not easy to come by. A careful recent study published by the State of Minnesota points to the comparative price advantage of black-market disposal. Landfilling "difficult-to-treat" hazardous waste costs $215 a ton. More than half (57 percent) of the identifiable hazardous waste generated in Minnesota was diverted into illegal channels. The best guess is that these wastes were poured clandestinely down sewers, spread on "unregulated land sites" for a dollar per ton, or added to ordinary sanitary landfills at a cost of five dollars a ton. State of Minnesota, "Interim Report, Hazardous Waste Management, Minnesota's Issues/Options," January 1979.

12. This analysis is adapted from Robert A. Leone, *Environmental Controls* (Lexington, Mass.: Lexington Books, D.C. Heath, 1976).

13. Ibid., pp. 8–11.

14. Cost increases will not have the same effect on foreign producers. Import competition will grow. Domestic firms competing in overseas markets will be handicapped for the same reason. The chemical industry, for example, is an international industry with significant imports of some products and significant exports of others. Patterns of international trade will be sharply affected by the regulations.

15. *Federal Register* Vol. 43 (18 December 1978):58948. Emphasis added.

16. Michael O'Hare, "Not on *My* Block You Don't: Facility Siting and the Strategic Importance of Compensation," *Public Policy* 25 (Fall 1977):407–458.

17. Hazardous-waste-disposal facilities are not isolated cases. For a classic study of similar difficulties in securing approval for a public-housing project, see Martin Meyerson and Edward C. Banfield, *Politics, Planning and the Public Interest* (Glencoe, Ill.: Free Press, 1955).

18. *Federal Register* Vol. 45 (19 May 1980):33405–33491. Proposed regulations do not present any sort of formula state officials are to use in deciding whether or not to grant the request.

19. For an example in a different policy area, see Bernard J. Frieden, *The Environmental Hustle* (Cambridge,Mass.: MIT Press, 1979). Frieden analyzes the impact of citizen participation on suburban-subdivision-investment decisions. Presenting data that were often contrived, environmental advocates were able to deter investment in modest subdivisions. Projects permitted after protracted hearings had run their course contained fewer residential units than originally proposed. They also went for a higher price. Parallels are clear and ominous.

20. For an extended account of the Wilsonville case, see U.S. Environmental Protection Agency, *Siting of Hazardous Waste Management Facilities and Public Opposition,* (Report SW-809 (Washington, D.C., 1979), pp. 303–316.

4

Equity Issues and Wilderness Preservation: Policy Implications for the Energy-Environment Tangle

James L. Regens

Since the early 1960s, the temporal dimension for public policymaking in the United States generally has lengthened while the spatial dimension has expanded. This reflects an awareness that policy decisions formulated within traditional contexts frequently affect individuals and groups outside those arenas. Once routine decisions are now subject to scrutiny by a larger number of participants in the choice process. Although greater participation may exert a positive effect on policymaking, it can also produce increased difficulty in establishing widespread support for courses of action if homogeneity of interest is diluted as the base of participation expands. In essence, if participants exercise a veto rule by articulating what not to do (frequently advocating conflicting positions), the process becomes less capable of establishing rapid consensus over what to do. When this occurs, not only does the time needed to arrive at decisions grow longer but often previously hidden equity trade-offs and interdependence across issue areas become more apparent.

This is illustrated nowhere more clearly than in the seeming conflict between energy needs and environmental quality.[1] In less than a decade, both have become major policy concerns. Each represents an expansion of the public sector's role along with new public–private-sector relationships, although the full extent of those institutional changes has not yet been determined. Linkages between policy decisions in both areas and their attendant equity trade-offs are increasingly more apparent. However, because technology, economics, resource allocation, and social goals all interact, it tends to be extremely difficult to resolve value conflicts through national consensus.

The controversy surrounding attempts by the U.S. Forest Service (USFS) to study potential expansion of the nation's wilderness lands provides a graphic example of this problem, with corresponding difficulty in achieving consensus

Portions of this chapter were presented at the 1979 Annual Meeting of the Midwest Political Science Association, Chicago, April 19–21. This study was supported partially by Oak Ridge National Laboratory, under a research fellowship with the U.S. Department of Energy. I am grateful to Helen Ingram, Dean E. Mann, Lettie M. Wenner, Mark Shields, and Alfred H. Voelker for their helpful comments. Data were collected by the Resource Analysis Group, Oak Ridge National Laboratory, under U.S. Department of Energy contract number W-7504-eng-26 with the Union Carbide Corporation.

over trade-offs. The USFS second Roadless Area Review and Evaluation (RARE II) project was intended to offer a systematic guide for allocation of selected areas for wilderness preservation.[2] An important goal of the RARE II program was the quick release of public lands lacking wilderness attributes to such multiple-use activities as recreation, wildlife habitat improvement, timber harvesting, road building, and resource extraction. Presumably, such an approach to land-use planning, with its emphasis on widespread public participation, would facilitate agreement over policy decisions. Instead, RARE II increasingly became embroiled in controversy, especially about the equities of specific tract allocations.

This suggests that establishing consensus about the acceptability of policy options involves reconciling disagreement over the equity of not only substantive but also procedural and perceptual outcomes of the policy process. In this context, *substantive equity* conceptually represents the empirical distribution of costs and benefits resulting from policy choices to affected parties. *Procedural equity* refers to the fairness of the decision or allocation process, and *perceptual equity* involves subjective assessments of adequacy on the part of interested parties. Thus, trade-offs and resultant equity issues involve the following elements: the decision process (procedural), the resultant effects (substantive), and cognitions about the process and effects (perceptual).

Using the USFS RARE II process as an illustration of the problems involved in accommodating these potentially conflicting views of equity, this chapter examines the extent to which such issues arise in the context of wilderness preservation versus energy-resource-development trade-offs as well as the implications of those issues for consensus formation.

An Overview of the Rare II Process

Efforts to designate selected portions of the nation's public lands for inclusion in the National Wilderness Preservation System (NWPS) are a relatively new policy issue on the agenda of government. The idea of preserving wilderness areas, in which man's impact on the environment is substantially unnoticeable, however, is not a new concept. Attempts to foster wilderness preservation formed the basis for the early conservation movement of the late 1800s and early 1900s, leading to the establishment of such groups as the Sierra Club. Nonetheless, although some wilderness areas were first established by administrative directive in the 1920s, the concept was not readily accepted.[3] As a result, comprehensive attempts to allocate roadless areas to wilderness status are a relatively recent phenomenon that was formalized by the Wilderness Act of 1964 (PL 88-577) which defines wilderness as:

... an area of undeveloped Federal land retaining its primeval character and influence ... and which (1) generally appears to have been affected primarily by the forces of nature, with the imprint of man's work substantially unnoticeable; (2) has outstanding opportunities for solitude or a primitive and unconfined type of recreation; (3) has at least 5,000 acres of land or is of sufficient size as to make practical its preservation and use in an unimpaired condition.

Congress further specified that within a wilderness there will be no roads, timber harvesting, use of motorized vehicles, or landing of aircraft. These prohibitions as well as subsequent administrative interpretations of the act essentially preclude significant resource exploration or development in wilderness areas.[4]

Clear benefits are perceived to accrue to society as a result of wilderness preservation. From a scientific standpoint, such areas are invaluable natural laboratories for ecosystems research. Their naturalness and solitude also provide opportunities for primitive recreational uses. Wilderness designation also enhances environmental protection: activities in adjacent areas that would impact adversely on air-quality levels in wilderness areas are restricted; and water quality is maintained, since prohibiting development within wilderness areas reduces the potential for watershed pollution. Finally, as Clawson has argued, wilderness also "satisfies certain cultural standards or values of its advocates."[5] Thus, wilderness, in the present context, has come to be viewed not merely as a specific geographical location but as an almost mystical link between modern man and his earlier, presumably more intimate relationship with the natural environment.[6]

Wilderness designation, however, also implies a willingness to accept social costs, at least in the near term. The total area being studied by the RARE II process involves over 62 million acres distributed in 2,919 tracts and located in thirty-eight states and Puerto Rico.[7] The overwhelming majority of those tracts are located in portions of the western United States that are prime candidates for domestic energy-resources development.[8] The implications for energy development are twofold. First, although the exact percentage of domestic reserves (especially oil) located within these areas remains uncertain, industry sources suggest that the current rate of resource depletion and our evolving understanding of resource-deposition processes may in the near future bring greater demands for entry of these areas into the development cycle.[9] More importantly, as noted, the effects of wilderness designation are not localized to the specific tract. Siting and construction of a variety of facilities such as minemouth power plants, slurry pipelines, or transmission corridors would be restricted, if not precluded, in adjacent public areas because of environmental standards and use restrictions for wilderness areas.

On the other hand, some forms of energy development might have such adverse environmental impacts that future wilderness preservation would be extremely difficult if not impossible in some areas. Production or facility siting might fundamentally alter an area's wilderness attributes. Thus, wilderness designation could affect both the scope and nature of energy development as well as environmental protection. Clearly then, the decision to designate specific areas for wilderness status carries with it implicit judgments about the trade-offs between energy and the environment. In fact, Senator Max Baucus (D-Montana) asserts that allocating the National Forest System's "remaining roadless areas in an equitable fashion . . . is the crux of the RARE II process."[10]

In the past, the USFS and other federal agencies responsible for public-land management have tended to answer the questions of where and how much wilderness and nonwilderness on an individual, tract-by-tract basis. Initial attempts at more systematic decision making can be traced to the USFS first roadless area review and evaluation (RARE I), conducted in 1973, which resulted in the selection of 274 study areas containing 12.3 million acres. RARE I soon became embroiled in controversy over both its scope and its rate of implementation. For example, it did not include the national grasslands or the national forests east of the Mississippi River (potential eastern wilderness areas). Groups that supported or opposed potential designations for specific tracts emerged as critics of the planning effort's equity. In fact, a federal court order currently prohibits development of the areas included in the RARE I inventory until an environmental-impact statement (EIS) is prepared and approved for each tract on a one-by-one basis. Under these circumstances, conflict would seem to be inevitable for efforts to accommodate developmentalist and preservationalist values within a single comprehensive planning process.

Nonetheless, starting in 1977, the USFS initiated its RARE II study to evaluate the wilderness, environmental, and resources potential of the entire 197 million acres in the National Forest System. In June 1978, the USFS issued a draft EIS based on that inventory as well as inputs from a public-involvement program completed in the fall of 1977. The draft EIS was designed to outline the choice process for assigning each tract to one of the following categories or status: wilderness, nonwilderness (multiple uses other than wilderness), and further planning for all uses, including wilderness. The number of tracts in the further-planning category were intended to be kept to a minimum. The USFS proposed allocating each tract within the overall study according to the following specific decision criteria:

> Alternative A. No other action than that presently being followed in land- and resource-management planning would take place with activities continuing as if RARE II did not exist.
>
> Alternative B. All roadless areas are allocated to nonwilderness areas.
>
> Alternative C. Emphasis is on high resource outputs, but consideration is given areas rated high in wilderness attributes.

Alternative D. Emphasis is given areas with high wilderness attributes, but any of those areas with significant resource-production potential are placed in the further-planning category.

Alternative E. Emphasis is on achieving an established minimum-level representation of landform, ecosystem, associated wildlife, and accessibility characteristics in the Wilderness System.

Alternative F. Emphasis is on achieving an established moderate level of the same characteristics as Alternative E in the Wilderness System.

Alternative G. Emphasis is on achieving an established high-level of the same characteristics as Alternative E in the Wilderness System.

Alternative H. Emphasis is on allocation of roadless areas on the basis of regional and local needs, as perceived by the Forest Service.

Alternative I. Emphasis is on adding areas with the highest wilderness attributes to the Wilderness System, with secondary consideration being given to areas of high resource-production potential.

Alternative J. All roadless areas are recommended for wilderness.[11]

The ten alternatives were supposed to be applied to each tract. The overall outcome of the process was perceived by the Forest Service as being a genuine attempt to balance energy-environment trade-offs on the basis of "resource opportunity costs, a rating of wilderness attributes and a series of criteria that reflect some components of a quality wilderness system."[12] Consequently, to identify the policy implications stemming from the USFS RARE II experience, it is first necessary to evaluate the substantive equity of that planning effort.

Assessing the USFS Planning Process

Substantive Equity

The tract allocations proposed by the USFS final EIS represent a synthesis of alternatives C and I, which emphasize high resource outputs and high-wilderness-attribute ratings "modified in response to public comment received on the draft environmental statement, existing laws and regulations, identified public needs, and professional judgment by Department of Agriculture decision-makers."[13] The final EIS recommended the following overall tract allocations: 15,088,838 acres in 624 tracts to wilderness status (24.3 percent); 36,151,588 acres in 1981 tracts to nonwilderness status (58.3 percent); and 10,796,508 acres in 314 tracts to further planning (17.4 percent). Empirically, such an allocation pattern suggests that the USFS did attempt to balance the trade-off between access for energy development as well as other multiple uses of forest areas with a desire to expand environmental protection. Although disagreement over the appropriate mix between wilderness and nonwilderness (for example, perceptual equity) or the extent to which USFS allocation choices complied with formal decision criteria (for example, procedural equity) may exist, the real pattern supports the conclusion that substantive equity concerns were addressed by the RARE II process.

Procedural Equity

As noted earlier, the 1964 Wilderness Act defined a wilderness as an area having natural integrity, opportunity for solitude, and opportunity for a primitive recreational experience. Such locales also might contain ecological, geological, or other features of scientific, educational, scenic, or historical value. To use these factors as evaluative criteria for allocating individual tracts under the RARE II process, the USFS developed an index that incorporated them into an indicator of each tract's wilderness attributes.[14] The draft EIS also included data for each tract on the known occurrence or likelihood estimates of geological favorability for reserves of oil and gas, coal, uranium, and, geothermal energy.[15] In addition, the presence in each tract of a number of other minerals considered critical for U.S. industry was assessed.[16] Thus, each tract received an individual appraisal of its wilderness attributes and of the presence or absence of energy and other critical mineral resources.[17] This raises the question of whether the USFS measures of wilderness attributes and resource potential guided tract-allocation decisions.

The case of the Idaho-Wyoming-Utah thrust-belt area, part of the Rocky Mountain Overthrust Belt, is an example of how important those factors were in guiding tract assignments.[18] The region has not only high wilderness potential but also high potential for both energy resources and critical minerals. For example, the Idaho-Wyoming-Utah thrust belt currently is one of the most important onshore regions for oil and gas exploration as a result of significant recent discoveries.[19] The region also contains more than one-half of the identified phosphate resources for the United States as a whole as well as other industrially or economically important critical minerals.[20] Moreover, its landforms, vegetation, and wildlife combine to create ecosystems possessing superior wilderness qualities.[21] As a result, it provides an ideal data base for testing whether or not tract allocations conformed to formal decision criteria.

Given the categorical measurement of the tract-allocation options, discriminant analysis provides an appropriate technique for assessing the importance of USFS estimates of tract-specific wilderness-attribute ratings, potential oil and gas resources, and potential critical-minerals resources in tract allocation.[22] In this case, two functions that represent a linear combination of the set of independent variables that distinguishes among the tract-allocation options are produced. The standardized coefficients for the independent variables measure their predictive capability and are similar in interpretation to beta weights, and the eta^2 coefficient is comparable to the R^2 value in regression analysis. Interpretation of the sign for each independent variable on the discriminant functions is keyed to the sign of the group centroids for the function. The group centroids are the mean values for each category of the scores that serve as an index to classify each case into the most appropriate category of the dependent variable. In this analysis, a negative sign of the centroids and, thus, for the independent variables on the first function was related to designating a tract as a wilderness area. Because the first function has maximum predictive capability for the model, interpretation focuses on the coefficients for that function.

The first function in table 4-1 distinguishes allocation under RARE II to a nonwilderness status from the other two options. The second function distinguishes the wilderness option from further planning and nonwilderness. Generally, the higher a tract's oil and gas or critical-minerals potential is, the more likely it is to be recommended by the USFS to nonwilderness status. Low wilderness-attribute ratings also tend to produce nonwilderness designation. Moreover, the analysis succeeds in classifying correctly USFS recommendations for a high percentage of the tracts (82.4 percent), with moderate overall predictive capability. Clearly, the USFS appears to have followed its decision criteria. Procedural compliance, however, does not necessarily guarantee public acceptance of the equitable nature of the underlying trade-offs.

Perceptual Equity

In addition to developing resource data for the various tracts, the USFS also attempted to obtain local input for the decision process primarily through public hearings, both before and after issuing the draft EIS. More than 264,000 replies from almost 360,000 people were received during the comment phase after the draft EIS was issued on 15 June 1978.[23] This tremendous outpouring of public reaction was encouraged and eagerly anticipated by the USFS as a means "to develop a sense of consensus or general public agreement."[24] In fact, the chief of the USFS, John R. McGuire, observed:

> One issue that has consistently blocked or diminished the effectiveness of our Land Management Planning on individual sites has been the entire roadless area controversy. To the extent we can settle this issue—or achieve a measure of resolution—then to that extent we can proceed more confidently with Land Management plans for these areas. . . . But, we need the public to let us know what broad bound it places on our actual decisions.[25]

Similar but somewhat more guarded optimism about RARE II's potential "to arrive at some final decision about the future use of the roadless areas in the National Forest System" is evident in congressional viewpoints.[26] Although recognizing that "expectations that RARE II will resolve the entire roadless area

Table 4–1

Standardized Discriminant Function Coefficients for Predictors of USFS Tract Allocations (Idaho-Wyoming-Utah Thrust-Belt Area)

	First Function	Second Function
Wilderness-attribute rating	−.421	.865
Critical minerals	.322	−.430
Oil and gas	.863	.470
Percent cases correctly predicted = 82.46%	eta^2 = .358	

issue in one fell swoop are unrealistic," Senator Baucus expressed the hope "that the current phase of the public evaluation of the program will generate enough information to foster consensus among forest user groups sufficient to settle, once and for all, a large portion of this total."[27]

Despite such official expectations, participation appears to have produced increased polarization among the major interest groups rather than fostered consensus about the equity of the USFS decisions. Most public response to the draft EIS as the USFS expected, was focused on outlining preferences for allocation of specific roadless areas. A significant volume of comment, however, concerned alternative approaches and decision criteria for land-use planning.[28] For example, environmentalist groups such as the Sierra Club claimed that the USFS substantially ignored their interests. They argued that preserving a high-quality wilderness system had become secondary to resource development, since, in their opinion, most of the USFS alternatives favored development interests. Consequently, they refused to acknowledge any of them. Instead, environmentalists proposed their own alternative—"Alternative W"—which allocates more acreage to wilderness than does the USFS final EIS.

Opposition to RARE II, however, was not limited exclusively to environmentalists. Wilderness areas differ from national parks, where motorized vehicles are allowed, and national forests, where grazing and timber or mineral development as well as camper-type activities can occur. As a result, although environmentalists have argued for more wilderness, industry and other development-oriented groups maintain that potential wilderness areas contain valuable natural resources that would be "lost" if those lands are given formal wilderness status. Similar reservations about reduced access are expressed by recreational groups such as skiers, hunters, snowmobilers, and four-wheel-drive-vehicle owners. In fact, the public response generated by the comment phase favored an "emphasis on economic values and jobs, timber production, and accessibility as reasons for allocating roadless areas to the nonwilderness category."[29]

Clearly, satisfying the demands of one interest coalition in the context of RARE II produces conflict because the demands of others go unanswered. Groups such as Friends of the Earth desire environmental protection; others like Americans for Energy Independence emphasize energy development. Each represents a legitimate response to a perceived public problem. The difficulty, in a policy sense, lies in the value assumptions and societal trade-offs that guide the selection of policy responses.

Contrary to what might be expected, substantive and procedural equities emerge as necessary but insufficient conditions for establishing policy consensus. Such consensus about policy decisions may be unattainable without a corresponding sense of perceptual equity in policymaking. The RARE II experience, at least, supports such an inference. Moreover, it should be apparent that the debate over wilderness preservation—as part of a larger national dialogue about energy-environment trade-offs—will not be resolved conclusively by the RARE II process.

Policy Implications

As this chapter illustrates, energy development and environmental protection appear to be highly interdependent, with obvious economic costs and benefits accruing to society regardless of which is emphasized. Moreover, this pattern is recurrent across the broad spectrum of energy-environment issues. Solutions to one question raise problems for other policy options whose benefits and costs may require major trade-offs among social goals. Selection of one option may reduce, if not eliminate, future opportunities to adopt others. Consequently, the potential for conflict is increased.

If, however, one projects a long-term as well as immediate dimension for energy policymaking, then the question of long-term environmental costs to fulfill immediate energy requirements becomes relevant. Under such circumstances, energy-development options that minimize lasting adverse environmental consequences would appear the most desirable socially. Adopting this perspective implies that policy options that foster energy development or environmental protection do not necessarily represent mutually exclusive choices. Instead, it seems reasonable to assume that their costs and benefits vary. Decision makers may select alternatives that maximize accommodation and minimize conflict, or they may adopt options that exacerbate conflict. Moreover, such a perspective not only emphasizes the consequences of action within either policy area but also focuses attention on the linkages between them.

The controversy surrounding the implementation of the RARE II process provides an excellent illustration of this phenomenon. Although wilderness designation is a national policy issue, tract allocation represents a question of land-use management for a specific site. Therefore, although the aggregate outcome of the process may be equitable, implementation occurs at the individual tract level. Each tract is assigned to either wilderness or nonwilderness.[30] Assuming subsequent development happens, allocation to nonwilderness essentially rules out future suitability for wilderness. On the other hand, designation as a wilderness reduces the likelihood but does not absolutely preclude future nonwilderness status. Thus, the outcome, although reversible (for example, nonzero sum) for protection, is potentially fixed for development.[31] Aa a result, even though avoidance of prolonged debate over tract assignment was the objective of the RARE II process (that is, to attain perceptual as well as procedural and substantive equity), such conflict was inevitable given the varying perceived costs and benefits for proponents and opponents of wilderness preservation on a tract-specific basis. This is the case in spite of the USFS's seeming compliance with its procedural decision criteria, which strive to balance energy-environment values in the substantive allocation of tracts.

Moreover, attempts to implement RARE II reveal that efforts to treat it as a comprehensive mechanism for policy choice isolated from the ongoing national debate over energy-environment trade-offs have been unsuccessful. This was especially true for efforts to build consensus about its equity through public participation. Such failure reflects the fact that the trade-offs are not uniform for all the interested parties. This lack of uniformity increases the problem of establishing perceptual equity and accommodating divergent interests in the absence of a common basis for compromise. In fact, expanding public participation (a central feature of RARE II) increased the potential for divergence rather than rapid consensus over desired outcomes.[32] Given the expansion of preferences articulated in the RARE II process, conflict over outcomes of decision making was inevitable and also understandable, since decisions on individual-tract assignment represent choices between competing as well as alternative value hierarchies.

The irony is that in spite of establishing substantive and procedural equity the RARE II experience may be mistakenly interpreted as evidence that systematic attempts at policymaking are doomed to failure. In reality, although comprehensive efforts often encounter tremendous scale problems vis à vis applying their decision rules to individual cases, the so-called error of Rare II appears to be one not of scope but rather of the assumption that such comprehensiveness automatically will minimize conflict. Instead, the very comprehensiveness of RARE II, with its emphasis on allocating all tracts at one time, although attractive from a rational perspective, was a primary source of difficulty in consensus formation (for example, attaining perceptual equity). Because the temporal dimension for bargaining opportunities was reduced, the appearance, if not reality, of a zero-sum game was created at the individual level even though the aggregate outcome may well be nonzero sum. Unlike incrementalism, comprehensive planning strategies may identify more clearly the likelihood that such barriers to policy agreement will emerge. Unfortunately, the analysis also reveals that attaining substantive and procedural equity through comprehensive planning does not necessarily guarantee consensus formation and its accompanying sense of procedural equity. Instead, such an approach serves primarily to highlight the effects of variable trade-offs, and the policymaking process (which inherently involves politics) merely represents a potential avenue for accommodating conflicting interests.

Notes

1. Precisely defining environmental quality is difficult—it encompasses a number of problems, including air pollution, water pollution, wildlife and wilderness protection, land use, solid-waste management, chemical use, noise abatement, radiation protection, and resource conservation. For a review of this conflict see J.L. Regens, "Energy Development, Environmental Protection and Public Policy," *American Behavioral Scientists* 22 (November/December 1978): 175-190.

2. U.S. Department of Agriculture, Forest Service, *Draft Environmental Statement Roadless Area Review and Evaluation* (Washington, D.C., 1978).

3. Ibid., p. 5.

4. The act, in establishing wilderness preservation as a national policy, created the National Wilderness Preservation System (NWPS), initially consisting of 9.1 million acres. The NWPS, as of April 1978, contains more than 16.6 million acres located in national forests, national parks, and wildlife refuges.

5. M. Clawson, *Forests for Whom and for What?* (Baltimore: John Hopkins University, 1975), p. 125.

6. For a discussion of the concept see R. Nash, *Wilderness and the American Mind* (New Haven, Conn.: Yale University, 1967).

7. U.S. Department of Agriculture, Forest Service, *Summary—Final Environmental Statement: Roadless Area Review and Evaluation* (Washington, D.C., 1979), p. 1.

8. See I.L. White et al., *Energy from the West: Policy Analysis Report* (Washington, D.C.: Environmental Protection Agency, 1979). A number of areas with substantial known or potential mineral deposits, including energy resources, such as large portions of the Rocky Mountain Overthrust Belt, are included for possible designation as wilderness areas.

9. Rocky Mountain Oil and Gas Association, "Petroleum Industry Estimates of 'Undiscovered Recoverable Hydrocarbon Resources' in Tracts Covered by the Forest Service 'Roadless Area Review and Evaluation (RARE II)'," (memorandum, 10 March 1978), mimeo.

10. M. Baucus, "The RARE II Process: Congressional Views, Cares, Concerns" in *Professional Perspectives on RARE II Decision-Making for the Western*

United States, R.E. Shannon et al., eds., (Missoula, Mont.: School of Forestry, University of Montana, 1978), p. 160.

11. This is the specific wording of the criteria for each alternative. U.S. Department of Agriculture, *Summary—Final Environmental Statement,* pp. 2–3.

12. U.S. Department of Agriculture, *Draft Environmental Statement,* p. 21.

13. U.S. Department of Agriculture, *Summary—Final Environmental Statement,* p. 3.

14. Three-member teams assigned numerical values ranging from 4 (lowest) to 28 (highest) to each tract, using as much objective or descriptive data as possible, to reflect each individual tract's overall wilderness-attribute rating. Emphasis was placed on conceptual consistency, reliability, and validity. See U.S. Department of Agriculture, Forest Service Wilderness Attribute Rating System Task Force, *RARE II Wilderness Attribute Rating System—A User's Manual* (Washington, D.C., 1977). For the actual ratings for specific tracts, see the supplements to the U.S. Department of Agriculture, *Draft Environmental Statement.*

15. First, tracts were assigned to one of the following categories of resource potential: (1) low—no favorable geology and no mineral occurences; (2) moderate—favorable geology, but few or no mineral occurences; and (3) high—known mineral occurences in the area and the geology is favorable for reserves. For each tract in the high-potential category, a simple yes/no coding format was then used to indicate the known and/or potential occurence of each energy resource. See the supplements to the U.S. Department of Agriculture, *Draft Environmental Statement.*

16. For RARE II purposes, forty-five nonenergy minerals considered critical were treated as a group. A simple yes/no coding format was used to indicate the presence or absence of any critical minerals within each tract. Ibid.

17. Because original tract-specific resource data would have been costly to generate, assessments previously developed by the U.S. Geological Survey (USGS) and the Department of Energy (DOE) of the proven or possible presence of the energy and critical minerals resources were used for RARE II. The USFS only provided final resources ratings derived from the more detailed USGS and DOE data without furnishing the supporting data used in RARE II.

18. The area is bounded on the north by the Snake River volcanic plain, on the east by a line projected northward along and beyond the trace of the crest of the Moxa arch, on the south by the North Flank fault of the Unita Mountains, and on the west by the Wasatch fault. Strictly speaking, the Gros Ventre Mountains and the Grand Tetons are not part of the Idaho-Wyoming-Utah thrust belt. The area comprises about 15 million acres, and the USFS identified sixty-three RARE II tracts totalling approximately 3.1 million acres within it.

19. *Oil and Gas Journal,* (13 March 1978).

20. J.B. Cathcart and R.A. Gulbrandsen, "Phosphate Deposits," in *United States Mineral Resources,* D.A. Brobst and W.P. Pratt, eds. (Washington, D.C.:

U.S. Geological Survey, 1973). Although the western-U.S. phosphate resources are important in their own right, they also contain significant low-grade concentrations of other critical mineral elements.

21. R.G. Bailey, *Ecoregions of the United States* (Ogden, Utah: U.S. Forest Service, 1976).

22. The entire Idaho-Wyoming-Utah thrust belt has some uranium potential, so this indicator of energy resources was excluded, since it is a constant. Coal was also excluded as a variable because only a few RARE II tracts contain outcrops of minable coal and lignite.

23. U.S. Department of Agriculture, *Summary—Final Environmental Statement,* p. 2.

24. Z. Smith, "RARE II: Status and Outlook," in Shannon, *Professional Perspectives,* p. 130.

25. J.R. McGuire, "RARE II: A Broader View," in Shannon *Professional Perspectives,* pp. 116–118.

26. Baucus, "RARE II Process," p. 159.

27. Ibid., p. 161.

28. See U.S. Department of Agriculture, *Summary—Final Environmental Statement,* p. 4. Formal statistical analyses of the public-comment data are not available at this time and were not provided in the final EIS.

29. Based on its own analysis of response content rather than the number of signatures, the USFS concluded that support for nonwilderness allocation exceeded responses supporting wilderness allocation by a margin of approximately 3 to 1. Ibid, p. 5.

30. As noted earlier, a small percentage (17.4 percent) were allocated to further planning, which represents a holding category that defers final decision making.

31. As the name implies, some outcomes are termed zero-sum because the costs and benefits of the policy options are arrayed in such a manner that their payoffs add to zero for the paritcipants (that is, one "player" wins whatever the other loses). In the nonzero-sum situation, the sum of the payoffs does not add to zero or any other fixed constant. This is the case because some outcomes will yield more joint costs or benefits to the participants than others. For a discussion of these concepts see R.D. Luce and H. Raiffa, *Games and Decisions* (New York: Wiley, 1957).

32. The public comment provides an excellent illustration of this phenomenon. Although an individual tract ultimately can be assigned to only one category, public responses often argued for allocating the same tract to both wilderness and nonwilderness.

5

Technology, Domestic Structures, and Ocean-Pollution Regulation

James. P. Lester

Despite the increased salience of marine-environment protection both within the United States and abroad, collective responses to the global problem of ocean pollution from ships and oil continue to lag far behind the need for such action. Although several nations (beginning in 1954) have proposed international conventions for dealing with such aspects of marine pollution as prevention, control, and liability, it is striking that half of these conventions have not received timely ratification by the requisite number of nations (see table 5-1). Moreover, the advanced industrial nations of the West, with control of much of the international shipping and oil interests, exhibit substantial variation in their ratification of these international conventions.[1]

This chapter explores the role and influence of domestic structures on international cooperation on ocean-pollution regulation. Most studies in this century have suggested that the nation-state lies at the root of international conflict and that its weakening, circumvention, or transcendence is necessary to strengthen international cooperation. For example, early proponents of international organization at the turn of the century advocated the direct transfer of national authority to international institutions, codified in various international legal instruments, such as the Conventions of the Hague Conference and the Covenant of the League of Nations. Functionalists subsequently foresaw the gradual circumvention of the nation-state through the growth of international tasks and organizations that dealt with practical rather than political issues. Neofunctionalists identified an inexorable logic and mechanism (spillover) whereby functionally related activities would eventually alter national attitudes and institutions and create new supranational political authorities. Most recently, transnational and interdependence theorists have emphasized the roles of non-nation-state actors and new international circumstances that constrain and limit the authority and options of national governments.[2]

Thanks are extended to the Texas A&M University Research Committee for a summer research stipend to support a portion of this research; to the Graduate Program in Science, Technology, and Public Policy at The George Washington University for providing me with clerical services and support; and to Henry R. Nau, James M. McCormick, Harvey J. Tucker, and Michael J. Stoil for their constructive suggestions. None of them bears any responsibility for my analyses and interpretations.

Table 5-1

International Conventions and Other Agreements for the Prevention and Control of Marine Pollution

Conventions, Treaties, Protocols, Regulations, and Standards	Pollutant	Responsible Body	Status May 1979
International Convention for the Prevention of Pollution of the Sea by Oil, 1954	Oil	IMCO	In force
Amendments to the International Convention for the Prevention of Pollution of the Sea by Oil, 1971 (Great Barrier Reef)	Oil	IMCO	Not yet in force
Amendments to the International Convention for the Prevention of Pollution of the Sea by Oil, 1971 (Tanks)	Oil	IMCO	Not yet in force
International Convention Relating to Invervention on the High Seas in Cases of Oil Pollution Casualties, 1969	Oil	IMCO	In force
International Convention on Civil Liability for Oil Pollution Damage, 1969	Oil	IMCO	In force
International Convention on the Establishment of an International Fund for Compensation for Oil Pollution Damage, 1971	Oil	IMCO	In force
International Convention for the Prevention of Pollution from Ships, 1973	Oil	IMCO	Not yet in force
Protocol Relating to Intervention on the High Seas in Cases of Pollution by Substances Other than Oil, 1973	Other substances than oil	IMCO	Not yet in force
Convention on the Prevention of Marine Pollution by the Dumping of Wastes and Other Matter, 1972	All wastes	IMCO	In force
Protocol of 1978 Relating to the International Convention for the Prevention of Pollution from Ships, 1973	Oil	IMCO	Not yet in force

Source: Intergovernmental Maritime Consultative Organization: Marine Environment Protection Committee, *Status of International Conventions Relating to Marine Pollution of which IMCO is Depositary or Is Responsible for Secretariat Duties*, XI/2/1, (May 4, 1979).

All these approaches share the view that the nation-state is antithetical to the growth and development of international cooperation. But is it? A few studies have suggested that a strong nation-state may be a prerequisite to effective international cooperation. In an insightful article in *Foreign Affairs,* Robert L. Paarlberg argued that "improved domestic policy leadership is the true precondition for effective welfare management abroad. Global welfare cannot be properly managed abroad until it has been tolerably managed at home. Without a prior exercise of domestic political authority, the global welfare crisis will not admit to efficient interstate control."[3] Others have emphasized national strength abroad as well as at home as a prerequisite for international cooperation. Historically, dominant or hegemonial states have fostered international cooperation, albeit to serve their own imperialistic or altruistic visions of global order.[4]

What are the determinants of international cooperation and, in particular, the role of the nation-state in such cooperation? Is there evidence that an internally strong nation-state inhibits or accelerates international cooperation?

This chapter explores these questions in the specific sector of ocean-pollution regulation. A growing body of literature suggests that, in this sector above all, the nation-state is being increasingly weakened both by the expanding scope of modern technology, which is global in its consequences, and by the deepening intensity of technological change, which particularizes interests and makes national consensus and decision making more difficult.[5] What evidence can we bring to bear to confirm, modify, or refute this proposition?

Out dependent variable is international cooperation. The independent variable of primary interest is the nation-state. The simple proposition is that a strong nation-state correlates with more international cooperation in ocean-pollution regulation and a weak state demonstrates a propensity toward less cooperation.

In other words, we contend that there is an important intervening variable between physical capabilities of states and international cooperation in ocean-pollution regulation. This variable is organizational capabilities, involving a state's capacity to mobilize its resources and to apply these resources to international cooperation. This variable is more closely attuned to a state's political and institutional as opposed to physical and resource strength. A state may have abundant resources (for example, as the United States is said to have in energy), yet not be able to mobilize these resources if its internal institutions and society are fragmented and weak (as the United States has shown itself to be in energy). On the other hand, the stronger a state's organizational capabilities are, the better that state may be able to mobilize its resources for international cooperation, even if these resources are relatively small.

Several concepts are helpful in analyzing a state's internal organizational capabilities. In the literature on political economy, the concept of *domestic structures* refers to governing coalitions and policy networks within a state that determine the degree of centralization in that state and influence the type of foreign economic strategies that states adopt.[6] *Policy networks* refer to what we call "organizational capabilities" (both formal and informal relationships) and differ depending on the degree of differentiation (or, conversely, centralization) that exists between the state and the society in a given country (public versus private sector) and the degree of centralization that exists within the state and within the society. Thus one way to test for the influence of organizational capabilities is to operationalize the concepts of centralization within the state and between the state and the society. This we have done in the ocean-pollution area to test the notion that centralized structures promote international collaboration.

In addition to the role and influence of domestic-resource capabilities (that is, economic development and technological capability) and domestic organizational capabilities, the comparative ocean-policy literature suggests some possible determinants of international ocean-pollution regulation. For example, John Gamble finds that the strongest factors associated with international agreements on oil pollution within the International Maritime Consultative Organization (IMCO) are GNP, GNP per capita, the literacy rate, and international-organization membership. He concludes that "prosperity" and "internationalism" are the major determinants of international ocean-pollution regulation.[7]

Based on this discussion then, the following hypotheses are postulated for testing. The first hypothesis reflects functionalist logic:

H-1: The greater the level of economic development and technological capability of a nation is, the greater is the tendency of that nation to cooperate on ocean-pollution regulation; conversely, a lesser level of resource capabilities means a lesser level of cooperation.

The next three hypotheses suggest that domestic structures influence international collaboration:

H-2: Nations with unitary (centralized) governmental structures are more likely to cooperate than those having federal structures.

H-3: Nations with centralized organizational structures for environmental policymaking are more likely to cooperate than those nations having fragmented organizational structures for environmental policymaking.

H-4: Nations with more centralized state-society structures for R&D are more likely to cooperate than those having decentralized state-society structures.

Our final hypotheses are derived from Gamble's findings with regard to the educational-attainment level of industrial nations, as well as their "internationalist orientation":

H-5: Nations with a more educated population are more likely to cooperate than those having a less educated population.

H-6: The greater the membership in international organizations concerned with ocean-pollution regulation, is, the greater is the cooperation.

To examine these fundamental propositions, two approaches are employed. The analysis begins with an examination of bivariate statistical relationships between several theoretical linkages to ocean-pollution regulation; thereafter, I supplement these aggregate data with a discussion of U.S. involvement (as an example of a highly fragmented domestic structure) in ocean-pollution regulation. This latter discussion details the specific nature of domestic structural factors that inhibit international support for ocean-pollution regulation.

Concepts and Measures

The concepts and measures for our aggregate-data analysis are shown in table 5-2. This analysis is applied to the Western European and other states (WEO) (which are the most active nations in ocean-pollution regulation within the Intergovernmental Maritime Consultative Organization) during the period 1974 to 1978.[8]

Our dependent variable, international cooperation in ocean-pollution regulation, is measured by the number of actual ratifications of ocean-pollution conventions divided by the total number of conventions in a given year under consideration within IMCO. This percentage would then indicate the degree of actual cooperation to potential cooperation. However, it is also necessary to weight this score to control for a given country's shipping interest in the regulation of ocean pollution. It is far more significant behavior when a country with 10 percent of the world's total oil-tanker tonnage ratifies conventions concerned with ocean pollution than when another country with minimal tanker tonnage ratifies the same number of conventions. Thus, a country's individual score is weighted by the percentage of the world's tanker fleet held by that particular country and calculated separately for each of the years 1974 to 1978. The data for the number of conventions ratified by each country for a given year were collected by IMCO and published as working documents for each IMCO Marine Environmental Protection Committee (MEPC) meeting, beginning in 1974. The data for each country's oil-tanker fleet within a given year are taken from *Lloyd's Register of Shipping: Statistical Tables* (1974-1978). Using these two sources of data, the country scores are computed for the years 1974-1978 and are presented in table 5-3.

The independent variables considered to be most important for explaining international ocean-pollution regulation are economic development, technological capability, educational attainment, internationalism, and domestic structural centralization. In this chapter, economic development is expressed as GNP per capita. The source for this variable is the *Statistical Abstract,* vols. 1974-1978.[9]

Technological capability in this functional area is represented by the percentage of the GNP devoted to gross national expenditures on environmental R&D. The data on environmental R&D are found in UNESCO, *Statistical Yearbook,* for the years 1975, 1976, and 1977.[10]

The level of educational attainment by each country is measured by the percentage of the adult population that entered the highest level of secondary education. This particular indicator is selected to allow a comparison with

Table 5-2
The Conceptual Model

Concepts	Description/Rationale	Operationalization
Dependent variable		
International collaboration	Nations cooperate as a consequence of domestic resource capabilities, internationalism, and domestic structures.	(percent of world tanker fleet $\times$ $r/R)^a$
Independent variables		
Domestic resources	Suggests resources available for international cooperation.	
Economic development		GNP per capita
Technological capability		Environmental R&D $\div$ GNP
Internationalism	Suggests a tendency toward international collaboration on the basis of community knowledge of, and interest in solving, global resource problems.	
Education		Number of persons entering highest level of secondary education $\div$ total adult population
IO membership[b]		Actual memberships $\div$ potential memberships
Domestic structures	Suggests resources mobilized for international collaboration.	
State centralization (overall)		Unitary versus federal structure
State centralization (specific)		Centralized versus fragmented structure for environmental policymaking
State-society centralization		Centralization of R&D Funding: 2 = government funding 1 = equally funded by government and private sources 0 = private-sector funding

[a]r = number of conventions actually ratified; R = total number of conventions considered within IMCO.

[b]Refers to memberships in international organizations concerned only with ocean pollution.

Gamble's findings concerned with the influence of education on ocean-pollution regulation. The data for this variable are found in UNESCO, *Statistical Yearbook: 1977.*

Table 5–3
Individual-County Scores for Ocean-Pollution Regulation,
1974–1978

Country	1974	1975	1976	1977	1978
Australia	.005	.006	.003	.003	.001
Belgium	.009	.008	.005	.006	.005
Canada	.010	.008	.006	.006	.005
Denmark	.076	.091	.089	.092	.082
France	.183	.292	.222	.260	.266
Germany	.023	.046	.059	.081	.097
Greece	.081	.201	.257	.269	.236
Ireland	.000	.000	.000	.000	.000
Italy	.038	.064	.108	.104	.080
Japan	.429	.375	.500	.484	.370
Netherlands	.027	.021	.066	.050	.048
New Zealand	.000	.000	.001	.001	.001
Norway	.692	.683	.719	.670	.563
Spain	.048	.041	.086	.116	.112
Sweden	.123	.181	.200	.195	.143
Switzerland	.000	.000	.000	.000	.000
United Kingdom	.571	.625	.664	.669	.575
United States of America	.155	.123	.127	.132	.149

Note: Countries were excluded that were not members of IMCO (for example, Turkey) or that had no oil-tanker tonnage (for example, Austria).

Internationalism is measured by the number of functional international-organization memberships held by a particular country. Gamble's research suggests that combined membership in the Food and Agricultural Organization (FAO), IMCO, the Intergovernmental Oceanographic Commission (IOC), the Intergovernmental Maritime Committee (IMC), World Health Organization (WHO), World Meteorological Organization (WMO), UNESCO, UN Environmental Program (UNEF), and the International Atomic Energy Association (IAEA) is an important predictor of cooperative behavior in ocean-pollution regulation. Each nation's score on this variable is based on the percentage of memberships held by each country in these nine functional organizations. The data are drawn from the *Yearbook of International Organizations: 1978* (Brussels: Union of International Associations, 1978).[11]

Domestic structural centralization is, as we have discussed previously, our central concept. To tap this concept, three single measures are used. The first measure is the degree of vertical centralization of authority for policymaking in general. A unitary system is representative of a highly centralized structure of authority, and a federal system reflects a decentralized structure. The source of this variable is Arthur S. Banks and Robert B. Textor, *A Cross-Polity Survey.*[12]

A more issue-specific measure of intragovernmental centralization of authority is provided by a nation's organizational structure for environmental policymaking. Nations were coded as being either centralized (1) or decentralized (0) in terms of their domestic organizational structure for environmental policymaking. Data for this variable are taken from several sources.[13]

A third aspect of the domestic structure relates to the structure of R&D funding between the state (public sector) and the society (private sector). The national R&D efforts of OECD (Organization for Economic Cooperation and Development) countries are almost exclusively financed by government and/or business enterprise. There are major differences, however, between countries in the respective roles of the two sectors. Broadly speaking, the countries belong to one of three groups in which R&D is (1) mainly government funded (55 percent and over); (2) financed equally by government and business; and (3) mainly business funded (55 percent and over).

Countries in which the R&D funding is mainly through business are considered to be decentralized state-society structures and are coded 0. Those nations in which R&D funding is mainly through the public sector are considered to have more centralized state-society relationships and are coded 2. Those nations in which R&D is equally financed by government and business are coded 1. The data for this variable are provided by OECD, *Patterns of Resources Devoted to Research and Development in the OECD Area.*[14]

Findings

Table 5–4 presents the findings for the rank-order correlations between two categories of our independent variables and ocean-pollution regulation. An examination of table 5–4 reveals that domestic resources are only weakly related to collective behavior in this policy arena; moreover, the relationships are in the opposite direction to the initial hypotheses, suggesting that the more prosperous, better educated, and technologically advanced nations are less likely to support ocean-pollution regulation than are less prosperous, less educated, and less technologically advanced nations. The findings that economic development and technological capability are inversely related to collaboration is consistent with the findings by Ruggie, who argues that " . . . as national capabilities increase and become sufficient to perform a given task, the propensity for international collaboration (in that instance) decreases."[15] Further,the magnitude of the relationship between technological capability and collaboration is extremely weak.

The finding that a nation's educational attainment level is negatively related to ocean-pollution regulation conflicts with the earlier findings by Gamble.[16] The present results suggest that as the percentage of the adult population entering secondary school increases, there is less support for ocean-pollution regulation. To some extent, this finding is explained by some intercorrelation between education and economic development, since the most economically developed nations are also the most educationally advanced ($r = .38$). In addition, in a recent case study of ocean-pollution regulation, it was observed that the most advanced nations perceived that they would suffer a greater relative disadvantage than the less advanced nations if these ocean pollution regulations were adopted. This case study describes several instances in which the wealthier, more capable,

Table 5–4

Spearman Correlation Coefficients Showing the Relationship between Selected Independent Variables and Ocean-Pollution Regulation, 1974–1978

Independent Variables	1974	1975	1976	1977	1978
Domestic resources					
Economic development	−.04	−.06	−.06	−.00	−.03
Technological capability	−.09	−.24	−.08	−.04	.01
Internationalism					
Education	−.24	−.28	−.28	−.32	−.32
IO membership	.03	.04	.04	.06	.08

Note: A visual examination of scatterplots, on which the actual amounts were plotted, showed the effect of one or two extreme values of countries, at both ends, in resources and in international ocean-pollution regulation. Therefore, the correlations reported here are based on rank orders, using the *rho* coefficient. In addition, correlations were also calculated on the basis of actual amounts; the results generally were lower but still negative.

and better educated countries perceived certain ocean-pollution regulations as an attempt by the poorer countries to promote economic (versus environmental) ends.[17]

The findings for the relationship between membership in functional international organizations and ocean-pollution regulation offer strikingly little support for hypothesis 6. It is true that the direction of the findings is generally consonant with the predictions advanced—that is, the greater a country's membership in international organizations concerned with ocean-pollution regulation is, the greater is the cooperation. Thus, the claim made for the importance of membership in international organizations concerned with ocean-pollution regulation is vindicated if one only considers the direction of the results.

However, it is obvious from the size of the correlations that the magnitude of the relationships is extremely weak, in most instances bordering on the trivial. The highest *rho* coefficient is .08 (in 1978). Thus, these results are so miniscule as to raise serious questions about the relevance of membership in international organizations as a predictor of international cooperation.

It could be argued that other measures of internationalism, such as a nation's total financial contribution to international organizations concerned with ocean-pollution regulation, would produce different results. This may be true, and this possibility should be examined in future studies. However, given the meager rank-order correlations reported here, it is doubtful if that impact will be particularly large.

Turning now to a discussion of the primary focus of this chapter, we examine the relationship between our three measures of domestic structure and ocean-pollution regulation. Table 5–5 presents the mean scores for each category

Table 5-5
A Comparison of Mean Cooperation Scores by Type of Structure,
1974–1978

Type of Structure	1974	1975	1976	1977	1978
Overall governmental structure					
Unitary	.175	.199	.224	.229	.199
Federal	.038	.037	.039	.044	.050
Domestic-agency structure					
Centralized	.252	.267	.260	.256	.223
Fragmented	.023	.041	.092	.072	.066
Public-private structure					
Centralized	.223	.261	.266	.267	.243
Neither	.102	.110	.122	.127	.111
Fragmented	.106	.114	.156	.152	.128

Note: The higher the mean score reported, the stronger the support for ocean-pollution regulation.

of our domestic structural variables. In every instance, we notice that nations having more centralized structures tend to promote foreign policymaking on ocean-pollution regulation to a greater extent than do nations having more fragmented structures, as evidenced by the higher mean scores. Thus, the findings in table 5-5 are consistent with our hypothesized relationships between each measure of the domestic structure and ocean-pollution regulation.

In addition, the magnitudes of these relationships are moderately strong, as shown in table 5-6. The highest positive eta coefficient is .56, and the highest partial beta is .88 [for state (agency) centralization]. The betas show that centralization of authority for environmental policymaking is the strongest positive influence on ocean-pollution regulation among the variables considered. As we discussed, this finding may be explained by the suggestion that centralization of authority may facilitate cooperation by minimizing interagency disputes, which could delay or block such cooperation. We will further explore this explanation in the concluding discussion.

In addition, the betas for public-private centralization range from .21 to .36, thus providing moderate support for hypothesis 4. This finding may also be explained by the suggestion that centralization of R&D further concentrates R&D resources, thus increasing the pool of available resources that might be readily applied to international projects concerned with ocean-pollution regulation.

The relationship between the measure of the overall governmental structure (federal or unitary) and collaboration was extremely weak for the years 1974 to 1976. Therefore, the findings show that during the period 1974 to 1976, a

Table 5-6
Multiple Classification Analysis Showing the Relationship
between Domestic Structures and Ocean-Pollution
Regulation, 1974–1978

Independent Variables	1974 Eta	1974 Beta	1975 Eta	1975 Beta	1976 Eta	1976 Beta	1977 Eta	1977 Beta	1978 Eta	1978 Beta
Domestic structures										
Overall governmental structure	.30	.01	.35	.09	.38	.06	.38	.44	.35	.27
Domestic-agency centralization	.56	.64	.55	.61	.44	.69	.43	.88	.43	.65
Public-private structure	.26	.22	.32	.31	.27	.36	.27	.30	.31	.21

Note: Eta is analogous to simple r and beta may be viewed as a standardized partial-regression coefficient.

nation's overall government structure was relatively unimportant in promoting policies for ocean pollution regulation. However, by 1977–1978, the influence of unitary structures increased substantially, suggesting that the overall governmental structure has a delayed effect on policymaking in this arena. Although not an immediate influence, this structural variable eventually exerts its influence as nations go about the lengthy process of policy formulation through ratification of ocean-pollution regulations. Every nation must present each convention to its home government for ratification, and nations having unitary structures are thus able to complete the process more rapidly. Centralization of authority provides for concerted action in the environmental sphere and apparently allows the central government the initiative and ability to intervene directly to promote policies in a particular area. Federal structures pose certain problems for the formulation (and coherence) of foreign policy. In such structures, foreign policy is often susceptible to undermining by provincial authorities, or constitutional and legislative procedures deny flexibility and rapid response vis-à-vis global problems.[18]

Finally, as table 5-7 illustrates, the domestic structural variables (as a separate category of factors) were better able to account for the variation in ratification scores than either of our two other categories of variables. As expected, domestic structures explained more total variation in ocean-pollution regulation than either domestic resources or internationalism for the years 1974 to 1976 and as much variation as explained by resource factors in 1977 and 1978. These findings suggest that domestic structures are at least equal to domestic-resource factors in their explanatory contribution toward ocean-pollution regulation; this contributes to our initial argument concerning the significance of domestic structures on foreign policymaking.

Table 5-7
Predictive Ability of the Three Categories of Independent
Variables on International Cooperation in Ocean-Pollution
Regulation, 1974-1978

Independent Variables	1974	1975	1976	1977	1978
Domestic structures					
Multiple R	.61	.62	.53	.52	.51
Total variance explained (R^2)	.37 (.35)[a]	.38 (.35)	.28 (.22)	.27 (.21)	.26 (.23)
Domestic resources					
Multiple R	.15	.14	.17	.52	.51
Total variance explained	.02	.02	.03	.27	.26
Internationalism					
Multiple R	.24	.28	.30	.34	.35
Total variance explained	.06	.08	.09	.12	.12

[a]The first R^2 value refers to the following two measures of domestic structures: overall governmental structure and domestic-agency centralization; the value within the parentheses refers to the following two measures: domestic-agency centralization and the public-private structure.

Conclusions

These findings carry rather significant policy implications. For the advanced industrial countries, it is found that nations with more centralized domestic structures are more likely to reach timely agreement on concrete goals of collective action concerned with the regulation of ocean pollution. This implies that nations with highly fragmented organizational structures for environmental policymaking might benefit from organizational centralization if their policy objective is ocean pollution-regulation. Before such conclusions are drawn, however, the precise mechanisms by which domestic structures frustrate multilateral attempts to regulate ocean pollution should be subject to analytical scrutiny through in-depth case studies that explore these relationships. Case studies selected to represent both highly centralized states (Denmark, France, United Kingdom, for example) as well as highly fragmented states (Canada, Germany, Switzerland, for example) should devote particular attention to the role and influence of several key domestic groups (especially Parliament, the bureaucracy, and the oil and shipping industries) on the policy responses of these states to ocean pollution.

Previous research by others, as well as on-going research by this author, have found U.S. involvement in this foreign-policy arena to be characterized by:

1. significant intervention by domestic groups (for example, Congress, the bureaucracy, and private industry); and

2. a basic dissensus between government agencies, between agencies and industry, and within agencies over the desirability of certain technical ocean-pollution-prevention, control, and liability measures.[19]

For example, the oil and shipping interests have consistently opposed measures that will cost the regulated industries additional expenses, either through the alteration of ship design and the reduction of cargo capacity or through the installation of additional equipment. The issue of double bottoms and segregated ballast (SBT) has been the most controversial issue in IMCO discussions, with private industry opposing retrofitting of SBT to tankers of any size—they believe that other measures (especially crude-oil washing) are just as effective; moreover, the industries are opposed to double bottoms on all new tankers.[20]

Secondly, U.S. interagency participation in ocean-pollution discussions has been characterized as a highly fragmented, adversary process. Federal marine science and other oceanic activities are conducted by more than twenty-one organizations in six departments and five agencies. Among these institutions are the departments of State, Commerce, Interior, and Treasury; the Environmental Protection Agency (EPA); the Coast Guard; the Executive Office of the President, including the Council on Environmental Quality (CEQ); the Office of Management and Budget (OMB); and the National Science Foundation (NSF). Each agency, like each government at the IMCO meetings, has often attempted to maximize its particular interests at the expense of the others. Moreover, significant disputes between agencies have continued to arise as the international negotiations generate pressure for trade-offs of interests.

For example, at the Tanker Safety and Pollution Prevention (TSPP) conference, a major agency conflict developed around the issue of SBT for existing tankers. The environmentalists, including CEQ, EPA, and NOAA were in opposition to the position held by the U.S. Coast Guard and the U.S. Maritime Administration. Specifically, CEQ and other environmentalists were in favor of SBT for all ships of 20,000 dwt and above. After TSPP, CEQ testified before Congress on that measure, much to the embarassment of the U.S. State Department.[21]

Another example of interagency conflict occurred in connection with the double-bottom issue and illustrated that the environmentalists themselves often disagreed. With regard to the double-bottom issue, EPA was itself divided. Prior to the TSPP Conference in 1978, EPA's International Affairs Office favored a unilateral approach that would result in tougher domestic standards than those being proposed at IMCO, and the Office of Water Programs (now the Office of Water and Hazardous Materials) supported the Coast Guard position favoring a substitute for SBT and double bottoms.[22]

The influence of the U.S. Congress on efforts to regulate ocean pollution from oil and ships may be described as a curious paradox. Congressional involvement exerts a positive influence in the sense that the underlying threat of national (domestic) action serves as a strong incentive for multilateral (and harmonious) action. At the same time, however, the Senate has inhibited efforts to regulate ocean pollution by its failure to give timely consent to ratification of the 1973 Convention for the Prevention of Pollution from Ships, the 1969 Convention on Civil Liability for Oil Pollution Damage, the 1971 Fund for Compensation for Oil Pollution Damage, and the 1978 Protocols to the 1973 MARPOL Convention.

Several alternative explanations may be advanced for the reasons behind the U.S. failure to ratify. First, under the assumption that the environmentalists (and environmental factors) are controlling, it can be argued that the conventions are simply too lenient in their standards for pollution prevention, control, and liability. The argument is that the Senate will not advance ratification until IMCO strengthens these regulations up to the standards proposed under domestic legislation currently pending before Congress. For example, the Senate opposes ratification of the 1969 Liability Convention because the upper limits are too low. Moreover, the Convention does not impose liability limits outside territorial waters. Essentially, it is believed by the Senate that this Convention establishes a weak liability regime.[23]

A second possible explanation is based on the assumption that political and economic factors are controlling. The argument is that, if the United States ratifies the 1973 Convention or the 1978 Protocol but adopts more stringent domestic standards, then ratification would give a commercial advantage to nations not serving U.S. ports. Two standards would be in effect—one for ships serving U.S. ports and one standard for ships serving non-U.S. ports.[24]

Finally, a third explanation holds that domestic structural considerations are controlling. It is argued that the U.S. ocean-policy process is complicated by its highly fragmented nature. Thus, the conventions have not been ratified in the United States simply because it takes a good deal of time to process these conventions. Moreover, the Senate Foreign Relations Committee has been heavily involved in more pressing matters than ocean pollution, and, consequently, the conventions were held up by deliberation over SALT, the Middle East situation, and African matters.[25]

Although each of these explanations may, in part, help to explain the failure of the Senate to ratify these conventions, the point is that these interactions have delayed international action to regulate ocean pollution. In other words U.S. foreign policymaking for ocean-pollution regulation has been inhibited by a highly fragmented domestic structure in the United States. Specifically, fragmentation has resulted in extensive interagency (and intraagency) conflict and intervention by other domestic groups. Multiple points of access to policymaking in a fragmented domestic structure thus facilitated intervention and delay by industry and congressional actors.

In summary, the finding that differences in domestic structures lead to differences in international support for ocean-pollution regulation is but a step toward a validated empirical generalization. What is needed now are more clinical and intensive examinations of selected countries' involvement (other than the United States) in ocean-pollution discussions. Such analyses would thus contribute to the theoretical understanding of international decision processes pertaining to marine affairs as well as promote the progressive development of the ocean through more coherent policy choices.

Notes

1. See R. Michael M'Gonigle and Mark W. Zacher, *Pollution, Politics, and International Law: Tankers at Sea* (Berkeley, Calif.: University of California Press, 1979).

2. See, for example, Quincy Wright, et al., *The World Community* (Chicago: University of Chicago Press, 1948); David Mitrany, *A Working Peace System* (London: Royal Institute of International Affairs, 1943); Ernst B. Haas, *Beyond the Nation-State* (Stanford, Calif.: Stanford University Press, 1964); and Robert O. Keohane and Joseph S. Nye, Jr., eds., *Transnationalism and World Politics* (Cambridge, Mass.: Harvard University Press, 1972).

3. See Robert L. Paarlberg, "Domesticating Global Management," *Foreign Affairs* 54 (April 1976):563–577.

4. See Henry R. Nau, *National Politics and International Technology* (Baltimore: Johns Hopkins Press, 1974).

5. See Eugene B. Skolnikoff, *The International Imperatives of Technology* (Berkeley, Calif.: Institute of International Studies, 1972).

6. See Peter J. Katzenstein, "Between Power and Plenty: Foreign Economic Policies of Advanced Industrial States," *International Organization,* special ed., 31 (Autumn 1977):587–606.

7. See John K. Gamble, *Marine Policy: A Comparative Approach* (Lexington, Mass.: Lexington Books, D.C. Heath, 1977).

8. The complete rationale for the selection of these variables is too lengthy for presentation here. The reader is referred to James P. Lester, "Technology, Politics, and World Order: A Cross-Issue Analysis of Functional Collaboration among Advanced Industrial Countries" (Ph.D. diss., George Washington University, 1980).

9. U.S. Department of Commerce, Bureau of the Census, *Statistical Abstract,* vols. 1974–1978 (Washington, D.C.: U.S. Government Printing Office).

10. United Nations Educational, Scientific and Cultured Organization, *Statistical Yearbook 1975–1977* (Paris: UNESCO).

11. See Gamble, *Marine Policy.*

12. Arthur S. Banks and Robert B. Textor, *A Cross-Polity Survey* (Cambridge, Mass.: MIT Press, 1963.

13. See Donald L. Kelley, ed., *The Energy Crisis and the Environment: An International Perspective* (New York: Praeger, 1974).

14. OECD, *Patterns of Resources Devoted to Research and Development in the OECD Area* (Paris: 1975).

15. See John G. Ruggie, "Collective Goods and Future International Collaboration," *American Political Science Review* 55 (1972):882.

16. See Gamble, *Marine Policy.*

17. See Lester, "Technology, Politics, and World Order," chap. 7.

18. See C. Robert Dickerman, "Transgovernmental Challenge and Response in Scandanavia and North America," *International Organization* 30 (Spring 1976):213-240.

19. See Ann Hollick, "National Ocean Institutions: Research Needs," *Ocean Development and International Law* 3 (1975):299-335.

20. See M'Gonigle and Zacher, *Pollution, Politics, and International Law,* pp. 260-263, and Lester, "Technology, Politics, and World Order," chap. 7.

21. Interviews with representatives of the U.S. Coast Guard, the U.S. Environmental Protection Agency, and the U.S. Department of State during May 1979. The Tanker Safety and Pollution Prevention (TSPP) Conference was held in 1978.

22. Interview with EPA Representative, 8 June 1979.

23. See U.S. Senate Committee on Commerce, Science and Transportation, *Oil Spill Liability and Compensation* (Hearings held 9, 10, and 20 June 1977) (Washington, D.C.: U.S. Government Printing Office, 1977). Also, interview with U.S. Department of State representative, 30 May 1979.

24. This explanation was suggested by a staff member of the House Committee on Merchant Marine and Fisheries during a telephone interview on 11 June 1979. See also letter from Frank N. Ikard, president, American Petroleum Institute, to U.S. Coast Guard, 11 May 1976, p. 5.

25. This explanation was offered by a senior staff member of the House Committee on Merchant Marine and Fisheries during an interview on 12 June 1979. See also comments by Senator Magnuson in U.S. Congress, Senate, Committee on Commerce, Science and Transportation, *1978 IMCO Protocols* (Washington, D.C.: U.S. Government Printing Office, 1978), pp. 119-120.

6

Interorganizational Coordination in Environmental Management: Process, Strategy, and Objective

Joseph J. Molnar and
David L. Rogers

An important issue in the management of environmental problems is the need for coordinated action among the myriad public agencies sharing new or expanded responsibilities for resource protection and management. Public laws and executive actions bearing on environmental policy invariably emphasize the necessity for interagency cooperation. The National Environmental Policy Act of 1979, for example, created new institutional arrangements to force interagency cooperation on environmental problems, in the form of the Council on Environmental Quality, as well as interagency participation in the environmental-impact-statement writing-and-review process.[1] A reorganization also brought together the pollution-control functions of ten agencies in the Environmental Protection Agency by the consideration that the individual agencies could never be fully effective because of their inability to mesh realistically with the behavior of natural systems.[2]

Following traditional patterns, American government has responded to the complex problems of the environment by fragmenting them among specialized agencies and by attending to them sequentially.[3] The resulting structure is one of mission-oriented agencies, each with a broadly stated but specialized mission and an authorized set of means by which to pursue it. Staffs are comprised of individuals trained in professions directly relevant to mission, and the agency's task is the achievement of the mission at the least public cost irrespective of other public values that might be affected by its activities.[4] As a consequence of specialization, a comprehensive response to environmental problems often requires an interweaving of agency missions, achieved through the process of coordination.

Because environmental problems do not always coincide with bureaucratic boundaries of authority or legitimacy, coordination plays a key role in resolving gaps and inconsistencies in agency roles and responsibilities. When different levels of government and jurisdiction are considered, the importance of interorganizational coordination becomes increasingly apparent.

We thank L.J. O'Toole for helpful comments on an earlier draft of this chapter and L.A. Ewing for valuable editorial assistance. Support was provided by the Alabama Agricultural Experiment Station, Auburn University.

The mobilization, mutual adjustment, and concerted action of interagency systems occur under a set of assumptions and motivations that are qualitatively different from the actions or internal deliberations of a single agency. The purpose of this chapter is to examine the special problems, disadvantages, and strategies of coordination in the environmental-management-policy sector.

We seek to explore some of the assumptions and motivations underlying efforts to promote as well as to avoid coordination, including ideas of resource dependencies, organizational exchange, and the larger political economy in which environmental management is accomplished. In the linkages, connections, and interfaces among agencies many of the conflicts, discontinuities, and gaps in environmental policy are confronted and resolved, underscoring the importance of coordination as an interorganizational process.

Coordination as a Process

Although coordination is a generalized interorganizational process found in all levels and areas of government, several concerns make coordination a distinct issue in the environmental sector. First, the relative youth of many of the environmental agencies suggests the many new missions, roles, responsibilities, and activities that must be installed and maintained in the broader administrative arena.[5] Second, as befits the institutionalized products of the several environmental social movements,[6] environmental agencies are pressed by numerous external constituencies and interest groups to expand (as well as curb) their activities in various directions.[7] Third, many environmental issues reflect an evolving scientific milieu in which taken-for-granted aspects of a resource or environmental problem may be suddenly placed in a new light by research findings that reveal an unforeseen health hazard, a new threat to the ecology, or new social values or practices, each making the loss or abuse of a resource an immediate concern.[8] In each case, a single agency may not be capable of making an adequate response without communication, consultation, or negotiation with other organizations possessing impinging legal authorities, administrative competencies, or knowledge bases. Thus coordination is an integral part of the process of environmental management.

Coordination Defined

The concept of *coordination,* as J. Pressman and A. Wildavsky note, is deceptively simple: "Policies should be mutually supportive rather than contradictory. People should not work at cross-purposes. The participants in any activity should contribute to a common purpose at the right time and in the right amount to achieve coordination."[9] Coordination has been variously viewed as "a structure or process of concerted decision-making . . . with some deliberate degree of adjustment, . . ."[10] sharing, communicating, and cooperating,[11] the act of bringing into a common action, movement, or system,[12] and as an admixture of interference and facilitation.[13]

Coordination is a process that requires some recognition of an interagency system accompanied by efforts to maximize the comprehensiveness, compatibility, and cooperation among the constituent units. Coordination occurs at policy as well as the operating levels and includes planning, action, and the joint evaluation of actions. The process implies some degree of timing, sequencing, and accommodation among the interrelated activities of a set of agencies. One national study of state officials in environmental management found coordination in the abstract to be a positive goal for most respondents.[14]

Some writers differentiate coordination from simple cooperation or resource exchange.[15] From this perspective, coordination strategies are based on joint planning or action toward some shared objective. Basic forms of resource exchange or cooperation do not necessarily imply the sharedness of goals of purpose implicit in the concept of coordination, but they do imply some level of mutual acceptance or legitimation of objectives that allows the transactions to occur.

On the operating level, coordination is evidenced in interagency responses to environmental events such as a wildlife kill, a chemical spill, or an air-pollution alert. Numerous agencies are called into play to respond to a periodically occurring situation requiring the orchestrated efforts of a variety of groups. Coordination is said to occur when organizations manifest expected responses at appropriate times. The process reflects successful efforts to establish mutual expectations and fulfillment of those expectations on a more or less sustained basis.[16]

Coordination in an interorganizational system is driven by some concept of desired performance.[17] Ideally, coordination is achieved when an external goal, condition, or situation contributes to order, consistency, pattern, or structure in the individual and mutual decisions, actions, and policies of the component organizational actors. Coordination occurs when institutional arrangements collectively respond to an environmental problem in a timely manner. Certain benefits are achieved, and adverse consequences avoided, thereby influencing judgment of the performance of the interorganizational system.[18]

An often unchallenged assumption is that coordination will bring about outcomes qualitatively superior to those obtained if the parties were to act alone. The concept of coordination assumes that non-zero-sum "games" predominate in interagency decision making (as opposed to zero-sum games with distinct winners and losers).[19] That is, a long-run series of coordinated efforts are expected to yield a higher average joint outcome and, consequently, a better approximation of the "public interest."

Coordination as Participation

Coordination also has been viewed as a process by which those who are not directly responsible for making a particular decision are provided the opportunity to influence the decision.[20] The participation of other agencies (and the public) in a decision is viewed as one mechanism for overcoming the tendency for officials to be insulated from nonagency viewpoints and the associated filtering of upward-bound information.[21] Three forms of formal interagency participation in decision making have evolved in the A-95 review, the environmental-impact statement, and the regional water-resource planning process. All are viewed as means for overcoming the intraagency tendency to stifle criticism and simplify information flows.[22]

As a broader effort to overcome the excesses of special-mission agencies with narrow frames of references, Office of Management and Budget circular A-95 was instituted as a regulation promoting coordination of federal programs with each other and with state and local plans and programs.[23] Tied to the concept of substate regionalism, the A-95 review coordinates programs through a clearinghouse function of review and comment. Operating on a project basis, A-95 review boards collect, classify, and distribute information among applicants and governments and agencies potentially affected by a proposed project. The A-95 process does not function on a policy or regulatory level, however, but serves primarily to improve coordination at the state-local level and among federal agencies within a particular locale.

More specific to the environmental arena, environmental-impact statements must be prepared for major federal actions significantly affecting the quality of the human environment.[24] The preparation of such statements requires review and comment by other federal agencies, providing some level of formal participation in planning. The exchange of information occurs, however, at a project administrative point generally far removed in time and hierarchy from the site of actual policymaking and project design. Both A-95 reviews and environmental-impact statements coordinate federal actions and generally not regulatory processes or broader policymaking.

A third mechanism of formal coordination operates under Section 208 of the Federal Water Pollution Control Act Amendments of 1972. Primarily a planning mechanism, the legislation is intended to promote coordination in the regulation of nonpoint pollution sources on a substate regional basis. Similarly, the Water Resources Planning Act of 1965 established a national-level Water Resources Council to coordinate river-basin planning and oversee other federal water-resource-development programs.[25] In the 1940s and 1950s numerous federal interagency-coordinating committees were organized in river basins to coordinate a broad range of development issues and the impacts of federal projects. Particularly in the Northeast and the West, regional efforts to coordinate water resources have suffered problems of political viability due to the many interests involved.[26]

Coordination as a Response to Overload

Coordination in environmental policy is complicated by the broad range of agency missions encompassed in the realm of environmental management. Increased amounts of administrative discretion have been delegated to agencies to develop solutions to complex problems. Reich asserts that one effect has been to transfer more and more of the legislative function from the legislature to administrative rulemaking procedures.[27] Consequently, the governmental agenda in the area of environmental protection has become seriously overloaded, and coordination has been one response of agencies without the capability to act on legislatively expanded responsibilities.

Andrews maintains that the environmental-protection agenda has been overloaded in at least four ways.[28] First, the number of governmental missions in the environmental-protection arena has increased. Second, increases in the responsibilities of each agency have not been equaled by an increase in resources. Third, resources and responsibilities have been increased but without time to absorb them effectively (crash programs). Finally, an increase in diversity and conflict among agency missions often constrains comprehensive decision making in the environmental arena. Coordination is a response to, and sometimes a consequence of, each type of overload.

Since 1970, the number of actors in environmental management has increased considerably. Pollution control, wilderness and historic preservation, coastal-zone management, energy, toxic-substance control, soil conservation, hazardous-waste management, and other missions have been added or expanded in the environmental agenda. Some states have additional missions involving land-use controls, agricultural-land preservation, and billboard control beyond the federally mandated activities. Decision making in any one area of environmental management inherently involves other organizations with related or overlapping missions, increasing overload by expanding the number of consultations needed for any one decision.

A second overload is the assignment of responsibilities in excess of a capacity to implement them. The promulgation of standards, permits, timetables, and oversight responsibilities, in addition to ongoing mandates for research and enforcement, create an overload problem common to many agencies. The Environmental Protection Agency, for example, as a young organization with many tasks to complete, was slow to fulfill environmental-impact statement requirements for its projects.[29]

New programs overload agencies with new demands for information, personnel, and administration. Substantial time and effort are required to absorb new individuals and their activities into the agency as a whole, and coordination allows a new mission to be incrementally installed in the spectrum of ongoing activities. Lack of coordination often is traced to a simple lack of knowledge about what is going on in other agencies. Developing new or more effective channels for the exchange of information often is viewed as a remedy, but this is a time-consuming process.[30]

Coordination can increase overload, however, when other agencies have clear channels for voicing performance expectations. Agency personnel develop psychological attachments to established ways of doing things, but coordination may require changes in these activities. It may be difficult to overcome old routines when new practices serve only to accommodate other organizations.[31] Internal resistance to coordination may be singularly intense when the other agencies' performance expectations are not perceived as contibuting to goal achievement in an existing overload situation.

The fourth source of overload is diversification of missions, a source of conflict within agencies, between agencies, and between levels of government.[32] The proliferation of environmental laws has increased the interpenetration of regulatory and planning missions among agencies. For example, the Forest Service traditionally managed forests according to professional standards of multiple use and sustained yield. Now, however, it must incorporate coastal-zone management plans where they apply, air- and water-pollution regulations of the Environmental Protection Agency, and Soil Conservation Service information into its decision making. Agencies and local government can no longer deal simply with their mission but must consider numerous laws, reporting requirements, and regulations in carrying out their work. Coordination is an integral part of resolving this type of overload and continuing the activity of the agency.

Coordination Strategies

Not all observers view a unified, comprehensive approach to environmental management as an achievable objective. Given the new awareness of the environment as an interconnected system, Charles Lindblom cautions against sole reliance on a comprehensive approach to environmental management:

> It is a system. We are deeply impressed as we have never been before with the interrelation of the parts. Believing, then, that everything is interconnected, we fall into the logical fallacy of believing the only way to improve those interconnections is to deal with them all at once.

> Clearly, everything is connected. But because everything is connected, it is beyond our capacity to manipulate variables comprehensively. Because everything is interconnected, the whole of the environmental problem is beyond our capacity to control in one unified policy. We have to find critical points of intervention—tactically defensible, or strategically defensible points of intervention.[33]

Some environmentalists object to an overemphasis on coordination, because it may divert significant attention and resources from more important substantive objectives of environmental programs. Others express concern that mechanisms for making major decisions through interagency coordination may not allow full opportunities for public participation in the setting of environmental priorities or may be dominated by economic or other special interests.[34] Coordination, however, does occur in various forms and to varying degrees within forms. C.L. Mulford and D.L. Rogers identify three major strategies for coordination: mutual adjustment, alliances, and corporate models, each representing an incrementally greater investment in the interorganizational relationship.[35]

Mutual Adjustment

Mutual adjustment may be considered the most pervasive or common model of coordination among agencies sharing common substantive concerns. When agency missions interpenetrate, obvious forms of mutual assistance and right-of-way evolve at the operating level and reflect more general arrangements at the policy level. Coordination by mutual adjustment, however, is fundamentally a voluntary political act, is frequently neither simple nor objective, and is not always perceived by potential participants as more efficient or desirable.[36]

Exchange is often a cumbersome form of mutual adjustment between agencies. Agencies can contract with private organizations to perform specifiable services or hire individuals to carry out a particular function. Both types of relationships rely on well-developed markets with legally enforceable contracts. These arrangements are not generally available for interagency transactions, and if they are employed they often represent the culmination of painstaking negotiation and counterproposal.[37] As Lawrence O'Toole and Robert Montjoy note, exchanges between agencies must often take place on the level of a barter economy, and even though side payments (program concessions, special considerations, logrolling on other issues, and so on) can sometimes be applied, the medium of exchange is often the terms of the interaction itself.[38]

Exchange is a more effective form of coordination when agencies deal with one another over extended periods and on more than one issue. Relationships are then likely to benefit from an accumulation of mutual bargaining experiences, interorganizational routines, and shared world views.[39] Agencies in infrequently activated relationships may have little incentive to negotiate. Ogle cites an example of successful coordination on the operating level among land- and forest-resource agencies in a remote western area, a result of close personal relations that developed over time from their common residence in a small rural community.[40]

Alliances

The alliance as a form of coordination involves not only common adaptation and coordinated action but also interaction in such a way as to form a network of relations in which actors grant power to each other. Some conception exists of a system of actors rather than a set of coincidentally related parts. The system begins to act as a unit and decision making may be centralized, but the units retain ultimate power. The intensity of participation in alliances varies from issue to issue, with some agencies initiating proposals, mobilizing support, and influencing implementation on a few issues directly within their missions, and on other issues participating only indirectly, perhaps by providing information or advice to other organizations.[41]

As the level of interdependence increases in an alliance, more communication and more decisions are needed, and the difficulty and cost of achieving coordination increases. Thompson[42] distinguishes three levels of interdependence: pooled, sequential, and reciprocal. Agencies in an alliance of pooled interdependence share a common district or domain of responsibility, but the operations of one unit are not directly dependent on the other. Because the organizations do not need each other, there is often little cooperation. Even if the total impact of their efforts would be enhanced by coordination, no one agency has an incentive to expend resources on coordination, particularly if one or more organizations would have to alter their routines.[43]

A lack of coordination in pooled interdependence situations has some positive aspects. Implementation of new programs does not have to wait upon agreement. Implementation is simplified as an intra-organizational problem. The resulting outcome may be less than the ideal associated with a fully coordinated effort. The impact, however, is likely to occur *sooner* and to a greater degree, at least for the near term, than if more intensive coordination were attempted.

An alliance based on sequential interdependence suggests an order or chain of effort among the agencies. Poor performance or delay at one point will affect subsequent operations. Performance expectations are much higher for one participant in this type of arrangement. O'Toole and Montjoy cite the Environmental Protection Agency as an example of sequential interdependence.[44] The Environmental Protection Agency is not dependent on any one organization for it to proceed. However, the project agency is dependent on the Environmental Protection Agency for approval before it can proceed. Coordination is likely to take place in the form of scheduling, but such coordination is not likely to be efficient from the applicant's viewpoint, for any delay in processing retards the whole project. From the Environmental Protection Agency's viewpoint, coordination is less of a problem, as there are many one-on-one relationships and all of them do not have to be coordinated at once.

An alliance based on reciprocal interdependence occurs when agencies cannot proceed without one another. The most difficult relationship to coordinate, reciprocal interdependence requires continuous mutual adjustment and bargaining and often engenders delay and communication problems. O'Toole and

Montjoy argue that this type of interdependence is most likely to force inter-organizational coordination and to generate long-term benefits through shared world views, routines, and trust.[45]

Corporate Models

Corporate models rely on authority, hierarchy, and administrative reform to achieve coordination. Creation of the Environmental Protection Agency was in the best tradition of the corporate model, incorporating ten previously separate programs under one roof. On the state level, environmental superagencies often bring coordination and decision making together under a single administrator.

Hierarchical coordination is often reluctantly imposed on the participants. The 1972 Coastal Zone Management Act details to states the responsibility for coordinating federal and local governments as a prerequisite to gaining coastal-zone-management control. The responsibility to coordinate, however, is not the same as the authority to coordinate. Gendler notes that, although some good has resulted from state-federal interaction, the more common result is an effort by both sides to protect or expand their authority, with the agencies being particularly slow to react to demands for new organizational processes.[46]

Hierarchical coordination is not always neutral or objective; all coordinative arrangements impose costs on some participants and confer benefits on others.[47] Although bargaining and negotiation are not eliminated, corporate models substitute coercion for voluntary participation in coordinative arrangements.

Superagencies combining pollution control, resource management, and other functions present special problems. Some have argued that pollution control is essentially consumer oriented and that resource management is basically producer oriented. The concern is whether diverse constituencies can be adequately integrated under one umbrella, or will stalemate and inaction be the result.[48]

One national study examined contacts among pollution-control, conservation, and development officials on the state level.[49] The research showed very little contact between pollution-control and conservation officials, moderate contact between pollution-control and development officials, with the most frequent contact among pollution-control officials themselves. The results illustrate a pattern of communication segmented by function, suggesting some level of cost or barrier to coordination across functional lines. Similar separations have been noted among federal agencies concerned with the protection versus the promotion of natural resources.

The costs to coordination across functional lines reflect the simple fact that different agencies, by and large, have different goals. The basic nature of the organizational process is to ignore many goals and focus on one or a few that can be effectively and efficiently achieved. Thus many employees of the Army Corps of Engineers value and enjoy fishing and hunting, but they usually are not paid to think extensively about these concerns in a professional capacity.

Different functional lines also may reflect fundamentally different world views and problem perceptions that would ordinarily require a great deal of preliminary clarification before coordination could occur. Thus two solutions to intractable goal difference are to minimize contact with the other agency as much as possible or to segment relationships to narrowly defined tasks.

Coordination as an Administrative Objective

All government agencies maintain a repertory of coordination strategies, but coordination will remain a central concern for environmental agencies for some time to come. The legislative agenda for the environment is no doubt incomplete, and yet-to-be-written laws and regulations will provide many ensuing opportunities for coordination. The timetable and increased stringency of enforcement guidelines will no doubt expand the need for communication and conflict resolution over procedures and the overlap of administrative rulemaking. Shifts in the issue-attention cycle of environmental management will make new demands on agency performance and place selected issues and enforcement areas under intensified public scrutiny.[50] Certainly, hazardous-waste disposal has emerged as such an issue in the 1980s.

Coordination arrangements that seek drastically to simplify or consolidate organizational structures in environmental management are unlikely to succeed. As coordination involves a temporary and changing set of interactions, any attempt to fully fix administrative machinery in a rigid structure will lose the flexibility to respond to evolving conceptions of environmental problems. The sheer breadth and complexity of environmental management precludes extensive coordination imposed through hierarchial integration, centralized control, or structural consolidation.[51] Efforts to coordinate will continue to rely on pervasive informal or "lateral" relations between skilled personnel who develop their own informational networks, at all administrative levels and all stages of program planning and execution.[52]

A potential danger lies in an overemphasis on coordination as a solution for or cause of administrative failures in environmental management. Coordination is a process of adjustment and not a mechanism for resolving fundamental differences in value or perspective. A simple prescription for more coordination often belies a recognition of incompatible structures and the need for a basic reordering of priorities and organizational arrangements that can be accomplished only through executive, legislative, or constitutional action.

Furthermore, full coordination may not be desirable to prevent the capture of environmental decision making by any one set of interests or perspectives. A diverse political economy of multiple environmental agencies may more effectively reflect and respond to the evolving environmental values of the American public than a rigidly coordinated, monolithic superagency. Coordination processes bring environmental agencies together in some type of moving average of regulation and protection, perhaps leveling some of the bureaucratic excess and zeal associated with an institutionalized social movement, as well as prodding along those agency outlooks and practices that are residuals of an era now passed.

Environmental management will doubtless continue to place a heavy reliance on the managerial techniques of voluntary cooperation and informal processes of interaction. These may, in fact be more meaningful avenues for cooperation than formal coordinative procedures and structures.[53] Coordination, however, will remain a value motivated by some standard of agency performance. Efforts to coordinate as a goal itself will lack purpose and direction, given that coordination is most usefully viewed as a sustained means for achieving an evolving set of ends.

Notes

1. Frederick R. Anderson, *NEPA in the Courts* (Washington, D.C.: Resources for the Future, Inc., 1973).

2. Lynton Caldwell, "Environmental Quality as an Administrative Problem," *Annals of the American Academy of Political and Social Science* 400 (1972):109.

3. D. Baybrooke and C. Lindblom, *A Strategy of Decision* (New York: Prentice-Hall, 1963).

4. Richard N.L. Andrews, "Environment and Energy: Implications of Overloaded Agendas," *Natural Resource Journal* 19 (1979):488.

5. Howard E. Aldrich, *Organizations and Environments.* (New York: Prentice-Hall, 1979).

6. Joseph M. Petulla, *American Environmental History* (San Francisco: Boyd and Fraser, 1977).

7. Anthony Downs, *Inside Bureaucracy* (Chicago: Little, Brown, 1967).

8. Anthony Downs, "Up and Down with Ecology—The Issue Attention Cycle," *The Public Interest* 28 (1972): Merrill Eisenbud, *Environment, Technology, and Health: Human Ecology in Historical Perspective* (New York: New York University Press, 1980), p. 38.

9. J. Pressman and A. Wildavsky, *Implementation.* (Berkeley, Calif.: University of California Press, 1973), p. 133.

10. Roland L. Warren, *The Structure of Urban Reform* (Lexington, Mass.: Lexington Books, D.C. Heath, 1974), p. 68.

11. B.J. Black, and H.M. Kase, "Interagency Cooperation in Rehabilitation and Mental Health," *Social Service Review* 37 (1963):26.

12. F.H. Parker, T.E. Peddicord, and T.L. Beyle, *Integration and Coordination of State Environmental Program* (Lexington, Ky.: Council of State Governments, 1975), p. 95.

13. Harold Guetzkow, "Relations among Organizations," in *Studies in Behavior in Organizations,* ed. R.V. Bowers (Athens, Ga.: University of Georgia Press, 1966).

14. Parker, Peddicord, and Beyle, "Integration and Coordination."

15. C.L. Mulford et al., *Assessment of Nature and Impact of Interorganizational Coordination between Organizations* (Ames, Iowa: North Central Regional Center for Rural Development, 1979); David L. Rogers and David Whettan, *Research Needs on Interagency Coordination* (Ames, Iowa: North Central Regional Center for Rural Development, 1979).

16. Richard E. Ogle, "Institutional Factors to Encourage Interagency Cooperation in the Management of Natural Resources," *Public Administration Review* 30 (1972):17.

17. Basil M. Sharp and Daniel W. Bromley, "Agricultural Pollution. The Economics of Coordination," *American Journal of Agricultural Economics* 61 (1979):594.

18. Charles L. Schultze, "The Role of Incentives, Penalties, and Rewards in Obtaining Effective Policy," in *Environmental Quality and Water Development,* ed. R.H. Haver and J. Margolis (Washington, D.C.: National Water Commission, 1970).

19. Roy Burke and James P. Heaney, *Collective Decision Making in Water Resource Planning* (Lexington, Mass.: Lexington Books, D.C. Heath, 1975), p. 82.

20. American Institute of Planners, *Coordinating State Functional Planning Programs: Strategies for Balancing Conflicting Objectives* (Washington, D.C.: U.S. Department of Housing and Development, 1978), p. 10.

21. Downs, *Inside Bureaucracy.*

22. Timothy O'Riordan, "Policy-Making and Environmental Management: Some Thoughts on Processes and Research Issues." *Natural Resource Journal* 16 (1976):55.

23. Jerome Stam, *Coordinating Federal Programs: The Case of the Office of Management and Budget Circular A-95* (Washington, D.C.: USDA-ESCS, 1980), Rural Development Research Report 20, p. 1.

24. Larry W. Canter, *Environmental Impact Assessment* (New York: McGraw-Hill, 1977).

25. Burke and Heaney, *Collective Decision Making,* p. 7.

26. Helen M. Ingram, "The Political Economy of Regional Water Institutions," *American Journal of Agricultural Economics* 55 (1973):10.

27. C. Reich, "The Law of the Planned Society," *Yale Law Journal* 75 (1966):1227.

28. Andrews, "Environment and Energy," p. 490.

29. Richard A. Liroff, *A National Policy for the Environment* (Bloomington, Ind.: Indiana University Press, 1977), p. 103.

30. Parker, Peddicord, and Beyle, "Integration and Coordination," p. 97.

31. Laurence J. O'Toole and Robert S. Montjoy, "The Implementability of Legislative Mandates" (Paper presented to the Annual Meeting of the Southern Political Science Association, New Orleans, 1977), p. 21.

32. Andrews, "Environment and Energy," p. 493.

33. Charles E. Lindblom, *Managing the Environment* (Washington, D.C.: U.S. Environmental Protection Agency, 1973), p. 84.

34. Parker, Peddicord, and Beyel, "Integration and Coordination."

35. C.L. Mulford and D.L. Rogers, "Coordination Defined: Elements, Linkages, and Models" (Ames, Iowa: Department of Sociology, Iowa State University, 1978), mimeo, p. 20.

36. Dennis A. Rodinelli, "Policy Coordination in Metropolitan Areas: An Ecological Perspective," *Administration and Society* 10 (1978):205; Joseph J. MOlnar and David L. Rogers, "A Comparative Model of Interorganizational Conflict," *Administrative Science Quarterly* 24 (1979):405.

37. E. Bardach, *Implementation Game* (Cambridge, Mass.: MIT Press, 1977), p. 225.

38. O'Toole and Montjoy, "Implementability of Legislative Mandates," p. 20.

39. Ibid., p. 29.

40. Ogle, "Institutional Factors."

41. Rodinelli, "Policy Coordination," p. 219.

42. James F. Thompson, *Organizations in Action* (New York: McGraw-Hill, 1967), p. 55.

43. O'Toole and Montjoy, "Implementability of Legislative Mandates," p. 33.

44. Ibid., p. 36.

45. Ibid., p. 39.

46. Mickey Gendler, "Toward Better Use of Coastal Resources: Coordinated State and Federal Planning Under the Coastal Zone Management Act," *Georgetown Law Journal* 24 (1977):246.

47. H. Seidman, *Politics, Position and Power: The Dynamics of Federal Organization* (New York: Oxford, 1970).

48. Stahrl Edmunds and John Letey, *Environmental Administration* (New York: McGraw-Hill, 1973), p. 382.

49. Parker, Peddicord, and Beyle, "Integration and Coordination," p. 17.
50. Downs, *Inside Bureaucracy*.
51. Rodinelli, "Policy Coordination," p. 227.
52. Seidman, "Politics, Position and Power," p. 170.
53. Rodinelli, "Policy Coordination."

7

Congress, EPA, the States, and the Fight to Decentralize Water-Pollution-Grant Policy

Richard T. Sylves

The Cleveland-Wright Amendment, contained in the Clean Water Act of 1977 (P.L. 95-217), represents a new phase in the evolution of the federal water-pollution–construction-grant program. The amendment mandates increased decentralization of federal grant-review responsibilities to the states.[1] For the general public and the major news media, congressional review and passage of the Cleveland-Wright Amendment (C-W) were not front-page news items, Yet, this seemingly obscure measure sparked considerable controversy and activity among political and administrative actors strategically affected by the U.S. Environmental Protection Agency's (EPA) water-pollution-control–construction-grant program. Conflict between public-works proponents and environmentalists was particularly pronounced.

Many federal grant-in-aid programs require that national objectives be carried out through state and local governmental processes. The current federal wastewater-pollution-control program is organized on this basis. Under the program, municipalities (cities, towns, counties, sewer authorities, and so on) may apply for federal grants that subsidize 75 percent or more of the cost of constructing new or improved wastewater-pollution-control facilities. The states occupy a central position in this program. State pollution-control officials are required to review the suitability of municipal-project plans, designs, and construction-grant applications prior to the EPA review.

Implementation of the federal sewer-grant program has been complicated by the extraordinary demands and problems of intergovernmental program management. For example, Robert D. Thomas indicated that EPA officials confront a basic dilemma. They must reconcile the principle of "national supremacy" with the principle of "noncentralized government."[2] To operate in accord with these contradictory principles, the EPA used program (and project) grants as tools of intergovernmental program management. The EPA not only was responsible for assessing state compliance and eligibility for program grants in the aggregate, but the EPA used its discretion in municipal-project–grant-application review for managerial purposes. In other words, discretionary project grants (as opposed to

The author gratefully acknowledges the editorial assistance of Dean E. Mann in the preparation of this chapter. Errors or omissions are the responsibility of the author.

formula grants) available to EPA officials gave the EPA a monetary sanction over states and municipalities. The threat of losing federal grant money was a primary tool in EPA coordination of state pollution-control activities.

Thomas stated that, "the EPA is unable to direct state activities toward national program objectives through the utilization of grants as a management tool."[3] He reasoned that the mere promise of federal grant money could not induce state administrators to follow the EPA's direction. Uncertainty regarding how much money was being promised was the chief justification given for this conclusion. Rather than confirm or disprove the validity of the Thomas findings, this research examined a legislative measure that had the effect of discontinuing EPA use of water-pollution-control grants as instruments of intergovernmental program management.

The original (1974) version of the C-W called for substantial decentralization of program authority in implementation of the federal water-pollution-control–construction-grant program. The EPA was to delegate major portions of its program authority to qualified states. Under the C-W scheme, state pollution-control agencies would replace the EPA in handling project planning, project design, and construction-grant-application review.

A major generalization undergirding this investigation is that, as EPA surrenders planning, design, and particularly construction-grant authority to the states, the agency will gradually lose its capacity to supervise and coordinate state water-pollution-control activities. If project grants were inadequate management tools before, the almost complete loss of this tool under the C-W proposal must be assumed a very serious erosion of EPA bargaining power with the states.

A second generalization presented in this chapter involves federal preemption of state pollution-control responsibilities. In separate works published in the mid-1970s, Bruce P. Ball and Charles O. Jones claimed that intergovernmental linkages have evolved through a number of distinct stages in both water- and air-pollution programs of the federal government. Ball traced the evolution of major federal water-pollution law over time to show that early federal involvement in this policy area (1948, 1956) represented not much more than encouragement of state and local pollution-control activity. He demonstrated that federal water-pollution policy has moved gradually and almost inexorably toward federal domination of state and local water-pollution-control activity. Ball argued that with establishment of a national water-pollution-control program, the federal government was moving toward complete preemption of water-pollution policy.[4] This chapter contends that the C-W amendment was a clear departure from this preemptive trend. The amendment stands as a congressional, particularly a House of Representatives, effort to diminish EPA's sewer-grant-program authority by transferring portions of it to the states.

In a sense, the C-W proposal was to bring a form of deregulation to this huge public-works endeavor.[5] It must be understood, however, that *deregulation* in this context does not apply to public-sector–private-sector relations. Rather, the word here refers to streamlining a complex intergovernmental regulatory network by delegating the functions and duties of one level of government to another. This entails more than administrative decentralization of authority because there was to be a devolution of decision-making power from the federal level to the state level, instead of a dispersal of authority within a federal bureaucracy. Deregulation is a necessary term in this analysis because congressmen endorsing the C-W expected that the measure would bring about a net reduction in the amount of administrative regulation in the sewer-grant program, once the states were assigned more federal responsibilities.

Intent of the C-W

The C-W was originally drafted in 1974 as H.R. 13910. Failing enactment in the 1974 session, it was reintroduced in three succeeding sessions. It was not until 1977 that House-Senate conferees finally agreed on a revised version of the C-W.

The amendment that became law specified that—under a mutual agreement negotiated with the EPA—state water-pollution-control agencies, subject to gubernatorial approval, could be certified to perform specific functions and tasks that were previously carried out by the EPA.[6] Prior to enactment of the 1977 law, the EPA possessed the statutory authority to delegate some of its functions in the construction-grant program to the states.[7] Yet, EPA officials were not required to, and did not, exercise this authority before passage of the C-W. Thus, the C-W not only reaffirmed existing EPA delegational authority but also served notice that the Congress wanted the agency to establish and activate a process for delegating more EPA responsibilities to the states.

Unlike the original 1974 C-W bill, the C-W that became law did not require the EPA to surrender actual program authority to qualified states in administration of the federal sewer-grant program. The EPA would still be ultimately responsible for the program, but it could confer as well as withdraw state certification of delegated functions, and it was to be free to issue new regulations and to continue supervision of state water-pollution-control activities.

To some this might suggest that the EPA was forced to substitute one set of management tools for another. That is, in surrendering certain types of construction-grant authority to the states, EPA was losing a management tool. However, in being free to negotiate the content of state certification agreements of delegated functions, in being allowed to issue new regulations even after certification agreements had been approved, and in being able to police state compliance with the terms of certification, the EPA became the possessor of some new management tools. It will be demonstrated that under provisions of the C-W, the EPA's new set of management tools are more cumbersome and less effective than EPA's old control-grant technique.

What purpose was the C-W designed to serve? Sponsors of the amendment hoped that it would unsnarl administrative knots caused by the Federal Water Pollution Control Act (FWPCA) amendments of 1972 and by the body of regulations it generated. More specifically, the C-W sponsors expected implementation of the measure to result in curtailment of protracted, redundant, and ultimately expensive (for municipal-project sponsors) EPA reviews of project applications. Under the FWPCA of 1972, state environmental agencies were to accept or reject municipal-pollution-project plans, designs, and grant applications, prior to the EPA review. Critics charged that the three-tiered set of state-federal reviews mandated by the 1972 law was duplicative, time consuming, wasteful, and unnecessary. Critics also alleged that the EPA very seldom rejected state-approved construction-grant applications.[8] Because the EPA only reviewed state-approved applications at each stage of the construction-grant process, the need for federal reviews was questioned. Many congressmen hoped that the administrative reform produced by the measure would result in a more expeditious expenditure of allotted sewer-grant funds unencumbered by what they considered excessive EPA regulation.

Origins of the C-W

The impetus for drafting the C-W amendment came from oversight hearings held by the Subcommittee of Investigation and Review of the House Public Works and Transportation Committee. In mid-1974 the subcommittee launched an investigation to determine why the EPA's waste-treatment–construction-grant program was moving so slowly. Congressmen were alarmed by the slow pace in the obligation and expenditure of federal program funds (see table 7-1) and by the paucity of approved and completed projects.

A staff study prepared for the Subcommittee identified nine key program difficulties[9]:

1. inadequate manpower in EPA regions,
2. inadequate guidance from EPA headquarters,
3. compliance with new statutory requirements under FWPCA of 1972, including the National Environmental Policy Act (referring specifically to the environmental impact statement process), "infiltration/inflow" regulations, and cost effectiveness analysis,[10]
4. presidential impoundment of construction grant funds,
5. late issuance of regulations by the EPA,
6. compliance with requirements from at least 27 other statutes,
7. "administrative strains" caused by erratic fluctuations in monthly obligations,[11]
8. inadequate manpower requirements on the state level, (the report claims that the states have been short an estimated 3,400 positions in their water pollution agencies),[12] and,
9. duplication of federal, state, and local reviews of construction grant applications.

Table 7-1
**Public Law 92-500 and Subsequent Amendments: Obligations
and Outlays**
(dollars)

Fiscal Year	Authority	Allotments	Obligated (Each FY)	Outlays
1973[a]	5,000,000,000	2,000,000,000	1,532,048,571	0
1974	6,000,000,000	3,000,000,000	1,444,443,360	158,816,688
1975	7,000,000,000	4,000,000,000	3,616,168,130	874,158,134
1976[b]	0	9,000,000,000	4,813,639,424	2,563,497,940
1977[c]	1,480,000,000	1,480,000,000	6,663,832,006	2,710,444,759
1978	4,500,000,000	4,500,000,000	2,300,916,959	2,959,897,559
1979	5,000,000,000	4,200,000,000	3,871,696,000	3,612,400,000
1980	5,000,000,000	3,400,000,000	1,765,000,000	3,274,100,000

Source: U.S. Environmental Protection Agency, Office of Water Program Operations,"
Clean Water Fact Sheet–Construction Grants Program," (Washington, D.C., July 1980, unpublished agency.
Note: Excluding the 1980 figure, outlays do not include reimbursable funds; the 1980 figure includes reimbursable and old-law projects.
[a]Contract Authority
[b]Includes Transition Quarter (July-September 1976)
[c]Includes $480 Million Under Public Works Employment Act

The C-W addressed the ninth problem on the list. In some respects, delegating
EPA grant-review responsibilities to the states could alleviate a few other program adversities. Because state certification agreements under the C-W furnished
2 percent of the state's allotted grant funds to cover the administrative costs of
assuming delegated functions, shortages of state environmental personnel might
be ended. However, the C-W did not directly address other program difficulties
listed.

In general terms, institutional lag in correcting environmental problems was
not a new phenomenon.[13] However, the sheer magnitude of the 1972 $18-bil-
lion program resulted in extraordinary managerial problems for the EPA, the
states, and municipal governments. Agency attempts to meet extremely ambitious national timetables set out in the 1972 law resulted in institutional chaos.[14]

EPA officials were criticized for being too timid in program implementation, for being insensitive to the business cycle, which allegedly needed faster
public spending, and for lax enforcement of pollution-control laws in the area of
municipal water pollution. On the other hand, EPA personnel were accused of
spending public funds too fast and before EPA had produced adequate management controls.[15] The General Accounting Office (GAO) declared that the EPA
sewer-grant program lacked safeguards against inappropriate and too-expensive

treatment facilities, excessive profiteering by consultants and contractors, faulty workmanship, and inattention to environmental impacts.[16]

For House subcommittee members investigating the program, solving managerial problems was not an overriding objective. Getting more municipal projects underway and prompting a more expeditious flow of grant funds through the EPA to state and local governments was of paramount concern. Delays and obstacles in program management impeded the flow of politically valuable federal pollution-control-construction-grant funds to municipalities located in home states or congressional districts.

A review of the program's financial track record since 1972 reveals why so many congressmen were dissatisfied with its progress. Figures displayed in table 7-1 document spending lags in implementation of the federal sewer-grant program. The FWPCA of 1972 authorized a three-year $18-billion expenditure, "... to launch a crash program of federal grants to upgrade municipal sewage treatment works."[17] Table 7-1 indicates that Congress authorized expenditures of $5 billion for fiscal year 1973, $6 billion for fiscal 1974, and $7 billion for fiscal 1975. The table also documents subsequent appropriations for the program through fiscal year 1980.

President Nixon's controversial impoundment of $9 billion in congressionally authorized construction-grant funds restricted EPA's state allotments to $2 billion in fiscal year 1973, $3 billion in fiscal 1974, and $4 billion in fiscal 1975. Several years after the action was taken, the U.S. Supreme Court ruled the impoundment illegal. The Court ordered EPA to allocate the impounded $9 billion in fiscal 1976.[18] The impoundment was reported to have had little effect on the progress of the program. This was because, given the extremely difficult transition that all levels of government experienced in complying with the 1972 law, it was highly unlikely that the EPA could have obligated any of the impounded money to approved projects during the 1973–1975 period.[19] Total obligations for fiscal years 1973–1975 sum to $6.6 billion, an amount far less than the original $18 billion Congress authorized and considerably less than the $9 billion that the president permitted to be spent. Consequently, the impoundment action alone was insufficient cause for the slow progress of the program.

What then accounted for the wide disparity both between allotments and obligations and between obligations and outlays? One EPA official blamed the lack of program progress on poor economic conditions confronting municipal governments during the mid-1970s.[20] Others attributed lags in grant spending to slow movement on the part of the EPA in approving projects and obligating funds.[21] In one attempt to accelerate the grant process, EPA officials fused Step II (design) reviews with Step III (construction-grant) reviews, only to be barred from doing so in a ruling by the GAO.[22]

These factors, as well as a number of others to be discussed later in the chapter, all contributed to serious lags in the record of outlays (or expenditures) of federal grant funds. Ironically, despite the low dollar volume of project work completed, in 1977 the program was running out of funding authority for future projects. A new allotment of funds was needed for new projects, even though final expenditures had not been made on old projects. By late 1977, all but $1.1 billion of the original $18-billion authorization had been obligated to approved projects, but only a third ($6.2 billion) of the full authorization had actually been paid out to contractors and builders for completed work. This meant that more than half of the nation's 16,700 municipal dischargers failed to meet a 1 July 1977 statutory deadline requiring secondary-level waste treatment.[23]

Debate concerning the inadequacies of the 1972 law and the poor performance of the construction-grant program could not be kept free of political concerns. The water-pollution-control program created by Congress in 1972 represented a politically powerful but uneasy marriage between "environmental idealism and pork barrel practicality."[24] The formula for allocating the program's $18 billion was drawn "with care to assure that the money would be spread evenly among the states and territories so that 75 percent matching grants might flow into every congressional district."[25]

The environmental goals of the program were constantly in danger of being displaced by the high-stakes political considerations associated with the program's economic and developmental potential. The location and size of sewage-treatment facilities had become a central determinant of the growth potential of cities and suburbs. More treatment capacity permitted more residential, commercial, and industrial growth. Furthermore, construction-grant projects provided jobs for constituents. EPA estimated that cash outlays in fiscal year 1977 alone, created either directly or indirectly over 130,000 jobs. The agency predicted that the $5 billion in fiscal 1979 outlays would generate 172,000 jobs.[26] Waste-treatment-grant pork barreling occurred when, in an effort to insure maximum future growth at maximum federal expense, communities agreed to construct more expensive facilities than were needed.[27] Engineering, architectural, and real-estate-development firms had a major economic incentive in promoting waste-treatment capacity overbuilding as well.

Yet, EPA efforts to prevent such abuse were not greeted kindly at the local level. A congressional staff report claimed that communities were being told in intricate, interrelated detail exactly what they must do and how they must do it. The report alleged that the resolution of practical problems by federal fiat had frequently proven to be wasteful of natural resources, economically inefficient, and socially disruptive.[28] But the report acknowledged that when EPA tried to display "trust and flexibility" in dealings with states, municipalities, and industry, the agency left itself wide open for attack by those who insisted on a strict interpretation of the law.[29]

This array of administrative, financial, and political problems with the 5-year-old (1972) sewer-grant program convinced many congressmen that reform of the program was essential. Representatives Cleveland and Wright proposed their amendment as a means of facilitating program implementation to the benefit of states and municipalities.

Interest Groups and the Cleveland-Wright Amendment

In various House Public Works subcommittee hearings during the period 1974 to 1977, affected interests presented their views on the federal water-pollution-control program and the need for C-W legislation. Federal, state, and local pollution-control officials testified, as did environmental and industrial interests.

State environmental agencies stood to gain the most by enactment of the C-W, so it is not surprising that state officials across the country endorsed the proposal, expressing dissatisfaction with the FWPCA of 1972 and subsequent EPA administration of the program. State officials declared that delay permeated implementation of the federal program. They said delays were encountered in simply obtaining guidelines and regulations from the EPA about the grant-application process.[30] State agency representatives claimed that they were often left confused because they got different EPA interpretations on the amount of funds they were eligible to apply for, on what could proceed under certain guidelines, and on what constituted acceptable planning.[31]

State witnesses deplored the complex grant process brought forth by the 1972 law. The construction-grant process instituted by the new law contained three discrete phases with approval plans and specifications required for each step. At least ten major categories of requirements applied to a Step I facilities plan alone.[32] State environmental directors testified that EPA red tape was not only causing delays in environmental progress but was costing money as construction costs escalated during the delays.[33] They alleged that the EPA was burying them in paperwork.

The most frequent criticism heard in official testimony was that administrative delays held up the flow of badly needed grant money. Several state environmental administrators argued that they had been in the pollution-control business longer than the federal government and were therefore more qualified than EPA personnel in directing their state's pollution programs.[34]

When asked about the C-W, state witnesses were highly supportive. Among all the states, only Wisconsin officials opposed the amendment, and this was because they believed it would jeopardize the good working relationship they had developed with their region's EPA office.[35] Several state witnesses argued that the C-W did not go far enough to curtail the EPA administrator's discretion or to restrict EPA's power to promulgate more rules. The hearings made apparent the states' bitter distrust of EPA. State officials were suspicious that the EPA might not implement the provisions of the C-W if it became law.[36]

Representatives of municipal governments mirrored the concerns of their state counterparts. As project sponsors and originators of grant applications, municipalities were extremely important. Municipal officials emphasized that problems with projects built under the pre-1972 program, skyrocketing construction costs, unexpectedly high project bids, and high borrowing costs had all been disincentives to new project development.[37] Although critical of regulatory delays in the grant program, representatives of city and county organizations were traditionally the most active lobbyists in support of the construction-grant program. The National Governors' Conference and the National Conference of State Legislatures joined the National Association of Counties and the National League of Cities in promoting liberalization and expansion of the federal construction-grant program.[38]

Both state and local officials overwhelmingly endorsed the C-W. It should be noted that states and localities were not enthusiastic about setting up user-charge systems, carrying out industrial-cost recovery, or filing environmental-impact statements. These duties were mandated in the 1972 law.[39] Given the choice, state and local officials much preferred preparing money-generating grant applications rather than carrying out these regulatory responsibilities. The EPA's use of construction grants as program-control grants meant that approval of grant applications was linked to satisfactory compliance with more onerous and less rewarding activities, such as those listed. If the C-W, through state certification provisions, decoupled grant review from other regulatory activities, state and municipal officials would have been no doubt elated.

In fact, the 1977 Clean Water Act's C-W did not completely decouple grant-application review from other regulatory activities. If states wanted to secure certification agreements with EPA, the EPA could make certification contingent on a commitment or plan to implement other regulatory activities. In other words, states that wanted to assume responsibility for federal grant functions might be obligated to carry out other less desirable and more controversial activities as the price of certification. Nevertheless, EPA surrender of the control-grant technique backed the agency out of selective day-to-day management and oversight of state pollution-control administration. EPA's enforcement tools became macro administrative under state certification because state noncompliance with certification agreements was punishable only by EPA withdrawal of certification—not an insignificant action. However, prior to the enactment of the C-W, the EPA had full responsibility for federal project-grant-application review; it possessed a strategic micro administrative tool. Delaying or rejecting each state's municipal project-grant application on a project-by-project basis enabled the EPA to exert considerable political and administrative influence on the states and on grant-seeking municipalities. Thomas correctly identified the inadequacies of the initial control-grant technique. However, delegating EPA responsibilities to the states through certification agreements has made it even more difficult for EPA to fine-tune and coordinate state actions in the interest of national objectives.

Industry interests were represented at the hearings particularly in the fields of engineering and architecture. Support for decentralization of the federal sewer-grant program was nearly unanimous among these designers and builders of municipal waste-treatment facilities.[40]

As the interest with the most at stake in the C-W controversy, the EPA cut a high profile in House subcommittee hearings at the C-W and related measures. In 1974, EPA policy was that no new delegational authority was necessary. EPA Administrator Russell Train declared that state involvement in the EPA's construction-grant administration was desirable in principle. However, he opposed immediate state certification, as specified in the C-W, because he believed most states were unprepared for such an assumption of responsibility. He insisted that if states were to be delegated EPA administrative functions, the delegation process should proceed on a gradual basis.[41]

Only a year later, in 1975 hearings, Train and other EPA officials modified their stand. EPA officials wanted to allow selective transfers of responsibility to those states that were qualified and interested. Train endorsed state certification and held that it simply amplified existing EPA policy.[42] He maintained that little red tape would be encountered in implementing the program, as "it would not take much time to turn certification over to the states."[43] He claimed that most states would not need new legislation to transact delegation agreements. He also indicated that the EPA would monitor state compliance with the agreements by spot checks, so that monitoring would not be paper generating. However, Train insisted that if a state were delinquent in meeting its delegated responsibilities, the EPA should be allowed to resume partial or total control of the program immediately, without having to first hold a public meeting to justify the action. Under the 1975 C-W proposal, EPA would have been required to hold a public hearing before taking authority back from a state[44].

In 1977 hearings on the measure, Douglas Costle, then EPA administrator, voiced support for the amendment and advocated that the proposed 2-percent-grant-formula allotment for state administrative costs be raised to 3 percent.[45]

In general terms, EPA's transition from opponent to proponent of the C-W can be understood as bureaucratic self-preservation. EPA officials acknowledged major administrative problems with the grant program but balked at surrendering program authority to the states. As long as the amendment conceded EPA's ultimate authority over the program, EPA officials were willing to pursue state-delegation agreements, to keep the states and influential congressmen satisfied. Moreover, since the revised C-W allowed the EPA to draft, alter, and circumscribe conditions of state eligibility for certification, as well as to nullify approved state agreements in an expeditious fashion, the agency presumably had little to lose under the final C-W.

Environmental groups were keenly interested in the federal construction-grant program. They formed a panel to testify at the House subcommittee hearings on the program and the C-W. The Natural Resources Defense Council, the

Environmental Defense Fund, the Conservation Foundation, and the League of Women Voters were the key groups comprising the panel. In 1975 hearings, all these groups went on record opposing the C-W.[46]

The environmental panel defended the FWPCA of 1972 and attributed program delays largely to President Nixon's impoundment of construction grant funds. Although acknowledging delays in the EPA's development of guidelines, panelists blamed the lack of program progress on local objections to certain federal requirements.[47] Panel members testified that state certification would lead to environmentally unsound projects. They argued that without tight EPA supervision there would be little incentive to effectively spend federal construction-grant money, that there would be too many opportunities to build inadequate facilities, to inflate costs, to invite fraud, and to build environmentally harmful treatment works.[48]

Panel members feared that once certification was granted, states would succumb to the influence of what they labeled the "sewage-industrial" complex. Somewhat less potent than its military counterpart, the sewage-industrial complex was said to frequently promote extensive sewer and sewage-treatment projects that were planned with little regard for environmental values.[49] Composed of land developers, contractors, the building trades, sanitary engineers, and state officials, the sewage-industrial complex was thought to be quite powerful politically at the state level.

Beyond this, the environmental panel feared that the EPA would be under considerable political pressure to certify states regardless of administrative capability.[50] Similarly, once certification was conferred, environmentalists believed the political costs of withdrawing certification would be too high for the EPA to take action.

Gradually, environmental groups moderated their opposition to the amendment. Spokesmen for these interests suggested that in certain areas states might be able to handle reviews of project plans and specifications but not more intricate responsibilities, like facilities planning. States would need time to develop the administrative machinery necessary to handle more complicated EPA functions. As the opposition of these groups softened, they expressed reservations about EPA's ability to enforce state-certification-program monitoring.

In many respects, it was the opposition of environmental groups that helped to stall passage of the C-W. As the advantages of decentralization became more obvious to environmental groups, their objections to the measure melted away. By 1977, the League of Women Voters and the Natural Resource Defense Council endorsed the state-certification provision.[51]

Implementation of the C-W

Table 7-2 lists the first thirty states to sign state-delegation agreements with the EPA under the C-W. Representative Wright's Texas was the third state to sign, and Representative Cleveland's New Hampshire was the fifth state to initial a certification agreement with the EPA.

Table 7–2
Rank-Order Sequence of States Signing Cleveland-Wright
Agreements with EPA by 1 October 1979

Rank	Date of Signing	State	State Participation in Eligible-Project Costs as of Oct. 1977[a] (percent)	EPA Region
1	8-3-78	Illinois	None	5
2	8-17-78	California	12.5	9
3	9-8-78	Texas	None	6
4	10-2-78	Wisconsin	5-15	5
5	10-6-78	New Hampshire	20	1
6	10-27-78	Georgia	None	4
7	12-7-78	Alaska	12.5	10
8	12-26-78	New York	12.5	2
9	1-10-79	Maryland	12.5	3
10	3-5-79	Idaho	15	10
11	3-14-79	Minnesota	15	5
12	3-15-79	South Carolina	None	4
13	3-29-79	Arizona	5	9
14	3-30-79	Michigan	5	5
15	4-6-79	South Dakota	5	8
16	4-16-79	Maine	15	1
17	5-11-79	Vermont	15	1
18	5-21-79	Wyoming	None	8
19	5-30-79	Missouri	15	7
20	6-1-79	Connecticut	15	1
21	7-2-79	Pennsylvania	None	3
22	7-9-79	Montana	None	8
23	7-11-79	West Virginia	None	3
24	7-31-79	Nebraska	12.5	7
25.5	8-17-79	North Dakota	None	8
25.5	8-17-79	Washington	15	10
27	9-21-79	Massachusetts	15	1
28	9-26-79	New Jersey	8	2
29.5	9-27-79	Colorado	5	8
29.5	9-27-79	Utah	None	8

Source: U.S. Environmental Protection Agency, Office of Water and Waste Management,"
Status of 205(g) State Delegation Agreements," *Annual Report—EPA Agreements* (Washington, D.C., October 1979).

Note: EPA expected three more states to sign before 31 December 1979 and eight more before 30 September 1980.

[a]Information presented in this column obtained from U.S. General Accounting Office, *EPA Construction Grants Program: Stronger Controls Needed?*, CED-78-24 (Washington, D.C.: U.S. Government Printing Office, 1978), pp. 42–43.

It is beyond the scope of this chapter to document the negotiations process and content of each state's agreement. Many variables affect the ability and willingness of states to achieve certification under the program. It is for this reason that the study draws no inferences concerning the sequence or timing of state agreements. A necessary point to be considered in future research is the experience of state environmental agencies prior to achieving certification. Are the most qualified states assuming responsibility for substantial administration of EPA functions?

From the viewpoint of fiscal federalism, can states that have assumed delegated EPA authority be expected to administer efficiently the distribution of federal grant funds to their municipalities? This writer contends that the environmentalists may be correct in asserting that without tight EPA supervision, states would have little incentive to spend "effectively" federal construction-grant money. Table 7-2 indicates that of the first thirty states to sign agreements with the EPA, ten had no state matching-grant contribution in the construction-grant program. In other words, these states did not contribute state revenue to match any fraction of the 75 percent federal share of grant assistance. Certification agreements have not, based on available evidence, forced these ten states to contribute matching grant assistance to their state's program.

Table 7-2 shows that the maximum matching state contribution in the federal program is 20 percent (New Hampshire). About half the states on the list match 5 percent or less in the grant program. These states have almost no financial stake in insuring that the federal grants are allocated economically and effectively. Because they have concluded certification agreements, the costs of state administration of the grant program is heavily subsidized. In a sense, for these states the federal construction-grant program was almost a costless activity. Among the first ten states to sign agreements are Illinois, Texas, and Georgia. However, these states paid out no state funds on a matching basis with the federal government. Consequently, as these states assume EPA grant-review responsibilities, they will be distributing only federal dollars to their municipal governments. Subject only to EPA monitoring spot checks, it seems highly probable that many states will attempt to spend every alloted federal dollar available under few constraints.

Summation

As with any new law or policy, the C-W had attendant costs and benefits. The amendment benefited those interests favoring expeditious construction of grant-assisted–municipal-sewage-treatment facilities. The amendment imposed serious costs relative to EPA's coordinated direction of state water-pollution-control actions. As demonstrated in this chapter, delegating EPA construction-grant responsibilities to qualified states meant that EPA had lost considerable managerial leverage in its dealings with states and municipalities.

Before enactment of the C-W, the EPA employed project-grant-application reviews as intergovernmental managerial tools that could elicit certain state administrative responses. The technique was not flawless, as Thomas demonstrated;

nevertheless, entrusting state officials with the responsibility for allocating funds alloted to their states through congressionally determined formulas carries considerable risk. If EPA surrenders project-by-project review functions to states under certification, there is little incentive for states to allocate economically and effectively these funds to project-sponsoring municipalities. This is particularly a danger in the case of states that commit little or no state funds as matching grants in the program.

The C-W reversed any federal environmental-preemptive trends detected earlier in the last decade. State officials, under C-W-type agreements, would be free to approve or reject municipal projects for federal as well as state grant assistance (where states match a percentage of the federal grant share). At the same time, the salaries of these state officials would be subsidized in whole or part by the federal government. Under this arrangement it will become increasingly difficult for the EPA to sanction or encourage certain state actions. In retaining program authority under the law, EPA may have won a legislative battle. In surrendering major portions of its grant-review responsibilities to the states it may ultimately lose an intergovernmental war.

Notes

1. The Cleveland-Wright amendment was originally introduced in 1974 in the House of Representatives as H.R. 13910. Failing enactment in 1974, it was reintroduced in 1975 as H.R. 9560. Passed by the House, H.R. 9560 died in House-Senate Conference Committee and was resurrected in H.R. 2175 in 1976, where it again passed the House and then died in conference committee. In 1977, it reappeared within H.R. 3199, which again passed the House, and after considerable conference-committee alteration, arose within the Clean Water Act of 1977, which passed the House and Senate and was signed into law by President Carter.

2. Robert D. Thomas, "Intergovernmental Coordination in the Implementation of National Air and Water Pollution Policies," in *Public Policy Making in a Federal System,* ed. Charles O. Jones and Robert D. Thomas (Beverly Hills, Calif.: Sage Publications, 1976), pp. 129–148.

3. Ibid., p. 133.

4. See Bruce P. Ball, "Water Pollution and Compliance Decision Making," in *Public Policy Making in a Federal System,* eds, Charles O. Jones and Robert D. Thomas (Beverly Hills, Calif.: Sage Publications, 1976), pp. 169–187. The Charles O. Jones work referred to is, "Federal-State-Local Sharing in Air Pollution Control," *Publius* 4 (Winter 1974):69–85.

5. The water-pollution–construction-grant program, at this writing, is the federal government's most expensive public-works program. See J. Dick Kirschten, "Plunging the Problems from the Sewage Treatment Grant System," *National Journal* 9 (5 February 1977):196–202.

6. For a detailed account of how the process is to be legally carried out, see U.S., Executive Office of the President, Office of Management and Budget, *1979 Catalogue of Federal Domestic Assistance* (Washington, D.C.: U.S. Government Printing Office, 1979), pp. 930–931.

7. See EPA Order 1270.3 (1/23/73) entitled, "Authority to Execute Certification Agreements with the States." The second order was EPA Order 1000.10 (1/23/73) entitled, "Policy with Respect to Delegating Certain Waste Water Treatment Facilities Construction Grant Review Responsibilities to Selected States."

8. See U.S. General Accounting Office, *EPA Construction Grants Program: Stronger Controls Needed?* CED-78-24 (Washington, D.C.: U.S. Government Printing Office, 1978), p. i.

9. U.S., Congress, the Library of Congress, Congressional Research Service, *Water Pollution: Amending the Federal Water Pollution Control Act of 1972,* Issue Brief Number IB77043, by Malcolm Simmons, Environment and Natural Resources Policy Division (Washington, D.C.: CRT Terminal Printer, 15 July 1977), p. 2. Hereafter cited as CRS "Issue Brief." Please note that footnotes appearing in the quotation were inserted by the author and do not appear in the original CRS document.

10. See U.S. General Accounting Office, *Stronger Controls Needed?* p. 40, for an assessment of the program's cost effectiveness.

11. Thomas, "Intergovernmental Coordination," pp. 132–135.

12. A congressional committee staff report asserts that ". . . it has been difficult for personnel in EPA . . . to cope with the massive new requirements. EPA has not had enough trained people to handle the workload placed on it by the passage of PL 92-500." See U.S., Congress, House, Committee on Public Works and Transportation, Subcommittee on Investigations and Review, "Interim Staff Report on the Federal Water Pollution Control Act Amendments of 1972" (Washington, D.C.: U.S. Government Printing Office, April 1975), pp. 1–20. Hereafter referred to as Committee on Public Works and Transportation, "Interim Staff Report."

13. Harvey Lieber's, "Public Administration and Environmental Quality," was one of the first publications to recognize this lag. (See *Public Administration Review* 30 (May/June 1970):277–286.)

14. Committee on Public Works and Transportation, "Interim Staff Report," p. 1.

15. Kirschten, "Plunging the Problems," p. 200.

16. See U.S. General Accounting Office, *Multibillion Dollar Construction Grant Program: Are Controls over Federal Funds Adequate?* CED-77-113 (Washington, D.C.: U.S. Government Printing Office, 1977).

17. Kirschten, "Plunging the Problems," p. 196.

18. Ibid., p. 199.

19. This view is supported in Committee on Public Works and Transportation, "Interim Staff Report," p. 4.

20. Kirschten, "Plunging the Problems," p. 200.

21. Ibid., p. 199.

22. Committee on Public Works and Transportation, "Interim Staff Report," pp. 10-11.

23. Kirschten, "Plunging the Problems," p. 196.

24. Ibid.

25. Ibid.

26. Ibid., p. 198.

27. For further investigation of waste-treatment-grant pork barreling, see the author's, "Objective Need versus Political Interference: The Administration of the New York State Pure Waters Program," in *Political Benefits: Empirical Studies of American Public Programs*, ed. Barry S. Rundquist (Lexington, Mass.: Lexington Books, D.C. Heath, 1980), pp. 117-136.

28. Committee on Public Works and Transportation, "Interim Staff Report," p. 7.

29. Ibid., p. 9.

30. U.S., Congress, House, Committee on Public Works and Transportation, *Implementation of the Federal Water Pollution Control Act of 1972*, H. Rept, 93rd Cong., 2nd sess., 1974, p. 2. Hereafter cited as Committee on Public Works and Transportation, *Implementation of Federal Act*.

31. Ibid.

32. Committee on Public Works and Transportation, "Interim Staff Report," pp. 4-5.

33. Committee on Public Works and Transportation, *Implementation of Federal Act*, p. 138. The hearings revealed that in just four states, 752 projects were awaiting federal approval (ibid., p. 86). It was shown that EPA was producing guidelines and regulations at the rate of two pages per minute and that a grant application once completed by a state averaged 26 inches in height.

34. See Robert F. Waldeck, "Cleveland-Wright Amendment: Origin, Support, and History" (Paper, University of Delaware, 25 October 1979), p. 3.

35. Ibid., p. 6.

36. Ibid., p. 18.

37. Committee on Public Works and Transportation, "Interim Staff Report," p. 5.

38. Kirschten, "Plunging the Problems," p. 202.

39. U.S., Congress, House, Committee on Public Works and Transportation, *To Amend the Federal Water Pollution Control Act*, 94th Cong., 1st sess., 1975, p. 132. Hereafter cited as Committee on Public Works and Transportation, *Amend Federal Act*. Considerable legal delays and controversies held up the implementation of the industrial-cost-recovery program for several years.

40. A General Accounting Office report discloses that ". . . most municipalities rely totally on consulting engineers for planning, designing and supervising construction of treatment facilities." This may explain why contractors in

the business of building waste-treatment facilities were as anxious as the states and local governments to see the federal program decentralized (see U.S. General Accounting Office, *Stronger Controls Needed?* p. 2.)

41. Committee on Public Works and Transportation, *Implementation of Federal Act,* p. 686.

42. Waldeck, "Cleveland-Wright Amendment," p. 9.

43. Committee on Public Works and Transportation, *Amend Federal Act,* p. 255.

44. Waldeck, "Cleveland-Wright Amendment," p. 9.

45. Ibid., p. 13.

46. Ibid., p. 8.

47. Committee on Public Works and Transportation, *Amend Federal Act,* p. 132.

48. Ibid., p. 131.

49. Ibid., p. 123.

50. Ibid.

51. Waldeck, "Cleveland-Wright Amendment," p. 13.

8

Central Policies And Local Environmental Decisions

Robert Eyestone

The response of local planning authorities in Scotland to the on-land develop-ment pressures of oil exploitation in the 1970s is the subject of chapter 8. Their decisions illustrate a broad range of political processes, in Britain and elsewhere, by which local governments make local environmental/economic choices that also have substantial national-policy implications. When will these decisions favor environmental values? What compromises are necessary between national goals and local environmental concern? These questions will be discussed as some of the general implications of the Scottish experience.[1]

North Sea Oil: Whose Boom?

The discovery of commercially exploitable North Sea oil deposits off Scotland's east coast opened up what could best be described as a bonanza. Following the offering of drilling rights by the British government in 1970 and 1971, oil companies rushed to secure the necessary supplies and sites. Company executives talked of long-term prospects, but they sought to avoid commitments very far into the uncertain future.

Between 1971 and 1978, oil companies, contractors, and land speculators submitted at least eighty applications for permission to begin major projects directly related to oil development.[2] These planning applications—which are the uses that constitute the data base for this chapter—were submitted initially to Scottish local planning authorities (usually counties), but, as will be seen shortly, the Scottish Office and the Whitehall government were also involved in the response to this development boom.

The aggregate value of the oil-development projects proposed between 1971 and 1978 was more than £1000 million, approaching 20 percent of Scottish gross domestic product at the time. Who would gain and who would lose from explosive development like this?

1. Developers would gain. High-technology and high-risk, North Sea oil also promised high profits, especially after the Organization of Petroleum Exporting Countries (OPEC) began pushing up world oil prices in 1973.

An earlier version of this chapter was presented at the meetings of the Midcontinent Regional Science Association, Lincoln, Nebraska, 24–26 April 1980. I wish to thank Oscar Lund for helpful comments on the chapter.

2. The national government would gain. Through taxation of oil-company profits, the Treasury hoped to reduce its chronic budget deficits. Government policy required that oil and gas from the British sector of the North Sea be brought ashore and refined in Britain. Valuable refined products of the light, low-sulphur North Sea oil, in excess of British domestic needs, could be used to build export-based prosperity and reduce Britain's balance-of-payments deficit. Construction itself, together with its multiplier effects, would boost employment and national-income figures and reduce the need for welfare spending even before the oil came ashore.

3. Scotland, represented by agencies within the Scottish Office, expected to gain. The Scottish Economic Planning Department was delighted at the prospect of major private-capital investment. The entire British economy, including Scotland, suffered from a chronic shortage of investment capital, and major development money for Scotland usually had to come grudgingly from the national budget. Improved employment and income figures might also encourage expatriate Scots to return to Scotland and end the alarming pattern of long-term population decline in the country. The Scottish Development Department, however, felt that benefits would be conditional on proper site selection. Scotland would gain only if it picked the sites that not only required the least sacrifice of productive agricultural land and coastline attractive to tourists but also could be supplied most efficiently with the additional roads, schools, hospitals, and other social infrastructure required by the expanded oil workforce.

4. Local governments and local communities might also benefit, depending on the nature of the project. The areas in Scotland to which oil developers were most attracted happened to be sparsely settled, with chronic unemployment and depopulation problems. The service expectations of the population and levels of infrastructure investment were low. Although eager to accept a certain amount of new industry, therefore, local planners felt the capacity of the area to absorb investment was definitely limited. They responded instinctively to local farmers whose land would be taken for development because farm families were the backbone of local society, and they were also sympathetic to local "amenity groups"—associations of vacation-home owners in the area.

Local governments stood to gain additional property-tax revenues, but they expected central-government "revenue-sharing" aid to drop a corresponding amount, leaving them no richer than before. Local land values and housing costs would be bid up, air and water resources would be polluted, and traditional local industry might be destroyed because it could not offer wages comparable to those in the oil industry. Finally, the construction boom was admittedly short-lived. When it was over, local communities feared they would be stuck with derelict land and a legacy of unemployment. In sum, local concern was environmental but it was also social. National-conservation and environmental-protection groups joined local communities in questioning the need for rapid and reckless oil development.

Table 8-1 summarizes the goals and implied policy preferences of these four sets of actors in the oil-development decision process. Because they differ so markedly from each other, it is necessary to analyze the formal authority and other resources available to each to understand the nature of the decisions that were actually made. In fact, no set of actors enjoyed sufficient authority to dictate decisions by itself. Informal and extralegal factors, especially the assertiveness and confidence of local authorities and the existence and credibility of policy guidelines from higher levels of government, played critical roles in the emerging pattern of development.

Developers as Free Agents

The oil companies, construction firms, and land speculators who descended on Scotland had one great advantage—they had the venture capital. It was also their technical and business judgment on which everyone else relied, at least at the beginning of the boom. When a contractor said, for instance, that he had several contracts almost lined up and that he needed immediate zoning approval to secure them, it was difficult for anyone else to say that this was not true. The oil companies also decided how rapidly new finds would be exploited, although they did react to changes in national taxation policy.

Table 8-1
Perspectives on North Sea Oil Development

	Organizational Goal	*Implied Policy Preference*
Developers	Make profits; expand the firm	Remove all barriers to rapid planning approval for sites of all types, preferably in advance of the actual need for them
Whitehall	Increase national economic growth; reduce oil importation; improve the balance of payments	Make a variety of designs and sites available as soon as possible
Scottish Office	Improve Scottish economic conditions; plan for efficient social investment	Develop the most appropriate sites, providing that the need for sites is fully met
Local planning authorities	Preserve the traditional social system and local life-styles; preserve the local natural environment; improve local economic viability	Accept only those projects compatible with local needs and conditions

National-Government Powers and Resources

The Department of Energy, in consultation with the oil companies, approved designs for drilling rigs and production platforms. Once this was done, the Department could urge local authorities to provide enough sites suitable to each approved design to meet the need projected from data provided by the oil companies.

From time to time central-government agencies exhorted British industry to respond more aggressively to opportunities to supply the new oil business. Creation of the Offshore Supplies Office (OSO) in 1973 (first in the Department of Trade and Industry, then in Energy) gave tangible expression to this new goal. Its task was to provide information for companies wanting to break into the oil business and to find British sources of supply for oil-industry needs. Using its central-government connections, the OSO was able to pressure the oil companies while encouraging reluctant suppliers and promoting vacant construction sites.

Most frustrating for national policymakers was their lack of direct control over local land-use-planning processes. In January 1974 the Heath government did introduce a bill to give compulsory site-acquisition powers to the Department of Energy, subject only to parliamentary approval. This bill (never passed) would have virtually eliminated local and Scottish Office involvement in land-use planning for oil, and it met with great opposition from the Scottish National Party, the Scottish press, and conservation groups. The Labour government elected in February 1974 did not immediately reintroduce this legislation, and when they did bring in their own Offshore Petroleum Development (Scotland) Bill in November 1974, it contemplated compulsory acquisition powers for the secretary of State for Scotland (not the Department of Energy) only after normal planning procedures had been followed. This second bill passed in 1975 after the government defeated House of Lords amendments that would have provided additional protection for local interests.

Lacking formal planning authority, Whitehall had to rely on a sense of legitimacy it derived from national purpose and national policy requirements and its supposed knowledge of national-level needs for oil-development sites. This legitimacy eroded by early 1975, however, as actual demand fell far below Whitehall predictions. Inflated production costs and uncertainties caused by national-government plans for stiff taxation and partial nationalization of the oil industry significantly slowed the rate of development originally expected.

Local Governments

Many local planning authorities (county councils prior to local government reform in 1975, districts and islands councils afterward) were unprepared for the flood of applications for planning permission that followed the OPEC oil-price increases in 1973–1974. Governments in urbanized areas with heavy concentrations of industry, accustomed to planning for large-scale development, received few applications because they had plenty of industry-zoned land but little useful coastline. Local authorities in the highland and island areas, unfamiliar with large development projects and lacking planning staff, were besieged by construction companies because they had the coastal land, but it was in agricultural or recreational use.

Faced with a reasonably complete and properly filed application, a local authority was essentially constrained to respond according to a statutory time-table that set forth mandatory public announcements, consultation with other government agencies, a period for objections, time and method for filing appeals, and so on. Local planning committees pleaded with the Scottish Office for guidance or for a moratorium on local decisions pending a regional public hearing on oil needs—formal powers the secretary of State for Scotland clearly had—but without success. In some cases, speculative applications were turned back or delayed for lack of specifics or the developer's failure to complete proper procedures. In a few cases the local authority bluffed the developer into thinking the local authority possessed powers it actually did not have—namely, jurisdiction on and beneath the surface of sea lochs in which the final fitting of drilling platforms was done.

The greatest source of strength at the local level was the subjective legitimacy enjoyed by local planning authorities because of local political support and the fact that their members were themselves locals. Because most development proposals were a mix of positive and negative elements, however, local consensus on specific proposals was harder to achieve. As they gained experience with oil development, or heard about the experiences of others, many local planning committees became more sophisticated about the tactics of developers, the interpretation of promises, the use of planning conditions to reduce environmental damage, and the timing of counterdemands for maximum effect. No local planning authority began with this information, however.

The Scottish Office as Intermediary

The Scottish Office has formal planning powers that allow it to supersede local planning responsibility or to threaten to supplant it if the local-agency decision would be unacceptable to the Scottish Office. The Scottish Office can also claim to represent Scotland-wide planning rationality, because its comprehensive knowledge allows it to identify the optimum use for a particular site. This resource is not inherent in the formal powers of the Office, however, but depends on public support. To gain this support, the Scottish Office would have to reveal its planning priorities to the public in advance of specific decisions, but it has usually been unwilling to do so.

In August 1973 the Scottish Office did issue an interim advisory document that categorized sections of the Scottish coastline according to their potential and recommended long-term-development status. Without wishing to prejudice its own response or that of local authorities to any specific planning applications, the Scottish Office did clearly outline its own environmental perspective in this document. In effect, it attempted to structure the ensuing case-by-case arguments for and against development at particular sites. Unfortunately, the document's tentative nature and the change of government at the February 1974 election undermined the usefulness of the report. In August 1974 the new Labour government reissued the document as a set of planning guidelines, with somewhat stronger language regarding the twenty-six conservation zones carried over from the earlier list, and it provided a useful guide to local planners from that date.

Under ordinary circumstances, the Scottish Office could expect to enjoy significant bargaining advantages over local planning authorities because it controlled their access to grants from the Treasury for social-infrastructure expenditures. In the case of oil development, local authorities had a countervailing advantage—they could threaten to deny development permission for an oil project (which developers might then take to Norway, Holland, France, or Ireland) or at least they could force the Scottish Office to take the politically unpopular step of overruling local objections. Local authorities had this advantage because the decisions of developers were unpredictable and essentially uncontrollable. International consortia like ANDOC had no country loyalties, and American firms like J. Ray McDermott and Chicago Bridge and Iron would go wherever development permission was easy to get and technical requirements could be satisfied.

In several cases local planners, sensing that the Scottish Office was more eager for a pending development than local planners were, neutralized Scottish Office pressure by threatening to withhold development permission until they had a guarantee of additional financial aid for the extra services they would have to provide when oil development began.

Interorganizational Patterns

The foregoing analysis of the perspectives and resources of the various sets of actors in Scottish oil and environmental policy provides the basis for an interorganizational analysis of the resulting pattern of decisions reached in the 1970s.[1] This section provides (in brief form) the remaining information needed, a description of the relationships between these sets of actors.

The local planning authority (LPA) is initially dependent on the Scottish Office (SO) for information and planning expertise, but the LPA may have political legitimacy based on mobilization of local political support. Therefore mutual dependence can be expected. The SO has potential powers to call in or supersede local planning decisions but must be able to invoke urgent national justifications for this, so this resource is conditional. Over time, nearly all LPAs develop internal sources of information that reduce their dependence on SO information and advice. Therefore, when the LPA is inexperienced the most likely relationship will be one of unilateral dependence of the LPA on the SO, and when the LPA is experienced or strongly politically mobilized the relationship will usually be one of mutual independence.

The LPA and the Whitehall government (WG) are mutually independent, at least in the sphere of land-use decisions. The WG has an initial monopoly on projections of need for sites, but the political legitimacy of the LPA with regard to planning matters is a countervailing advantage. In any event, the LPA and the WG interact in a formal sense only through the SO as an intermediary.

Because the SO has the planning leverage over LPAs that the WG lacks, but the WG has knowledge of the need for sites and control of national policy regarding the rate of exploitation of oil reserves, these two agencies are at first mutually dependent on each other in gaining the benefits of oil development. As the credibility of national-need forecasts erodes, however, the relationship shifts gradually to unilateral dependence of the WG on the SO. The WG may still dictate development of particular sites, but only by supplying the needed venture capital directly through the Treasury.

Decisions

The British government, in its quest for rapid exploitation of North Sea oil, lacked coercive authority over local planning bodies in Scotland—such as the provisions of the unsuccessful 1974 land bill—and it could not legally impose selective sanctions on uncooperative local governments. Revenue-sharing funds, for instance, a potential source of Treasury leverage, were distributed by formula and could not be cut off or reduced arbitrarily.

A general prediction of interorganizational theory is that an organization lacking "hard" bargaining options (coercion or selective incentives) will shift to "soft" bargaining approaches (information and persuasion). It may also work through an intermediary organization if that intermediary has useful hard bargaining options it can be persuaded to employ. In British oil development, Whitehall lacked effective powers over Scottish local planners and therefore had to persuade and exhort them to act in the national interest. Whitehall also worked through the SO because the SO did have hard bargaining options— general planning powers plus the powers of the 1975 land act—in dealing with Scottish local planners. While pursuing an informational strategy, the SO could— and did—take development land into public ownership, offer direct monetary compensation (side payments) to local governments, impose extensive planning conditions on developers, and use elaborate and lengthy procedures to assure local opponents that their objections had been fully and fairly heard.

Whitehall, for its part, continued to use persuasive efforts on the SO and on Scottish local governments, and in a few cases it also made side payments that represented compensation to the SO for the political liabilities it incurred in allowing risky development projects to go forward. The aggregate result was a compromise of sorts—development occurred more rapidly and extensively than local governments wanted, but local governments won more concessions than they otherwise might have.

Table 8-2, showing the relationship between the local attitudes toward a development project and the subsequent SO action, demonstrates that local preferences were not overridden very often. The τ_b statistic, summarizing the reduction in errors predicting project approval or rejection, confirms that the overall relationship is quite strong.[3] Further, the decision procedures followed in the eight cases where local planning decisions were overruled were more lengthy and elaborate on average than those for other cases. In half of these eight cases the secretary of state for Scotland called a special public hearing to gather objections and hear expert testimony, whereas there were only three other instances of formal public hearings on oil projects. In half of these cases, also, the secretary of state for Scotland imposed stringent planning conditions on the developers over and above what was done at the local level, whereas there were only three other cases in which stringent conditions were added.

Decision time, reflecting bureaucratic processes of consultation, summarizing, and weighing of the evidence within the SO, is another measure of the attention given to a development decision. The average decision time for the eight deviating cases, after the local authority had acted, was 9.6 months as compared with the overall average for all oil cases of 5.9 months, and the average total decision time for the eight deviating cases was 10.7 months as compared with the overall average for oil cases of 6.4 months. Thus, on average, decisions going against local preferences did require more elaborate and lengthy decision procedures than would otherwise be expected.

Table 8-3 shows the relationship between previously announced SO planning guidance and the ultimate planning decision made in each case. Obviously planning guidelines are useful, both in identifying projects likely to be accepted and in discouraging the proposal of projects in areas that should be conserved in the name of a public larger than just the local residents.

Table 8-4 analyzes applications by time period. Before 1975 the national government was pushing for rapid development, urging the SO and local planners to approve more sites so that the production targets for 1980 oil independence could be met. Firms contracting for the North Sea were given a special 3-percent grant against interest rates on capital borrowing, and they were exempted from the three-day week imposed during the 1973–1974 coal strike. At the beginning of 1975 the Department of Energy revised its estimates and announced that

Table 8-2
Final Planning Decisions

Local Attitude toward Project	Scottish Office Action		
	Accept	Accept with Changes	Reject
Positive	9	3	1[a]
Neutral/mixed	2[a]	3[a]	0
Negative	1[a]	1[a]	18
		$\tau_b = .48$	

[a]Among eight cases in which local planning decisions were overruled.

Table 8-3
Relationship of Prior Planning Guidance to Project Approval

	Scottish Office Action			
	Accept	Modify	Reject	No Action–Proposal Withdrawn
Prior explicit statement on this project	5	5	2	1
Prior statement on this site in general	1	2	11	8
No statement or no planning guidelines in existence	2	3	9	3
			$\tau_b = .10$	

Table 8-4
Relationship of Central Guidance to Speculative Applications

	Nature of Application			
Application Date	Successful	Speculative	Redundant	Inappropriate
Prior to August 1974	25	8	5	12
August 1974 through December 1974	6	7	4	2
January 1975 and after	4	1	0	1
		$\tau_b = .06$		

there were already enough sites available. Prior to August 1974 local planners received little guidance on site selection, and the SO appeared to give tacit support to national-government projections of the need for development sites. With the August 1974 development guidelines, however, the SO emphasized conservation of the coastline and the planned grouping of projects in populated areas already involved with oil.

Projects in table 8-4 are classed as follows: *successful* applications are those approved and subsequently built, *speculative* applications are those where a developer did not seek a further site after being denied once, *redundant* applications are those where approval was granted but the project was not constructed, and *inappropriate* applications are those where a developer applied at a second site after being turned down initially.

Activity of all sorts is heavily concentrated in the early period. In terms of relative emphasis, however, the early period shows the highest concentration of applications made at the wrong site. During this period many developers applied simultaneously at several sites, evidence that they could not confidently predict the outcome of the local planning process. The most common type of application in the middle period was a one-time speculative proposal put forward by a developer with only a tangential interest in North Sea oil. This, together with the high proportion of projects approved during this period but not actually built, suggests that the planning guidelines were channeling proposals to the right sites but that national pressure for rapid development was still encouraging applications in numbers beyond what was actually needed by the industry. Finally, in the last period very few applications were submitted, but those that were submitted were more likely to be appropriate for site and need.

Concluding Observations

Because the British national government had no direct control over Scottish local authorities, central-government impact on land-use planning for oil development in the 1970s scarcely ventured beyond the "indicative" stage: the central government set forth production targets and then exhorted industry and local governments to act in ways that would help meet the target figures. Several oil rigs were purchased on a speculative basis by the Department of Energy, partly as a political gesture by the Labour government to laid-off shipyard workers and partly as compensation for Scottish politicians and their support of rapid oil exploitation. In further compensation for SO help, the Treasury provided direct financing for two Scottish construction sites, but when these failed to gain a single platform order the experiment was written off. The indicative planning targets did have a considerable impact on local land-use decisions, however. They created a sense of national obligation in some local authorities. Together with early financial incentives, the planning targets also stimulated a large volume of private development proposals. As a result, they contributed greatly to the degree of irrationality—overcommitment of scarce environmental resources of agricultural and scenic land to possible oil development—in local planning decisions throughout much of 1974.

The central government's "mistake" was to encourage the oil boom (which necessarily was based on nongovernmental technology and capital investment, and thus not directly controllable by government planners) with favorable terms at the outset. As oil began to flow, the central government imposed a heavy burden of taxation and partial nationalization of oil-company assets while scaling down its estimates of investment needs. This policy change, along with rapidly increasing exploration and production costs, caused oil companies to reconsider their development timetables and redesign their production strategies to reduce the capital intensity of their North Sea operations. The change also greatly reduced the decision load on local planners and it improved the chances that the few applications that were made would be well thought out. If planners had gotten better advice earlier, or if planning guidelines had been available to them when applications were coming in most rapidly, they would have been able to achieve a more suitable balance of environmental and development values.

The British experience with North Sea oil development shares many characteristics with related policy areas: energy policy, especially the exploitation of known natural resources; local enforcement of all kinds of environmental-protection policies, especially those relating to the exploitation of common-pool resources like air and water; and policies of economic management and stabilization, especially as they relate to the efforts of local and regional governments to inflate or deflate local economies. All these areas, and perhaps others, share a dependence on joint decisions by two or more governmental levels possessing interests that diverge in the short run although they may be seen to converge over the long term. Since political reactions occur (and policies are implemented) over the short run, the lesson for analysts is that short-run interorganizational relationships may be an essential component of an explanation for the outcomes in this broad set of policy areas.

Notes

1. Terminology used throughout the chapter draws on interorganizational theory, although there has not been space enough for a formal exposition. See Kenneth Hanf and Fritz W. Scharpf, eds., *Interorganizational Policy Making: Limits to Coordination and Central Control* (Beverly Hills, Calif.: Sage, 1978).

2. The early history of British North Sea oil is reviewed in D.I. MacKay and G.A. MacKay, *The Political Economy of North Sea Oil* (London: Martin Robertson, 1975). Data presented in this chapter were gathered by the author from primary sources and newspaper accounts.

3. The number of cases varies from table to table because of missing data. In every instance, however, the data represent at least a 40-percent sample of all cases, generally the larger and more controversial projects.

Incentive Systems in Environmental Regulation

Barry M. Mitnick

When critics of the performance of public regulation of strip mining complain, they sometimes refer to the absence of *incentives* for mining companies to reclaim mined property. Or, in discussing the quality both of personnel in state agencies regulating this activity and of the regulation performed by such personnel, they may refer to the absence of incentives—for high-quality personnel to stay with the agency and for personnel to remain free from the subtle influences of the industry. Policy prescriptions, that is, solutions to such perceived problems, however, are usually cast in the form of structural or institutional regulatory solutions: create or reorganize a regulatory agency; write sterner regulations; enforce stiffer conflict-of-interest laws. But if the problems can be understood in terms of incentives, perhaps the solutions— regulatory designs—also can be formulated through a basic focus on incentive systems and their manipulation.

A focus on incentive systems can be a particularly useful tool in the design and analysis of regulatory systems. In this chapter, I shall discuss the concept of incentive and its relevance to environmental regulation, develop a typology of regulatory means, and analyze the structure of the incentive systems faced by individual regulators. The discussion of regulators will employ the results of a study of inspectors in a midwestern state reclamation agency.

The Concept of Incentive and Environmental Regulation

Agents, Control, and Incentives

Regulatory problems can often be understood as *control problems*: the public or legislature faces a problem in insuring that the regulatory body adheres to public or legislative desires; the regulatory body faces a problem in insuring that private behavior affecting the environment realizes those public or legislative goals. Within the regulatory body, there is the problem of controlling the individual behaviors of the regulators. For the case of controlling individual regulators, most of the relevant regulatory literature focuses on the top-level

I would like to thank Dean E. Mann for his helpful comments on an earlier version of this chapter.

officials—that is, commissioners and directors, although much regulation is done by lower-level personnel, such as inspectors. The control problems for each level conceivably may differ.

Control problems of these kinds are in many respects similar to the general problems faced by *principals* in trying to control their *agents*.[1] The public or legislature as principal delegates the regulatory task to a regulatory body as agent; the regulatory body then acts as a principal in attempting to create agents in the private firms subject to its regulation. Thus, in seeking to identify and discuss the basic possible means of regulation, we may fruitfully examine the basic types of controls available to principals.

Abstractly, two basic means of control can be identified: (1) control through direct specification or instruction of the agent's behavior (for example, put scrubbers on smokestacks); and/or (2) control through rewards that encourage the agent to behave as the principal desires (for example, subsidies that may be used to build pollution-control facilities).

In general, the first alternative, through direct specification, circumscribes choices of actions available to the regulatee. The second alternative, on the other hand, increases the attractiveness of certain actions that may be chosen from among others by the regulatee. Clearly, if the regulatee does not wish to perform the behaviors required by direct specification, the efficacy of direct specification will depend on the threat of application of penalties (that is, negative rewards). Furthermore, the control-through-rewards alternative may not actually require transfer of a reward; provision of information to, or persuasion of, the regulatee may allow the regulatee to recognize rewards that were not perceived earlier. For example, a strategy of providing consumers with information on the risk of use of a product (rather than regulating production or use of the product through direct specification) may allow them to perceive more correctly the rewards associated with the product's consumption. Information can therefore alter the regulatee's perceived-reward system.

The two means of control can be linked: rewards may be supplied contingent on the performance of explicitly specified activities (for example, subsidies supplied to support construction of only specific kinds of waste-treatment facilities). Compliant behavior by the agent is, moreover, often not assured unless these two control means are linked; adherence to emission standards depends not only on the official promulgation of such standards but also on the use of fines or penalties backed by the ultimate coercion of the state.

This allows us to identify two basic varieties of regulatory means in the context of incentive systems. Both of the general types of means of control just discussed presume the existence of a relation between principal and agent (for instance, regulator and regulatee) in which either directives or rewards (or both) are manipulated to control the agent. This suggests the identification of the concept of incentive (which may then be applied to describe this control situation) as a relation rather than as some isolated property or object actually transferred between the principal and the agent.[2] Two basic kinds of incentive relation then exist in regulation: (1) a *directive* one, in which direct specification of regulatee behavior is backed by negative rewards (for example, coercion), and (2) what I shall term an *incentive* one, in which positive rewards bias or encourage the regulatee's particular choices of behavior. As discussed, I include information-based control means under the incentive category. Analysis of regulatory means for achieving environmental and other social goals can therefore proceed comfortably within a general framework of incentive systems.

Social-Choice Processes

Thus far I have identified two alternative means of regulation from consideration of basic control possibilities in agent-principal relations. Social action vis-à-vis the environment need not, however, be the result of explicit, manipulated, control attempts. Where superior principals seek to control subordinate agents, we have what is generally referred to as the social-choice process of "hierarchy." But other pure-type social-choice processes for making decisions regarding environmental or other regulation (and other forms of public action) exist, of course. These include the market, bargaining, and voting.[3] Mixed forms of these pure types not only exist but also are probably the most common observed forms. For example, it is not unusual for at least some bargaining to be present even where decision is formally hierarchical, for example, enforcement of air-pollution-control standards.

Much discussion has appeared recently in the literature regarding the substitution of so-called market forms of regulation for traditional standards or regulations-based forms.[4] These market forms include effluent charges, in which an attempt is made to price marginal units of pollutant expelled to the environment (and thereby price the use of, and damage to, the environmental resource), and auctions of permits or rights to use specified amounts of the environmental resource (that is, air, water). Effluent charges, however, are not really a pure market alternative, since they are to be set and possibly manipulated in a hierarchical control relationship. Permit auctions are not pure markets, since the aggregate level of pollution is set hierarchically through governmental limits on the size and number of permits to be sold. Both charges and permit markets are subject to hierarchical policing of compliance. Thus charges may be considered essentially as an incentive form under a hierarchical social-choice process and permit markets as a mixed form in which hierarchy sets limits within which the market is allowed to function. Both charges and permit markets do possess the market-like advantage of allowing subject parties some autonomy in choice of their behaviors.

I will limit my discussion in this chapter to hierarchical social-choice processes. Then directive means of regulation include rules and standards, and (positive) incentive means include tax incentives, subsidies, and effluent charges. Also included under incentive means are information/persuasion strategies, since they aim at changing perceptions of the relative attractiveness of potential actions; apparent positive rewards are thereby created or increased.

A major question in regard to choice among regulatory means (and among basic choice processes) is that of *quo warranto*—by whose warrant or authority is the regulatory decision made? In any formally democratic society, questions of public action are in theory linked to the ultimate authority of its citizens. Reliance on hierarchical means usually means that an administrator is delegated such decisions. But, as Edwin Haefele has argued forcefully, other social-choice processes—for example, innovative combined processes including representative voting—may actually better serve democratic theory.[5] With this caveat, I will, however, focus on hierarchical means.

Dimensions of Regulatory Control: Basic Regulatory Means,
Regulatory Target Levels, and Regulatory Enforcement

How can we systematically characterize the possibilities of regulatory control in the context of incentive systems? Regulatory mechanisms may be classified according to the basic regulatory means employed, the target levels at which they are directed, and the provisions made for regulatory enforcement.

Basic Regulatory Means. Incentives and directives have already been identified as basic alternative regulatory means. We can identify a number of aspects of these basic types to further classify or describe regulatory means. In particular, the parts of the incentive relation suggest some additional dimensions.

A simple incentive relation consists of an incentive message specifying behavior desired by the principal of the agent, information to the principal that the behavior was performed, and transfer of the reward from principal to agent.[6] In practice, of course, these steps may not be completed or follow this order, and complex incentive relations may be composed of multiple simple relations or their components. The basic control alternatives of specification of behaviors and of rewards are apparent here in the incentive message and in the transfer of rewards. The identification of basic types of regulatory means—incentive and directive—follows. We could also, for example, examine the explicitness, the completeness, and the restrictiveness of the specification in the incentive message and the kinds of rewards and reward-transfer mechanisms operative in the relation. Such dimensions could then be used to array regulatory means.

Regulatory Target Levels. We could also discuss aspects of the targets of the incentive message. In environmental regulation, standards may be set regarding ambient quality of the environment as well as regarding the quality of the effluent discharged into that environment. Furthermore, the level of the target of effluent standards (or, potentially, incentives) can vary—emissions from particular processes or sources, from a plant or facility as a whole, or from a region containing a number of facilities. Below any of these target levels, regulatees may have autonomy in designing their operations or in bargaining or trading in the pollutants with other regulatees. This autonomy can be reflected in the establishment of market-like adjustment or trading systems (which will be discussed further). Since the standards (or incentives) are set for a given target level (for example, some amount of particulate emissions from a whole plant), they do not apply to any individual emission sources (for example, individual smokestacks within the plant) below that level; it is only the overall result that matters.

In the past, both traditional command-and-control directive regulation and incentive forms like effluent charges largely have been designed for and directed at the individual-source target level, for instance, individual smokestacks or effluent sources. At the plant or facility level, the U.S. Environmental Protection Agency (EPA) has recently developed the so-called bubble policy under which plant owners can choose which sources to control as long as the plant's overall emissions of the particular pollutant (that is, what passes through an imaginary bubble placed over the plant) do not exceed a given level.[7] This could permit owners to reduce plantwide emissions in the most efficient—and least costly—fashion.

At the regional level, the EPA has been developing offsets and banking policies. Offsets permit new sources of pollution in areas that have not met clean-air standards. They do this by requiring the new pollution sources to be balanced by reductions in existing pollution in the area. In effect, trades are permitted that should encourage the most efficient means of control at a given pollution level while allowing economic growth. Offsets should occur where it is cheaper to reduce an existing source's emissions than to implement control of the same amount of pollutant in the new facility. In banking, offsets can be created by firms with relatively lower control costs, banked, and then either sold to other firms in the future or used in their own expansion.[8] Banking thus simply allows offset trades to occur over time, facilitating growth in individual firms and in the region as a whole. Note that the higher the target level, the more that market-like trades or adjustments can be made to meet the hierarchically set standard; the overall pollution-control system looks more like a mixed social-choice process.

In permit or rights auctions, the overall level of pollution in a region is set through the sale by auction of a limited number of pollution rights, or permits. Firms are permitted to trade these rights, setting up a market in them.[9] Although it is ultimately a mixed social-choice process, since the scarcity of these rights is hierarchically set, the rights auction and trading system looks fundamentally like a market. It is, however, obviously an extension and formalization of the sort of constrained trading system that could exist under offsets and banking.

Regulatory Enforcement. Since in all hierarchical means of regulation questions of compliance arise, especially where compliance is costly to the regulated party, identification of the enforcement system accompanying incentive and directive means (with any target level) would seem pertinent. In particular, in the context of incentive systems, we may be concerned with the negative rewards that are threatened for noncompliance. Fines and/or penalties typically accompany enforcement of noncompliance to traditional command-and-control standards. If the costs of compliance to the polluting firm are greater than the fines it may suffer (and/or the costs of opposing enforcement through the administrative process or the courts), it may be rational for the firm simply not to comply.

The so-called Connecticut Enforcement Plan, tried first in that state and subsequently by the EPA, attempts to deal with this problem. In essence, non-compliant firms are subject to fines equal to the amount they apparently benefited through noncompliance over the period of noncompliance. For example, a firm that had a net gain of $1 million through refusal to comply during the time since compliance was demanded would be fined this amount. In this way, the incentive for refusing or delaying compliance would be removed.[10]

A Typology of Regulatory Means

The varieties of environmental regulatory means discussed are depicted in table 9-1. Regulatory means in a hierarchical setting are characterized as to basic type (incentive versus directive), level of target (process/individual source, facility/organization, region/system), and level of penalty for noncompliance (less than gain from noncompliance; equal to or greater than gain from noncompliance).

From table 9-1, it is evident that some of the logical possibilities in regulatory design from the perspective of incentive systems have not been tried or even discussed by policymakers or analysts in the environmental area (the less or undiscussed possibilities are indicated in parentheses). Both incentive and directive means may be applied to targets of any level and with or without Connecticut-type enforcement provisions. Of course, this lack of discussion of some types may simply be due to problems in feasibility or implementation. It is, however, only recently that bubbles, offsets, banking, and other new means (which at first may have seemed administratively difficult) have even been proposed.

Consider, for example, an incentive means at the regional target level; one possibility is a regional-level effluent charge. In theory, a tax would be set on each unit of a region's collective discharge—for example, the discharges from an air or water basin—with the incidence of the tax on individual sources in the region left to assignment by a political authority established for the region. In this way, pressure may be placed on regional or state authorities to devise effective (and, possibly, efficient) control means in their area.[11] The

Table 9-1
Regulatory Means by Basic Type, Level of Target, and Level of Penalty for Noncompliance

Basic Type of Regulatory Means	Level of Target					
	Individual Source/Process		Facility/Organization		Region/System	
	Penalty < Gain	Penalty > Gain	Penalty < Gain	Penalty > Gain	Penalty < Gain	Penalty > Gain
Incentive	Effluent charge; subsidy; tax incentive or credit	(Effluent charge; subsidy tax incentive or credit with Connecticut plan)	(Effluent charge); subsidy; tax incentive or credit	(Effluent charge; subsidy; tax incentive or credit with Connecticut plan)	(Effluent charge; subsidy; tax incentive or credit)	(Effluent charge; subsidy; tax incentive or credit with Connecticut plan)
Directive	Rules and standards	Rules and standards with Connecticut plan	Rules and standards with bubble	Rules and standards with bubble and Connecticut plan	Rules and standards with offsets and banking	Rules and standards with offsets, banking, and Connecticut plan

Note: Items in parentheses are Connecticut-plan-incentive examples.

difficult questions of equity regarding which individual parties should pay how much of the tax would be left to local choice rather than mandated for all regions through federal action. Local, not national equity standards could govern. Such a charge might be viewed as a technique for dealing with situations in which one region creates externalities for another, such as when acid rain from Ohio, West Virginia, and western Pennsylvania damages lakes and vegetation in eastern Pennsylvania and New York. Of course, establishment of such a regulatory scheme might require state or regional compacts as well as federal legislation and could raise serious federalism questions.

Similarly, subsidies or tax credits might also be created at the regional level. It is possible that feasibility or implementation problems with many of these higher-level regulatory mechanisms would be no greater than with currently discussed bubbles and offsets, which are concerned with directive means at these levels. The point again is that the possibilities for regulatory controls are much wider than usually considered and include both incentive and directive means at several target levels.

In table 9-1, I have listed some sample types of means in each of the categories. Given the EPA's espousal of Connecticut-plan type penalties, I have listed rules and standards at each level (individual source/process, facility/organization, and region/system) both with and without this enforcement system. Since extension of such enforcement to incentive means is less clearly part of currently discussed alternatives, I have placed the Connecticut-plan incentive examples in parentheses. There is no basic design reason (as distinct from political feasibility or implementation reasons) why such enforcement could not also extend to incentive means, which, like directive means, employ the threat of negative rewards to assure compliance. For example, effluent charges are a positive incentive means because firms gain positive rewards from reducing discharges. Compliance through payment of the effluent tax and accurate reporting of discharges may require, however, threats of negative rewards.

The benefits of systematic knowledge of the logical possibilities in regulatory design should facilitate choice of appropriate means. Ideally, the aim would be development of a contingency theory in which particular means are linked to particular situations, with the efficacy of each means in each situation well understood. Knowledge of this kind, however, is not now available; even the systematic identification of regulatory possibilities has been rare. There have been a number of recent comparisons of alternative regulatory means, but few works have attempted such systematic identification and comparative analysis. Most discussions, even if insightful and of value for design purposes, are little more than catalogues or lists.[12] At any rate, a general incentives approach does allow us to systematically classify potential regulatory means.

Thus, with a general classification of regulatory means through use of the incentives framework, and identification of some general means by which regulators control regulatees, I turn to the relationship between the public or legislature as principal and the regulators as agents. As discussed earlier, analysis of regulatory control proceeds in two parts: control of regulatees and control of regulators.

Controlling the Regulators: The Incentive System of Regulators

Incentives and the Environment of Regulatory Bodies

As with control of regulatees, control of regulators can be effected both through manipulation or specification of desired behaviors and through manipulation of rewards. Similarly, means of control of regulatees may be divided into incentive and directive means. For regulators in an organizational setting, control can be exerted through whatever incentive relations exist between the individual regulators and the organization, and between the individual and elements of the organization's environment (for example, the regulated industry).

Formal control of regulators is normally exerted through directives distributed within the contractual bounds of the employment relationship. In exchange for salary, the regulator agrees to perform tasks within some zone of reasonableness; the tasks are specified by the directives of higher-level regulators (or the public or legislature as principal) that may have existing regulations and statutes as sources.[13] The regulator is policed through negative rewards associated with noncompliance with his or her employment contract; these may be administered through formal civil-service and other procedures.

In the regulator's general organizational setting, there may be in practice a variety of incentives and directives that may be manipulated to influence behavior. They may, however, be scarce; the controlling principals may face an economy of incentives in which necessary inducements must be carefully distributed and balanced with contributions received in return.[14] The inducements would include status rewards, coveted assignment or task rewards, organizational support resources (that is, more budget to spend), better physical facilities, threats of removal of any of these, and so on. This internal incentive system is, as described here, similar to that in any organization.[15]

But regulatory organizations, unlike many other organizations, are centrally concerned with management of their environments as part of their formal purposes or goals. Although business organizations may exist formally to make a profit and may seek to manage their environments (for example, form cartels) instrumentally, regulatory organizations, at least formally, exist *primarily* to manage some environment—for example, to control prices; police business practices; guard entry and exit; regulate the impacts of private firms on the physical environment, their workers, and their customers. Thus, to understand the particular behaviors of regulators through an incentive-systems framework, we should include as a central concern the incentive relations of regulators with components of their environment.

The incentive system faced by regulators is discussed in several places in the literature, both in systematic and more casual ways.[16] Most discussion has focused on the top regulatory officials, for example, regulatory commissioners. Often the aim is explanation of how the regulator may end up serving the goals of the regulated industry (sometimes referred to as "capture") rather than those of public or legislative principals. In essence, the regulated industry tends to possess or gain control of certain rewards important to regulators, such as status, friendship, convenience in task performance, and promise of a lucrative future job.[17]

But much regulation—particularly environmental regulation—is performed not solely (or at all) by some top-level official such as a commissioner. Of key importance is the behavior of what may be termed "line" regulators, for instance, air-pollution-emission or strip-mine-reclamation inspectors. Conceivably, the incentive system faced by such lower-level regulators may differ from that faced by the top-level officials. I will discuss the incentive system facing state-level line regulators through reporting some results of a study of the inspectors in a reclamation agency of a large midwestern state.[18]

The Reclamation Inspectors

The Surface Mining Control and Reclamation Act of 1977 provides for regulation of coal strip mining through minimum federal standards to be implemented largely through state agencies. Direct federal regulation substitutes in the absence of an approved state program. The numerous provisions of the act include substantial support for the state agencies involved: grants of up to 80 percent the first year, 60 percent the second, and 50 percent for succeeding years. A federal agency in the Department of Interior, the Office of Surface Mining, administers the program at the federal level. Final regulations under the act were in the process of being promulgated at the time the present study was undertaken, in early 1979.

The study of the state regulators was based on a questionnaire sent to all the inspectors and inspector supervisors in the agency, together with other background information obtained through interviews with agency officials. A small number (three responses) of inspectors who left the agency very recently were also included; this resulted in a slight variation in the number responding to certain of the questions. The head of the agency wrote a cover letter, sent with the questionnaires, encouraging response and permitting subjects to fill out the questionnaires during the work day. Responses were clearly indicated as voluntary, however, and strict assurances of confidentiality of individual responses were made. The data reported are based on twenty-nine responses, a response rate of about 85 percent. Some parts of the questionnaire were adapted from that used by Hal Rainey to permit comparisons at a later date.[19]

Of course, only one agency was investigated; the results should therefore be taken as only illustrative and suggestive.

To analyze the incentive relationships of the state reclamation inspectors, we need to examine the nature and sources of the rewards received (and sought) by the inspectors. As other scholars have described, regulators, like other public employees, may value: salary (both present and that to be received from a future job and through promotion); job security (both present and future); status/ prestige/recognition; friendship ties in the work setting; convenience in job performance (that is, reduction in or reasonable level of work load); ability to engage in interesting and fulfilling work; and ability to engage in meaningful public service, that is, achievement of public or programmatic ends through task performance.[20] Other possible rewards exist and are doubtless valued; these seem, however, among the most frequently discussed.

Current salary is of course provided through the inspector's employment relationship with the agency. Future salary (and job security) could come from the agency, with increases because of longer tenure and/or promotion, or from organizations outside the agency that the inspector may join. Since there are no recent departures from the agency because of failure to pass the civil-service exam or through discharge related to poor performance, all recent departures have been voluntary. Inspectors who remain with the agency receive job security through the civil-service system.

The major future sources of rewards for the inspectors appear to lie outside the agency. Turnover has been 15 to 20 percent per year. A study of a dozen recent departures reveals a median tenure of about three years. The data clearly reveal that there are two major future sources of rewards: the regulated mining industry, and the federal Office of Surface Mining; these are the two places the state inspectors go when they leave the agency. Of the last twenty inspectors or inspector supervisors to leave the agency (as of March 1979), 40 percent went to a regulated coal company, 40 percent went to the Office of Surface Mining, 10 percent retired, and 5 percent went back to school.

The inspectors were asked their perceptions of where their colleagues who left the agency tend to go to work. The subjects could choose "all," "most (more than 50 percent)," "some (20 to 50 percent)," "a few (0 to 20 percent)," and "none" for each of several destinations. Responses clustered in the "most" and "some" categories of the mining-company (34 percent and 59 percent) and federal-inspector (48 percent and 52 percent) alternatives. Furthermore, 80 percent of the inspectors perceived that most or some of their colleagues took their present jobs because they thought they could get a good future job in the mining industry, and 89 percent were anticipating the possibility of federal inspector jobs. All the inspectors thought their training in the agency would be useful for a position with a mining company or for a federal inspector's job or similar job. Asked whether they had ever talked, formally or informally, with anyone working in a number of relevant areas regarding a possible position, the inspectors gave the largest (and identical) responses for mining-companies and federal-inspector positions (62 percent).

The chief reason for the high rate of turnover, and for the mining-company-federal-agency loci to which departures flow, appears to be salary. Mining companies and the federal Office of Surface Mining are the two places in which the learned skills of the inspectors can be most amply rewarded. The federal office provides job security as well, of course, through civil service. The salaries of inspectors in the state agency (as of March 1978) were significantly lower (about 20 to 80 percent) than salaries in the federal Office of Surface Mining and in the mining industry. State salaries have since been increased, but federal and mining-company salaries remain significantly higher. The situation is similar for reclamation inspectors in a number of other states. The flat hierarchy of the state agency in question severely restricts promotion; the questionnaire indicated that inspectors perceived lower pay possibilities in the agency as compared with other possible positions. And all of the inspectors said they perceived that a "higher-paying job" was a major reason for those leaving the agency.

Consider now the other rewards listed. The inspectors were asked to indicate (on 7-point scales) the importance they attached to various rewards and, separately, the availability of these rewards within the agency. The percentages of inspectors responding to "important" and "extremely important," and to "mostly" and "extremely available" are combined and listed in table 9-2. The columns in table 9-2 are not strictly comparable, of course, although the questions were displayed to respondents in a parallel fashion. In general, we would expect subjects to leave the agency where rewards important to them are not being received and to go to organizations where such rewards are available, transition costs permitting.

The situation with regard to pay and promotion is apparent. Recognition and status/prestige are neither readily available nor highly important. Respect/friendliness is both important and available; but we may speculate that it may also be available in other work settings (more on this later). Job security is also both important and available; it would also be readily available in the federal civil service. The dead-end character of work as a state inspector may be reflected in the responses to "sense of worthwhile accomplishment," "development of abilities," and "exerting an important influence on your organization." Of course, both the federal service and mining employment offer greater promotion and commensurate job-growth possibilities. "Meaningful public service" and helping other people seem both important and available to a moderate extent; they would also be available in the federal service.

On a 7-point scale from extremely unfriendly to extremely friendly toward mining-company people, twenty-eight out of twenty-nine respondents were at least "a little friendly," and nineteen were "extremely" or "moderately friendly." Furthermore, 31 percent reported off-the-job social contacts with mining-company people, with an average of eight such contacts per month.

Table 9-2
Importance and Availability of Selected Rewards to Reclamation Inspectors in a State Agency ($n = 29$)

Questionnaire Item (Reward)	Percent "Important" and "Extremely Important"	Percent "Mostly" and "Extremely Available"
Recognition from your organization (awards, praise, etc.)	27	10
Higher pay than you now make	86	7
Promotion	72	14
Job security	75	73
Respect and friendliness from your colleagues or coworkers	79	72
A sense of worthwhile accomplishment in your work	100	58
Development of your abilities through your work	100	62
A good feeling about yourself, as a result of your work	93	66
Engaging in meaningful public service	38	44
Making a good deal of money	38	3
Doing work that is helpful to other people	69	42
Making important decisions and exerting and important influence on your organization	58	21
Achieving status and prestige	10	10

Note: Columns represent summation of percentages responding to top two items on 7-point scales. Columns are not strictly comparable, of course, although questions were displayed to respondents in a parallel fashion.

Such friendships could be the vehicles of postagency employment, of course, as well as of the growth of inspector perceptions of industry problems similar to those held by industry members. They could be part of any mechanism of capture.[21]

Friendships could also facilitate the transfer of information from regulated to regulator, increasing the inspector's convenience on the job. Although 94 percent of the inspectors had college majors generally relevant to their work in the agency, all inspectors are normally trained on the job. Friendships among inspectors and with the regulated parties may therefore play a major role in increasing regulator convenience. Both school and job training, of course, tend to limit the loci of future highly desired jobs.

The analysis of inspector rewards and reward sources therefore tends to confirm the existence of two major external incentive relations: one between the inspector and mining companies and one between the inspector and the federal Office of Surface Mining. These relations, which center on future job rewards, clearly dominate the inspector's relation with his or her agency. The incentive messages presumably transmitted in these external relations would of course differ: the industry would prefer less restrictive regulation; the federal office would prefer regulation consistent with federal standards (as against state preferences, or the preferences of the industry). Depending on the intensity of the inspector's non-self-interested preferences for public service, the performance of inspectors may be affected by these relations; there is, in effect, an incentive competition for the inspectors.

The incentive system just described for the inspectors—line regulators—may very well differ from that often faced by top-level state regulators. We have no countrywide data for top-level state reclamation officials. It is possible that top-level appointed state regulators in general may be constrained by accountability to elected officials to be more responsive to official policy (or unofficial political) goals; or they may be genuine advocates for their unit's program.[22] Regulatory officials dependent on governors and state legislatures for reappointment may behave differently from those who are elected. Of course, the existence of promotion ladders to the industry or to federal agencies may dominate, as it does for the lower-level line officials. For the case of upper-level state regulators in general, there is some historical evidence of a promotion ladder—or, more accurately, a trickle—to the federal agencies.[23]

The Interaction of the Means of Controlling Regulators and Regulatees

To design workable regulation, we of course need to know both what mechanisms (for example, incentive or directive) are appropriate to given contingencies and what regulator incentive systems are likely to insure proper administration of the selected regulatory means by regulatory personnel. Will use of certain regulatory mechanisms make it more or less difficult to control the regulators (thus reducing the on-paper efficacy of the particular regulatory mechanism)? For example, are there any factors to suggest that incentive means like subsidies are more likely to be well-administered than directive means like rules and standards?

Such questions only become relevant, of course, because some discretion exists and is always likely to exist in the management of regulatory mechanisms. Reclamation inspectors, for example, may always retain some discretion in judging whether coal companies are or are not in compliance—for example, in scheduling their inspections, in examining the whole of the mined property, in overlooking minor violations, and so on. Some areas of regulation permit more discretion than others, depending on the original legislative mandate and on rules made by the regulatory body to implement it. In addition, the costs of policing the regulators may simply not be worth the compliance gains thereby achieved.[24] Thus we expect some variance in actual and in permissible discretion across agencies.

An argument may be made, however, that incentive means are less likely to be problematic in this regard. Firms receiving purely positive incentives may exhibit better compliance, since compliance can be in the firm's self-interest. Even where the means of regulation are mixed, the incentive component may mean better compliance than under a purely or chiefly directive form. Consequently, firms subject to incentive regulation may place less pressure on regulators to deviate; they may have less reason to try to influence regulators through such rewards as information increasing regulator convenience and future jobs. In addition, the administrative process characteristic of directive regulation may provide many more opportunities for firms to provide dependent regulators with such rewards as information and prestige. At any rate, adequate regulatory design must consider the whole control problem—the incentive systems created both for regulators and regulatees.

Conclusions and Policy Consequences

In this chapter, I have presented the incentive systems approach as a way of structuring and integrating analysis of regulatory means and control in environmental (and other) regulation. Control is discussed at two levels: control by regulators over regulatees and control of the regulators themselves. I illustrated the case of control of the regulators by reporting some results of a study of state reclamation inspectors and argued that regulatory means with substantial incentive components may reduce control problems in both areas.

A major argument inherent in this chapter is that design of regulatory means can and should be more systematic and more variable, subject to situational contingencies, than it is usually presented. For example, a recently popular argument has been that market mechanisms would work better than traditional rules-and-standards regulation. The analysis in this chapter rejects such a flat statement. Regulation almost always has a hierarchical component to it, reflecting the control attempts of regulator principals over their regulatee agents, and it is usually backed by a hierarchical enforcement system. What we can see are mixed systems, in which market-like adjustments can occur at different levels within a hierarchical framework. Systematically identified and studied contingencies should select that regulatory means appropriate to the situation, whether the means is old-fashioned rules and standards (a directive means) or more recently proposed effluent charges (an incentive means).

The analysis of the incentive system facing the reclamation inspectors has some intriguing policy consequences. The inspectors face a dual external incentive system—to the industry and to the federal Office of Surface Mining. Were there no federal office, or no salary differential between the state agency and that office, the inspector incentive system would be dominated by the industry incentive relation alone. That, of course, would appear to be a recipe for capture. Thus the ladder to the federal level may police inspectors who desire promotion to that level to regulate according to federal standards. The federal ladder can thus prevent or decrease the degree of any capture behaviors among inspectors. Furthermore, this is done more cheaply than if federal inspectors were to do the work themselves. And it perhaps retains a myth of state control, which may deflect opposition to the regulation from the federal to the state level. Although there is substantial federal budget support for the state implementing agencies, this technique can also expand, through state budget contributions, the total resources devoted to regulatory control in this area. I suggest that such an incentive "safety valve" may be a useful design tool in any cross-level regulatory program in which some top-down control is desired.

Notes

1. The theory of agency, a theory of social relationships of "acting for," is currently a major area of research in finance and accounting. As far as I can tell, the utility of such a general theory was first proposed by Stephen A. Ross in "The Economic Theory of Agency: The Principal's Problem," *American Economic Review* 63 (May 1973): 134–139, and by this author in "Fiduciary Rationality and Public Policy: The Theory of Agency and Some Consequences" (Paper presented at the 1973 Annual Meeting of the American Political Science Association, New Orleans, La.), and in "The Theory of Agency: The Concept of Fiduciary Rationality and Some Consequences" (Ph.D. diss., Department of Political Science, University of Pennsylvania, 1974). On regulation and agency, see Barry M. Mitnick, *The Political Economy of Regulation: Creating, Designing, and Removing Regulatory Forms* (New York: Columbia University Press, 1980); Victor P. Goldberg, "Regulation and Administered Contracts," *Bell Journal of Economics* 7 (Autumn 1976): 426–448.

2. On this definition of *incentive*, see Barry M. Mitnick, Robert W. Backoff, and Hal G. Rainey, "The Incentive Systems Approach to the Study of Public Organizations" (Paper presented at the 1977 Annual Meeting of the American Political Science Association, Washington, D.C.).

3. On social-choice processes, see, for example, Robert Dahl and Charles E. Lindblom, *Politics, Economics and Welfare* (New York: Harper and Row, 1953); Charles E. Lindblom, *Politics and Markets* (New York: Basic Books, 1977); Stephen Elkin, "Political Science and the Analysis of Public Policy," *Public Policy* 22 (Summer 1974): 399–422; Otto A. Davis and Morton I. Kamien, "Externalities, Information and Alternative Collective Action," in *Public Expenditures and Policy Analysis* ed. Robert H. Haveman and Julius

Margolis (Chicago: Markham, 1970), pp. 74-95; Robert L. Bish, *The Public Economy of Metropolitan Areas* (Chicago: Markham, 1971).

4. For example, see Allen V. Kneese and Charles L. Schultze, *Pollution, Prices, and Public Policy* (Washington, D.C.: Brookings Institution, 1975).

5. Edwin T. Haefele, *Representative Government and Environmental Management* (Baltimore, Md.: Johns Hopkins University Press, 1973).

6. Mitnick, Backoff, and Rainey, "Incentive Systems Approach"; see also Mitnick, *Political Economy of Regulation.*

7. U.S. Environmental Protection Agency, "Regulatory Reform Initiatives" (Washington, D.C., October 1979).

8. Ibid.; Daniel J. Fiorino, "Implementing Regulatory Reforms—An Agency Perspective" (Paper presented at the Symposium on Strategies for Change in Regulatory Policy, Loyola University of Chicago, Chicago, Illinois, 3-4 December 1979).

9. On rights auctions, see, for example, J.H. Dales, *Pollution, Property and Prices* (Toronto: University of Toronto Press, 1968); Susan Rose-Ackerman, "Market Models for Water Pollution Control: Their Strengths and Weaknesses," *Public Policy* 25 (Summer 1977): 383-406.

10. On compliance to environmental regulation, see, for example, Alfred Marcus, " 'Command and Control': An Assessment of Smokestack Emission Regulation," Working Paper WP-308, Graduate School of Business, University of Pittsburgh, Pittsburgh, Penn.

11. Imposition of taxes on subunits has been discussed elsewhere in the context of obtaining performance closer to that desired by the monitor or policing principal (see Barry M. Mitnick, "The Theory of Agency: The Policing 'Paradox' and Regulatory Behavior," *Public Choice* 24 (Winter 1975): 27-42). In the context of managerial discretion and the theory of the firm, see Oliver E. Williamson, *The Economics of Discretionary Behavior: Managerial Objectives in a Theory of the Firm* (Englewood Cliffs, N.J.: Prentice-Hall, 1964).

12. For comparisons of environmental regulatory means, see, for example, Mitnick, *Political Economy of Regulation*; Kneese and Schultze, *Pollution, Prices, Public Policy*; William J. Baumol and Wallace E. Oates, *The Theory of Environmental Policy: Externalities, Public Outlays, and the Quality of Life* (Englewood Cliffs, N.J.: Prentice-Hall, 1975); U.S., Congress, Senate, Committee on Governmental Affairs, *Study on Federal Regulation*, vol. 6 and vol. 6 Appendix, 95th Cong., 2d sess., 1978; Congressional Research Service, *Pollution Taxes, Effluent Charges, and Other Alternatives for Pollution Control*, report prepared for the U.S. Senate Committee on Environment and Public Works, 95th Cong., 1st sess., 1977; Stuart S. Nagel, "Incentives for Compliance with Environmental Law," *American Behavioral Scientist* 17 (May/June 1974): 690-710; Davis and Kamien, "Externalities."

13. See Herbert A. Simon, "A Formal Theory of the Employment Relation," in Simon, *Models of Man: Social and Rational* (New York: Wiley, 1957): 183-195.

14. Chester I. Barnard, *The Functions of the Executive* (Cambridge, Mass.: Harvard University Press, 1938); James G. March and Herbert A. Simon, *Organizations* (New York: Wiley, 1958); Peter B. Clark and James Q. Wilson, "Incentive Systems: A Theory of Organizations," *Administrative Science Quarterly* 6 (September 1961): 129-166.

15. For a review of the literature on incentive systems, see Mitnick, Backoff, and Rainey, "Incentive Systems Approach."

16. For a review, see Mitnick, *Political Economy of Regulation*; see, for example, Roger G. Noll, *Reforming Regulation: An Evaluation of the Ash Council Proposals* (Washington, D.C.: Brookings Institution, 1971); Ross D. Eckert, "On the Incentives of Regulators: The Case of Taxicabs," *Public Choice* 14 (Spring 1973): 83-99; Louis DeAlessi, "An Economic Analysis of Government Ownership and Regulation: Theory and the Evidence from the Electric Power Industry," *Public Choice* 19 (Fall 1974): 1-42; Barry M. Mitnick and Charles Weiss, Jr., "The Siting Impasse and a Rational Choice Model of Regulatory Behavior: An Agency for Power Plant Siting," *Journal of Environmental Economics and Management* 1 (1974): 150-171.

17. On the "revolving door," see, for example, William T. Gormley, Jr., "A Test of the Revolving Door Hypothesis at the FCC," *American Journal of Political Science* 23 (November 1979): 665-683.

18. I would like to thank Robert W. Backoff, Charles Call, Steven Cover, Lori Hunter, Margery M. Mitnick, Hal G. Rainey, Rebecca Roberts, Bert Rockman, Charles Stubbart, and, especially, Jeffrey L. Wilson for their helpful comments and/or assistance in performing this study. Background material on the state agency, the inspectors, and the Surface Mining Control and Reclamation Act of 1977 is based on personal communication with members of the state agency. On this study, see also Mitnick, *Political Economy of Regulation*.

19. Hal G. Rainey, "Comparing Public and Private: Conceptual and Empirical Analyisis of Incentives and Motivation among Government and Business Managers" (Ph.D. diss. School of Public Administration, Ohio State University, 1977).

20. See, for example, Noll, *Reforming Regulation*; Eckert, "Incentives of Regulators"; DeAlessi, "Government Ownership and Regulation"; Mitnick and Weiss, " Siting Impasse"; Rainey, "Comparing Public and Private."

21. On capture, see Mitnick, *Political Economy of Regulation*. There was no evidence collected to determine whether such perceptions, such a process, or such capture existed in the agency studied.

22. See Anthony Downs, *Inside Bureaucracy* (Boston: Little, Brown, 1967).

23. See, for example, Mitnick, *Political Economy of Regulation*.

24. Mitnick, "Policing 'Paradox.' "

10 Charges to Control Aircraft Noise

Donald C. Cell

Introduction

The noise made by commercial aircraft operating over neighborhoods around metropolitan airports is now subject to the same kinds of direct regulations that have been applied to most other forms of pollution. Another way to deter such noise making would be to charge airlines according to the noise their aircraft emit during approaches and departures at these airports. This chapter describes how such noise charges could be calculated and administered, and shows why noise charges would be more efficient than the present regulations and also would probably be easier to administer.[1]

One useful way of comparing the efficiency of emission charges with that of regulations is to consider whether adoption of charges would improve the flow of information that provides the basis for decisions about abatement. Three arguments will be advanced. First, charges would tend to reduce the cost of noise abatement by shifting the choice of abatement methods to the airline industry, which has considerably more information about these methods than do regulators. Second, charges would generate more information about the benefits of abatement, which is needed to establish an appropriate level of abatement. Third, the cost of acquiring the information needed to administer aircraft-noise charges would be unusually low.

The Aircraft-Noise Problem

Economic theory distinguishes between two efficiency goals: promoting the least expensive methods of abatement and achieving the right level of abatement. To clarify this distinction in the case of aircraft noise, imagine a single monopoly airline that operates all the aircraft making the noise around an airport and also owns all the property subject to the noise. If this airline wishes to maximize its total wealth, from both operation of aircraft and rental property, two things may be predicted. First, among the many steps that the airline can take to

Among those who have helped in the preparation of this chapter, special thanks are due to the editor Dean Mann and to Edward Cell, Daniel Hart, William Hendley, T. Hardie Park, Robert Park, Arnold Reitze, and Fred Smith. Continuing discussions with John Morrall and James Brown have stimulated the author's interest in the aircraft-noise problem.

increase the rental value of its property by reducing the noise-purchase of quieter aircraft, rescheduling of noisier aircraft, changes in the operation of its aircraft near its property, noise-insulation of its buildings, and so forth—it will want to adopt only those steps that are cost-effective. Thus to say that cost-effectiveness is a goal of the airline means that the airline wishes to minimize the costs it must incur to achieve whatever reduction of noise it finds to be profitable and that the airline will therefore exploit all steps it expects will cost less before resorting to any methods of noise control that it expects will cost more.

Second, since the airline benefits as noise control increases the demand for its property and its rental revenue, the airline will continue to invest in noise control up to the point at which the cost of additional efforts begins to exceed the increased rental revenue. To the extent the increased rent that renters are willing to pay to the property-owning airline corresponds to the increased benefits of quiet the renters experience, the airline, in its incentive to acquire more rent, will tend to promote an allocatively efficient level of quiet.

This hypothetical case also serves to indicate, by comparison, why real-world airlines lack the incentive to pursue these efficiency goals, this lack of incentive being a major cause of governmental intervention.[2] For our purposes, the big difference between real-world airlines and this hypothetical airline is that the property around airports is owned by many individuals rather than by the airlines that generate the noise. Since the benefits of quiet would go to these property owners but not to the airlines, the airlines lack the incentive to incur the costs of abatement. The result is not only a conflict of interest but an excessive, inefficient level of noise.

Pressure to abate the noise is brought to bear directly on the hypothetical property-owning airline through market transactions, as renters are willing to pay more to live in homes that are quieter. By contrast, pressure has in fact been brought to bear indirectly on real-world airlines indirectly, from property owners through court litigation and action by government agencies.

In describing how noise charges would work as one governmental response to these pressures, it will be helpful to separate the discussion of charges designed to be cost-effective (minimizing the cost of any given level of abatement) from consideration of charges designed to be allocatively efficient (achieving a desirable level of abatement). By postponing consideration of how the noise-abatement target is to be determined, the next section will focus on the goal of cost-effectiveness, the question being whether to pursue the target through specific regulations or by means of charges. In this section *lower cost of abatement* will mean lower cost per unit of noise abatement. The result of a cost-effective policy may be to achieve more noise abatement at the same cost, or to achieve the same level of noise abatement at lower cost, or more likely to achieve some combination of these two goals. A discussion of the use of charges to determine the level of noise abatement and a comparison of the role of the courts with the administration of noise charges will follow.

Noise Charges for Cost-Effectiveness

This section compares charges with a few of the more important noise regulations to show why charges would be more cost-effective and probably less
burdensome to administer. The argument falls short of showing that such
charges would be advantageous to the airline industry, since we neither compare
the burden of the charges collected with the regulatory sanctions the charges
would replace nor consider how noise charges might redistribute the total
burden—abatement costs plus charges—within the industry. Still, from the
standpoint of the airlines, cost-effective charges may prove more attractive
than they might appear, in three respects. First, the purpose of charging for
noise is not to penalize airlines for the noise their aircraft make; rather, the
purpose is to establish a reward for noise abatement that is then considered
successful to the extent the charges remain uncollected as the airlines proceed
to abate the noise. As will be explained more fully later, charges would need
to be collected only so long as airlines, following prior notification of when
the charges would begin, continued to make noise that is considered excessive
at certain airports. Second, any charge burden is a transfer of money from
the airlines to the collecting agency; how this revenue is used, and who should
benefit from it, is a separate policy decision, which airlines would influence.
Third, as we shall now show, a shift away from inefficient regulations toward
charges would work to the benefit of the airlines by reducing their real-resource
costs per unit of noise abatement.[3]

Noise Regulations

FAA and airport regulations bypass a set of cost-effective abatement steps that
airlines could take had they the incentive to do so and call on airlines to take
other actions that are not cost-effective. The regulations, although they are
called "specific," are actually designed to control whole classes of abatement
actions that appear on the average to be cost-effective. The reason for the
imprecision of the regulations is that regulators cannot get inside airline management to acquire the detailed information about each airline's operations and
circumstances that they would need to segregate and omit particular actions
within the class that are not cost-effective and to pinpoint by-passed actions outside the class that are cost-effective.

Consider the rule calling for the retrofit or replacement of noisier aircraft,
first issued in 1969 and upgraded in 1977, on which federal policy largely
depends. Congress provided that the standards for aircraft should be "economically reasonable . . . and appropriate for the particular type of aircraft, aircraft
engine, . . . or certificate to which it will apply."[4] Accordingly, the noise standards vary according to an aircraft's weight, the number of engines that affect

approach and departure slopes, when the aircraft began its career, and when aircraft of the type were first designed. Since the cost of noise reduction varies among these classes, the finer-tuning aims to make the regulation more cost-effective than a single standard for all commercial aircraft would be. Yet such discrimination among classes of aircraft fails to minimize costs simply because the incremental cost of reducing sound emissions varies considerably within the classes that the regulations have been able to distinguish.

Probably the biggest disability of the regulation from the standpoint of cost-effectiveness is that the regulation is designed to control the sounds aircraft make rather than to control the harmful effects of those particular sound emissions that people actually experience. A noisy 707 operating in daytime freight service between two sparsely settled communities will make the same sound emissions as a 707 makes in a nighttime freight service between New York and Boston, but there is a lot of difference in the harmful effects. The federal rule applies the same standard to sound emissions in the two situations by calling for the retrofit or replacement of both 707s. Yet the same degree of harm reduction can be achieved at less cost to the airline, which (let us assume) operates both aircraft, if the first 707 continues to operate while the 707 on the New York–Boston run is replaced by an aircraft that is even quieter than the rule specifies.

The Federal Aviation Administration (FAA) has, however, issued guidelines for administering the regulation that recognize that it is impossible to tell whether an expenditure by an airline to retrofit or replace an aircraft is cost-effective without considering how much harm it would prevent: "In evaluating petitions for an exemption, the FAA will consider ... whether the petitioner is able to operate the airplanes ... into airports where a significant noise problem does not exist. ..."[5] Deciding which airports are free of "a significant noise problem" requires some kind of evaluation of the harmful effects of noise at different airports, which will vary by degree, particularly with the numbers of people who experience the noise. What if the FAA further fine-tuned the aircraft-noise standards by classifying airports according to the size of nearby populations? Nonetheless, to exclude all operations of all noisy aircraft at all airports just above the threshold while freely permitting all such operations at airports below the threshold would prove costly to the air-transportation industry and its customers. A comprehensive measure of the harmful effects of noise that weights the relative importance of both population size and aircraft-noise emissions and other relevant factors as well and a system of sanctions that deters aircraft operations at an airport in proportion to the harmful effects are what is needed.

The harm caused by the sounds from a particular aircraft at a particular airport depends also on the time of day the sounds occur. The efforts by National in Washington and Logan in Boston to deter nighttime operations illustrate why such airport regulations are not cost-effective. Despite the presence of two other regional airports that remain open at night, National's 10 p.m. curfew for scheduled landings is set at a fairly late hour; although it would probably be cost-effective to exclude some earlier flights during sensitive evening hours, it is not cost-effective to exclude them all, and the airport lacks the information it would need to discriminate intelligently. Logan Airport, having decided that exclusion of all night operations would be too burdensome, levies fines that deter some night operations by noisy aircraft. But Logan authorities generally permit freight operations at night by noisy aircraft such as 707s on grounds that the loss of their service would be too costly for both the commerce of the Boston area and the airlines. Logan lacks the information it would need to determine which of these operations are justified and which are not.[6]

Noise Charges

As the hyphenated term implies, cost-effectiveness is a ratio of two quantities: dollars of cost and the amount of the good provided. "Abatement of the harmful effects of noise" is the good that noise-control policy aims to provide. The commonly used abbreviation "abatement of noise" may be misleading unless we remember that *noise* always refers to a harmful experience, not simply to decibels of sound.

The preceding survey indicates that FAA and airport regulations do take some account of the fact that cost-effectiveness depends on both effectiveness in reducing harm and the cost outlay. But the survey also suggests that whatever level of noise abatement the regulations achieve could be accomplished at less cost if controls could be devised to deal with the many variations—particularly among aircraft, airports, and time of day—in cost per unit of harm prevention. We now describe a system of charges that would (1) overcome the disability of the regulations by shifting the burden of cost analysis from regulators to the airlines and (2) be inexpensive to administer.

First, the basis for the charge must be the amount of noise that each aircraft makes measured in terms of its harmful effects, in the following sense: the measure must at least roughly capture the differences in the degree of harm caused by the various aircraft operations so that the charges paid decrease in proportion as the harmful effects of the noise decrease (such a measure will be described). Second, the charge must be collected for all departures and landings (noise events) at a flat, constant rate per unit of harm, making it worthwhile for each airline to identify and pursue all abatement actions the costs of which are less than the charge. It is the flat rate of the charge that makes it unnecessary for the regulating agency to attempt the costly, impractical task of identifying and directly controlling each cost-effective action that airlines can undertake. Thus a flat rate capitalizes on the airline's greater expertise about the costs of a multiplicity of possible abatement actions. The rate or level of the charge is immaterial as far as cost-effectiveness is concerned; the level of the charge will determine the level of abatement, as discussed in the next section.

Taking other conditions as given, the harmful effects of the noise made by a particular aircraft during its landings and departures varies with three factors over which airlines exercise considerable control: the sounds the aircraft emits, the time of day it makes the sounds, and the number of people who hear it as this varies with the airport being used. Accoustical experts have developed a subjective measure of the sounds made by a single aircraft, called effective perceived noise (EPNdB), which takes account of loudness, duration, and shrillness of the sound. The total noise that a person near the airport experiences is measured by a noise-exposure forecast (NEF) at that person's location, NEF being a function of three variables: the EPNdB sounds made by particular aircraft, the number of aircraft making these sounds per day, and the time of day the sounds are made. Thus NEF contour lines are drawn around an airport indicating zones in which people experience different levels of cumulative EPNdB, night-time sounds being given 12 times the weight of daytime sounds. Finally, the noise impact made by a particular aircraft, given its EPNdB and the time of day, varies with the number of people located within each NEF contour at each airport as may be estimated from census data.[7]

Most people located outside NEF 30 are thought to escape significant harm, NEF rising to a maximum of about 45 at the inner borders of heavily used airports. Noise control is, then, needed at perhaps thirty airports where noise levels exceed NEF 30 to deal with aircraft whose EPNdB and time of landing or departure contribute to NEF levels between 30 and 45 at these impacted airports.

Accordingly, suppose each commercial aircraft faces charges that are roughly proportional to (1) that aircraft's contribution to noise levels in excess of the NEF 30 threshold level of noise and (2) the numbers of people within these noise contours. As a result of the charge, payments by an airline will decrease proportionally as the amount of noise the airline makes decreases, noise being measured according to its harmful effects. Such a charge is a flat rate per unit of noise in the sense that two units of noise should represent roughly twice the harm of one unit of noise and so cost twice as much. Cost-minimizing airlines will therefore attempt to discover and undertake all noise-abatement steps the cost of which, per unit of noise avoided, is less than the charge.

Airlines will have the incentive to reduce noise cost-effectively regardless of whether the average level of the charge is set above or below the numbers shown in tables 10-1 through 10-3.[8] It is not the level but rather the differences in the charges that gives airlines the incentive to adjust the combination of airport (table 10-1), type of aircraft (table 10-2), and time of day of the flight (table 10-3). Without attempting to list all the options that airlines may develop, we may predict that they will take various combinations of such steps as

Table 10–1

Average Noise Charge per Operation for Twenty-three Major Airports
(*dollars*)

Airport	Charge
Boston-Logan International	120.18
Atlanta	13.04
Buffalo	36.55
Chicago-Midway	45.57
Chicago-O'Hare	73.29
Cleveland	53.26
Denver	52.11
Dulles	5.64
J.F. Kennedy	113.07
LaGuardia	196.67
Los Angeles	53.54
Miami	70.55
Minneapolis-St. Paul	43.60
Newark	137.99
New Orleans	15.39
Philadelphia	25.96
Phoenix	13.04
Portland	0.82
San Diego	102.86
San Francisco	28.37
Seattle	64.49
St. Louis	29.45
Washington National	6.06

Source: Calculated by the Council on Wage and Price Stability based on data from Department of Transportation, *Aircraft Noise Reduction Forecast*, vol. I, *Summary Report for 23 Airports*, DOT-TST-75-3 (Washington, D.C., October 1974).

Note: The average noise charge is calculated from the total loss of property value around the airport due to the noise, based on an estimated depreciation of 1 percent per NEF unit over 30; this capital loss is expressed as an annual loss of rental value, divided by the total number of aircraft operations during the year, and allocated between day and night operations.

replacing or retrofitting aircraft that continue to use noise-sensitive airports; rescheduling the noisier aircraft that for a time remain in operation to keep them away from such airports, at night especially; shifting some flights to an outlying airport in the same metropolitan area; forgoing some stops now being made at such airports enroute and taking different routes; cancelling flights that are no longer profitable; adopting different operating procedures around the airports; and so on. The charge structure will induce airlines to weigh, compare, and rank all such steps according to their contribution to reducing the harmful effects of the noise.[9]

Conditions are unusually favorable both for monitoring the incidence of aircraft noise around the airport for each landing and departure and for

Table 10-2
Noise Levels of Aircraft by Operation
(*in EPNdB*)

Aircraft	Operations	Nonretrofit	New Type of Aircraft in Service	Full Retrofit
707–320B	Takeoff	113.0		102.2
	Approach	116.8		104.0
DC–8–61	Takeoff	114.0		103.5
	Approach	115.0		106.0
727–200	Takeoff	101.2		97.5
	Approach	108.2		102.6
737–200	Takeoff	92.0		92.0
	Approach	109.0		102.0
DC–9	Takeoff	96.0		95.0
	Approach	107.0		99.1
747–100	Takeoff	115.0		107.0
	Approach	113.6		107.0
DC–10–10	Takeoff		99.0	
	Approach		106.0	
L–10–11	Takeoff		98.0	
	Approach		103.0	
BAC–11	Takeoff		103.0	
	Approach		102.5	
Concorde	Takeoff		115.4	
	Approach		114.5	

Source: Based on data from Federal Aviation Administration, *Aviation Noise Abatement Policy* (Washington, D.C., 18 November 1976), p. 38 and U.S. Environmental Protection Agency, *Project Report: Noise Standards for Civil Subsonic Turbojet Engine-Powered-Airplanes* (Washington, D.C., December 1974), pp. 11–14.

administering the charges. Three facts account for this: (1) the noise is localized around the airport where aircraft operate near the ground; (2) the methods for recording noise levels are relatively well developed and the noise-monitoring equipment is inexpensive; and (3) administratively, FAA or the airport authority can easily assign charges to the relatively few airlines that operate aircraft into the airport.[10]

It may be asserted that such a cost-effective charge policy is nonetheless unrealistic because noise monitoring is still imperfect, because the day-night differential is somewhat arbitrary, because not all airports that have a noise problem may be induced to adopt the same rate of charge per unit of noise, and so forth. But such assertions ignore the point that any noise-control policy that aspires to cost-effectiveness must cope with these same problems to the best of its ability. So long as success is a matter of degree, any approach must be evaluated by whether it achieves the goal but rather by its degree of success in moving toward the goal.

Table 10-3
Schedule of Noise Charges for Logan International Airport
(*dollars*)

EPNdB	Day Charge	Night Charge
97	0.00	0.00
98	31.13	373.50
99	35.74	428.50
100	41.09	493.02
101	47.19	566.23
102	54.20	650.26
103	62.26	747.00
104	71.60	859.05
105	82.15	985.67
106	94.36	1,132.08
107	108.39	1,300.53
108	124.52	1,494.00
109	143.04	1,716.23
110	164.30	1,971.33
111	188.74	2,264.53
112	216.79	2,601.05
113	249.04	2,988.00
114	286.08	3,432.47
115	328.61	3,942.67
116	377.48	4,529.96
117	433.61	5,202.48

Source: Calculations by the Council on Wage and Price Stability, "The Noise Charge Approach to Reducing Airport Noise" (Washington, D.C., April 1977), pp. 14–27.

Note: The total loss of rental value around Logan, which is estimated to be $23.4 million in 1977 prices, is allocated among aircraft operations according to the charge formula $F_n = (A)2^{0.2n}$, where n is the aircraft's EPNdB and A is a constant. The $2^{0.2n}$ component is based on the estimate that at the typical airport the number of families subjected to the noise tends to double when NEF increases by roughly 5 units. Substituting for F_n the $70.53 average day charge and for n the 5.9 NEF units over 30 experienced by the average household, the constant A = $31.13 for a day operation and 12($31.13) = $373.50 for a night operation. Charges begin at a noise level of 98 EPNdB, which is the difference between 104, the estimated average noise per aircraft operation, and 5.9, the number of NEF units over the threshold experienced by the average household.

Noise Charges for Allocative Efficiency

The preceding section described a system of noise charges designed to achieve cost-effectively some level of noise abatement. But through what procedures, and on the basis of what criterion, is the level of abatement itself to be determined? We should first distinguish three alternative procedures through which the level of abatement may be determined. Some unspecified reduction in the harmful effects of noise at airports will result if policymakers continue to rely on the present array of FAA aircraft-noise standards, airport curfews, and other such regulations. Alternatively, policymakers could perhaps, through the legislative-regulatory process, set explicit noise-control targets for airports (on what basis?). These targets could then be approached either through the various specific regulations or through cost-effective charges, by adjusting the regulatory standards or the charge rate, as the case may be, as necessary to attain the targets.

A third approach would be for policymakers to let the level of noise control be determined through the charge system itself. By designing a more ambitious system of charges based on the social benefits of noise abatement, the idea is to build into the charges the incentive for airlines to reduce noise to a level which is socially desirable in the sense of being allocatively efficient. This section describes how such charges could be designed and administered.

The key difference between a partial version of charges, which aims only for cost-effectiveness, and a full version, which also aims for allocative efficiency, may be stated in terms of the base and the rate of charge. Cost-effectiveness is promoted by making the base for the charges as comprehensive as possible so that the same degree of abatement pressure is brought to bear on all noise events of the same magnitude, as discussed. Of course the rate of charge cannot help but affect the level of noise abatement, but the rate may be adjusted to move toward an abatement target that has been determined independently of the charge system. Alternatively, the level of noise abatement may be determined by setting the rate of charge equal to some measure of the benefits of abatement.

The argument for charges based on the best estimate of the social benefits of noise abatement is that policymakers, whether they proceed through the regulatory process or through charges, cannot avoid making judgments, or at least tacit assumptions, about the benefits of abatement. The imposition of costs on airlines and their customers, and the reallocation of resources that will result, cannot be justified apart from the benefits that people around the airport will experience as the noise is controlled. Without making any claims to precision, a systematic way to decide what cost burden is justified is to set the rate of charge equal to the best estimate of the social benefit of one less unit of noise. The purpose of the charge is to internalize the social benefit of noise abatement in the accounting of the airlines. The model is a competitive-resource price, which limits the use of the resource to those willing to pay for that resource's opportunity costs, as the opportunity cost of noise is the benefit of quiet. Thus the charge systematically links the airline's interest in reducing its charge expenses with the property owner's interest in reducing the noise.

Probably the most promising basis for estimating the benefits of quiet, or noise abatement, is the difference between the higher prices people have actually paid for property free of aircraft noise compared to the lower prices paid for the same kind of property subject to the noise. Assuming that the buyers of homes subject to the noise could have purchased quieter homes by paying higher prices, and that they are aware of the noise so that they can compare the relative value they place on the quiet they are sacrificing and the money (other goods) they are gaining, then the difference in the two prices reflects the average value these home buyers have in fact placed on quiet. Statistically, such valuations of quiet may be approximated by comparing the prices paid for two sets of homes that are similar in value-determining characteristics except that one set is subject to aircraft noise and the other is not. From studies of property values around nine metropolitan airports, it has been estimated that the value of property in 1970 had depreciated by a rate of 0.7 to 1.0 percent for each NEF-unit increase in noise above the annoyance threshold.[11] For example, a 1-percent rate of depreciation indicates that, in 1977 prices, an average buyer who paid $65,000 for a home subject to 37 NEF would have been willing to pay about $5,000 more—equivalent at a 10-percent rate of discount to a rental difference of about $40 per month—had that same home been subject to a threshold noise level of NEF 30. Based on the estimated depreciation rate for the airport, the average price of impacted property, the number of properties, and the NEF-noise pattern at the airport, we may estimate the total expected gain in property values due to noise abatement. Since NEF is a cumulative measure of noise derived from individual noise events (EPNdB), this total gain that noise abatement will produce may be distributed in terms of the noise created by individual aircraft.[12]

Since it is based on the present value of additional quiet—the marginal price of quiet, the rate of charge may need to be adjusted when the level of noise changes substantially, much as relative prices in dynamic markets will change. But such adjustments are not unique to charges; unless the regulatory process were to remain oblivious to new information about benefits and costs, regulations and their enforcement will be adjusted over time as well.

It should be noted that such noise charges would in some ways follow a common-law theory laid down by some courts. In an important case brought by property owners against Los Angeles International Airport, decided on appeal in 1974, the court required the airport to pay damages for the reduction of value of 581 properties ranging from $400 to $6,000 per parcel as estimated by expert appraisers. The court in return granted the airport a noise easement—the right to make noise.[13] The money damages were like charges in that they were based on estimated depreciation in property values. But unlike a charge system, the damages were awarded as a one-time compensation to property owners for their loss of capital values. Courts reason that they lack the administrative capability of assessing and collecting money damages on a continuing basis. This is a major disadvantage of the judicial approach as compared to the continuing administration of charges insofar as the social objective is to deter the noise by rewarding, as through reduced charges, continuing efforts to abate the noise.

If we are correct that policymakers must decide, either explicitly or implicitly, about the benefits of noise abatement, then policymakers also must judge the reliability of property values as compared to the reliability of alternative sources of information about the benefits.[14] In a political setting, the policymaker is concerned particularly with the feelings of the people who experience the noise. The policymaker will therefore compare the reliability of data from property values with that of alternative sources of information about the subjective effects of noise. The policymaker will also be influenced, probably to a lesser extent, by information about any delayed health effects of which people may, at least for a time, be unaware. Whether home buyers fully appreciate, or whether they exaggerate, the harmful effects of noise we cannot be sure. But the data presented in table 10-3 do indicate that home buyers have placed a substantial money value on quiet.[15]

The fact that charges are based on a money evaluation of benefits, although sometimes cited as a disability of the charge concept, is probably not a fundamental consideration. After all, the role of money here is simply to serve as a common denominator for the purpose of comparing costs and benefits, a task that policymakers can hardly avoid. Even to attain cost-effectiveness, which requires the comparison of different noise events, the effects of noise must be measured by such a common denominator. The struggle is chiefly over how the valuation process shall be controlled. This policy struggle over the level of abatement of aircraft noise is part of a broader problem concerning the allocation of resources between environmental quality and other goods and the setting of our social priorities.

Conclusion

Regulations and charges both establish procedures for comparing the costs and benefits of steps to improve environmental quality. Unlike the regulations, emission charges would establish a rule for systematically measuring, monitoring, and rewarding contributions to environmental quality by industry, and they would shift analysis of the costs of abatement methods to industry, which has the comparative advantage.

In the particular case of aircraft noise, methods for measuring and monitoring contributions to noise abatement have been so developed that the administration of charges would probably be less burdensome to government and individual airports than administration of specific noise controls has been. Being administratively workable in this sense, one version of charges would reduce the costs of reaching a noise-abatement target established through the regulatory process. Another version would take the additional step of basing the level of noise abatement on a measure of the valuation of quiet derived from the choices of the property owners.

We should not assume, however, that the advantages claimed for aircraft-noise charges apply equally to all other pollution problems. The measuring and monitoring of emissions according to their harmful effects, and the administration of charges, will be more difficult and costly where the harmful emissions are hard to measure and widely dispersed and where on-site administrative organizations such as airports are lacking. In some such cases, the specific regulation of equipment and processes may be much less costly to administer and, on balance, more effective. This case study of aircraft noise therefore suggests that the standard regulatory approach may have been applied to different pollution situations indiscriminately.

Notes

1. This chapter is based on the writer's authorship (with John Morrall) of a Council on Wage and Price Stability (CWPS) report, "The Noise Charge Approach to Reducing Airport Noise" (Washington, D.C., April 1977); statements the writer presented at Federal Aviation Administration hearings on aircraft-noise rules; and discussions with officials, industry people, and economists in Washington, D.C., during 1976–1977.

2. In addition to their lack of incentive to reduce the noise, airlines also lack control over some methods of noise relief that can only be carried out by property owners, such as insulation of buildings and sale of the property to others who are less bothered by the noise. The analysis in this chapter is incomplete in that it compares only those regulations that are directed at the airlines with charges that are also directed at airlines. Being directed entirely at airlines, charges conform with the theory of strict liability in tort law except that because of the absence of compensation, property owners retain incentives to take preventive actions. I am indebted to William Hendley for the point that the lack of coordination between abatement actions by airlines and noise-averting actions by property owners will nonetheless to some extent prevent a cost-effective solution.

3. A longer version of this chapter, presented at the June 1980 meetings of the Western Economic Association, gave more consideration to the effect of charges on the airline industry.

4. Noise Control Act of 1972, 86 U.S. Statutes 1241. See Federal Aviation Administration, "Notice on Phased-Compliance with FAR Part 36 Rule," *Federal Register* 41 (December 1976): 56046; and "Preamble to Amendments, Federal Aviation Regulations Part 36," *Federal Register* 42 (March 1977): 12360.

5. Department of Transportation, "Aviation Noise Abatement Policy" (Washington, D.C., November 1976), p. 7.

6. See "Logan International Airport Noise Abatement Regulations," *Noise Regulation Reporter* 69 (3 January 1977): D-1 to D-5. These detailed rules were never fully implemented.

7. William Lake, "Noise: Emerging Federal Control" in *Federal Environmental Law*, ed. Erica L. Dolgin and Thomas G.P. Guilbert (St. Paul: West Publishing, 1974), pp. 1150–1231, surveys the development of noise measurements as well as the history of noise regulations. The two-part day-night division should be broken down further.

8. Table 10-3 presents an illustrative charge system designed to be cost-effective. In addition, the base rate of these charges, which is derived from property-value data, is designed to be allocatively efficient. The data were developed by John Morrall, senior economist at CWPS and coauthor of the CWPS report in which the methodology is more fully explained.

9. For further discussion of the options see Council on Wage and Price Stability, "Noise Charge Approach." The list of ways to reduce the harmful effect of noise could be extended by experts in air transport operations. See for example the long list of steps that airlines have taken recently in response to the rising price of fuel, reported in the *Wall Street Journal*, 22 August 1980, p. 17.

10. Since FAA has rated the sound emissions of each type of commercial aircraft in standardized tests, all that is required is to record an airline's operations by type of aircraft and time of day. Or, to provide an incentive to reduce the noise by adjusting landing and departure procedures, microphones may be installed to record each aircraft's sounds at designated points. The annual cost of a system of twelve microphones installed at Dulles Airport amounts to about 0.5 percent of the airport's operating costs.

11. Jon P. Nelson, *Economic Analysis of Transportation Noise Abatement* (Cambridge, Mass.: Ballinger, 1978), chap. 6, provides perhaps the best survey and evaluation of the studies. The depreciation rate varies somewhat among airports, probably being, for example, on the high side in Boston where incomes are relatively high. The depreciation rate around an airport should be updated before it is used as the basis for charges.

12. See tables 10-1 through 10-3; the data for Logan Airport were developed to illustrate a method by which charges may be calculated and do not purport to be the final word.

13. The case referred to is Aaron v. City of Los Angeles, 40 Cal. App. 3d 471 (1974). For a survey and analysis of court decisions on aircraft noise, see William F. Baxter and Lillian R. Altree, "Legal Aspects of Airport Noise," *Journal of Law and Economics* 15 (1972): 1–113. Courts have held liable the municipal governments that own and operate the airports, reasoning that these authorities can act to control the noise making.

14. One group of economists would challenge this way of putting the problem. They contend that benefits data are simply too unreliable to be used. What threshold level of reliability is thought to be required, and the nature of the alternatives, is not clear to this writer. See Baumol and Oates, *Quality of Life*, pp. 355–357; William Baumol, "On Taxation and the Control of

Externalities," *American Economic Review* 62 (1972): 307–322. Organization for Economic Cooperation and Development (OECD) economists argued vigorously against the attempt to establish allocatively efficient charges in the case of aircraft noise, in an exchange of letters with the writer and his colleague at CWPS. On the OECD position see A. Alexandre and J.P. Barde, "Aircraft Noise Charges," *Noise Control Engineering* 3 (1974): 54–59. The OECD economists have done a lot of important and imaginative quantitative work in their advocacy of noise charges for the purpose of promoting cost-effectiveness.

15. The data on home valuation do omit the effects of noise on the people who spend time near an airport but live elsewhere; offsetting this omission is the tax subsidy to home ownership, which inflates the valuations somewhat. See Nelson, *Transportation Noise Abatement*; National Resources Council of the National Academy of Sciences, *Noise Abatement: Policy Alternatives for Transportation*, vol. 8 (Washington, D.C.: National Academy of Sciences, 1977), chap. 7; A. Myrick Freeman III, *The Benefits of Environmental Improvement: Theory and Practice* (Baltimore: Johns Hopkins University Press, 1979), chaps. 1 and 6; Mark E. Tomassoni, "The Economic Impact of Air Pollution and Aircraft Noise on Residential Property Values: A Selected Bibliography, 1969–1977," Council of Planning Librarians, Exchange Bibliography 1530 (Chicago: May 1978).

11

Converting Thought to Action: The Use of Economic Incentives to Reduce Pollution

Alfred A. Marcus

For many years economists have advocated using economic incentives instead of direct regulation to control pollution.[1] Since 1978 the Environmental Protection Agency (EPA) has been making various efforts to replace direct regulation with incentives.[2] Under authority granted to it by the 1977 Clean Air Amendments and in response to initiatives taken by its administrator Douglas Costle the agency has been conducting a series of regulatory-reform experiments. These experiments "use elements of the private market, and not the government to allocate the costs to society of controlling pollution."[3] The purpose, in Costle's words, is to unite "the equity of public administration with the efficiency of private enterprise."[4]

To what extent has EPA converted the incentives idea, advocated by economists, to action? This chapter argues that current efforts to develop incentive mechanisms are fragmentary and exploratory in nature and are not likely to have a major impact on existing EPA practices. The economists' idea, although theoretically compelling, overlooks compatibility and various technical and political problems that prevent its complete realization.

Economic Incentives versus Direct Regulation

One of the leading spokespersons for the economists' point of view, Charles Schultze, argues that the government can interfere in private-market activities to achieve regulatory objectives in two ways: (1) by grafting a "specific command-and-control module" onto the system of private enterprise, and (2) by modifying "the information flow, institutional structure, and incentive pattern" of the private system.[5] The first manner of control he calls direct regulation; the second, the use of economic incentives. According to Schultze, incentives have the following advantages over direct regulation: they minimize the coercion and emotional appeals needed to obtain compliance; reduce the need to obtain hard-to-get information from companies; allow for flexibility of company response to changing economic circumstances; increase production efficiency; and direct innovation into socially desirable directions.

Four schemes that use economic incentives to control pollution are commonly discussed: (1) effluent charges, (2) markets, (3) bubbles, and (4) noncompliance penalties. Economists generally consider effluent charges to be the best of these tools for reducing pollution. The underlying logic—the "pollutor-pays principle"—is simple and compelling. The government determines the damage caused by different concentrations of pollution, and the pollutor, through some mechanism, has to pay .for the damage. The government, for example, can set a price equal to the marginal damage caused by a unit of pollution. The pollutor then would have an incentive to decrease pollution up to the point where the marginal cost of reducing pollution was less than the price of discharging.

Even when the damage function is not known, which is the usual case, a similar system can be used, but less perfectly, with a politically determined environmental-quality standard replacing the unknown-damage function. To compensate for the problem of the unknown-damage function, the economist J.H. Dales has proposed establishing markets in pollution rights.[6] The government would set an upper limit to the amount of pollution that the environment of a particular region could absorb. It then would issue pollution rights, or licenses, and put them up for sale, requiring anyone who discharged in the area to hold these rights. If the pollution rights that the government issued were less than the actual waste discharged, then the rights would command a positive price, and a continuous market for rights would develop in response to the competition among buyers and sellers.

Giandomenico Majone writes that this proposal:"achieves an efficient allocation of resources, . . . it provides a planning tool that utilizes . . . the flexibility provided by the price mechanism; and it reduces administrative costs. . . ."[7] It removes from administrators the need to change charges to reflect economic growth.

Bubbles and noncompliance penalties, in contrast to the former schemes, were developed by government officials, not economists. They developed these schemes, not in the course of theorizing about the optimal method of abatement, but in the course of carrying out specific bureaucratic duties. Various economists and pollution-control experts have advocated integrated waste management and other forms of planning, but the bubble idea was the specific creation of EPA bureaucrats. The bureaucrats took the efficiency argument—that more pollution reduction can be achieved for less expense by joint action, and applied it to actual program needs under the 1970 Clean Air Act. To maintain air-pollution standards while decreasing the total cost to society of achieving these standards, agency bureaucrats have placed hypothetical bubbles over regions or groups of sources and permitted trade-offs between similar forms of pollution.[8]

The law now says how much pollution is allowed in the air—for example, an annual average of no more than 75 micrograms of particulates per cubic meter. In the hope of reaching these standards, EPA has limited the pollution from each source that it seeks to control—blast furnaces, boilers, paint sprayers, and so on—in an industrial complex. Under the bubble concept, the regulators could replace these "stack-by-stack" rules with a single limit applied to the whole plant. In either case, the total pollution would be the same. But by operating under an imaginary bubble, the plant's engineers would have the flexibility to find the most cost-effective mix of pollution controls to meet the standards.

The final scheme, noncompliance penalties, is also the work of bureaucrats trying to find a workable solution to an immediate problem. The problem in this instance was nonachievement of air-quality goals because of the considerable noncompliance of regulated industries, particularly industries that made the largest contribution to the total amount of pollution emitted. It made good economic sense for these companies with large pollution emissions to litigate and to delay compliance by legal tactics, bluffing, and other maneuvers, so long as the cost of compliance was more than the fines and penalties they would incur if they did not comply. To eliminate this money companies could save by not complying, the Connecticut Department of Environmental Protection (under the tutelage of Douglas Costle, who in 1977 became EPA administrator) first developed a series of gradually escalating penalties based on an estimate of the sum a company saved.[9] The Connecticut plan then was incorporated into national policy, when 1977 air-pollution amendments included a provision requiring EPA to impose fines on violators equal to sums that could be saved by not complying.

The economic theory that justifies the use of economic incentives does not justify the use of noncompliance penalties. Charges and markets give pollution a price and therefore correspond to the theory propounded by economists. Bubbles, although they do not give pollution a price, have the same basic intent, that is, to maximize economic efficiency by giving plant managers the discretion to reduce pollution in an economically efficient manner. Compliance penalties, on the other hand, deviate from the economic theory that justifies the use of economic incentives. They maximize goal achievement, not overall efficiency. Ann F. Friedlaender writes,

> . . . unless the marginal damages are equal to the marginal costs of cleanup, the two systems (charges and compliance penalties) will lead to different results. In particular, if marginal costs of cleanup rise rapidly as zero discharge is reached and if marginal damages rise slowly with movements away from zero discharge levels it is likely that the Connecticut plan will lead to more cleanup than the standard-fee plan because the penalties for noncompliance will be greater under the former than the later.[10]

Compliance penalties are an enforcement tool, not a cost-efficiency mechanism. Achieving enforcement goals without regard to economic efficiency may lead to less-than-desirable outcomes—too much pollution control at too high a price for society.

Authority for Isolated Initiatives

A proposal authored by EPA policy analysts to have Congress pass a "regulatory-experiments" bill was intercepted by environmentalists and the press before it got off the ground. The bill would have given the EPA across-the-board freedom to try policy experiments with some safeguards so that the agency did not utterly disregard congressional intent. Instead of authority for broad regulatory reform, EPA has vague authority for isolated initiatives. In a booklet entitled *Regulatory Reform Initiatives* (December 1978), the agency listed twelve alternatives and supplements to direct regulation that it has been considering.[11]

For the purposes of this chapter, nine of the EPA reform initiatives were examined (see table 11-1). Two of the reform initiatives belong in the category of charges: charges on solid-waste products and charges on nitrogen-oxide auto emissions. Two belong in the category of markets: "controlled trading" in emission rights in areas where "significant deterioriation" of existing air quality has to be prevented and controlled trading in areas where the attainment of air-quality standards still has to be achieved.[12] These reforms correspond in some respects to the measures that have been advocated by economists. (The reforms that were not examined were marketable permits for the control of chlorofluorocarbon emission, federal-procurement incentives, and noise-emission labeling. The latter two initiatives do not fit into the categories of charges, markets, bubbles, or noncompliance penalties, which are the concern of this chapter.

The other initiatives were authored by EPA bureaucrats. Two of these bureaucratically initiated reforms belong in the category of bubbles: a hypothetical bubble placed over manufacturing facilities, so that plant managers can make trade-offs among alternative sources of pollution and still achieve emission-reduction goals; and a hypothetical bubble placed over regions where air-quality goals have not been met, so that local government officials can make trade-offs among competing sources of new pollution.[13]

Table 11-1
Divisibility and Reversibility

	Likely Adoption
Charges	
Solid waste	no
Nitrogen oxides	no
Markets	
Clean-air regions	no
Nonattainment regions	no
Bubbles	
Manufacturing facilities	yes
Nonattainment regions	yes
Noncompliance penalties	
Stationary sources	yes
Heavy-duty engines	no
Operation and maintenance	no

The final reform initiatives were not efficiency generating but enforcement mechanisms. The 1977 Clean Air Act Amendments required that EPA assess noncompliance penalties against stationary-source violators of air-pollution laws. It also gave the agency the right to impose noncompliance penalties against heavy-duty-engine manufacturers if they failed to meet emissions standards.[14] An agency task force, in addition, was considering imposing noncompliance penalties to insure the proper operation and maintenance of pollution-control equipment. The purpose of these measures was to take away the money a company could save by not complying with the law.

The author discussed the reform measures with thirteen EPA officials in the spring of 1979. His discussions were with those who were coordinating the regulatory-reform program as a whole at EPA and with those who were taking the lead in developing specific reform initiatives. EPA officials who were interviewed for this chapter admitted these reform efforts lacked coherence. The pieces were "looking for a structure."[15] They had not reached a "critical mass" in regard to their development.[16] Commitment to them was only provisional. It could be retracted if further analysis and practice demonstrated that the reforms were not worth pursuing. The ideas were subject to conditions that scholars of innovation call divisibility and reversibility.[17] Divisibility means that new ideas are often divided into numerous units and many scaled-down versions are tested and evaluated. Reversibility implies that the fragmented and reduced versions of the idea, if not able to prove compatibility, technical superiority, or political feasibility, may be abandoned. Questions were asked about the compatibility, technical superiority, political feasibility, and likely adoption of the reform initiatives. Compatibility refers to the "goodness of fit" between the idea and the existing program and situation.[18] Technical superiority refers to the relative advantage the idea appears to have over other ideas and the status quo. Finally, political feasibility refers to the political support the idea receives from relevant actors. Without compatibility, technical superiority, and political feasibility, an idea is likely to languish and may ultimately perish.

Table 11-1 summarizes the responses about likely adoption. Of the nine regulatory-reform initiatives, only three were likely to be adopted. The survival rate among initiatives was likely to be 33.3 percent. The extent to which EPA was converting thought to action was that it was using mostly bubbles and to some extent noncompliance penalties, not markets or charges. The analysis that follows endeavors to explain in a general way why EPA has favored only a few of these schemes and rejected the others.

Incompatibility with the Existing System

A theme running through comments of the EPA officials was that markets and charges, although theoretically commendable, were not compatible with the existing regulatory system. Implementing regulatory reform introduced an element of uncertainty. Businesses, for example, had certain expectations about the current system; that it was amenable to court delays and congressional amendment and could be modified. Markets and charges, however, could generate new uncertainties for the business corporation and upset a familiar pattern of business-government interaction.

In addition, markets and charges did not guarantee achievement of goals Congress had established. Under the 1977 amendment, healthy air was to be accomplished by 1987; and the best conventionally available pollution equipment was to be installed by 1983. The introduction of incentives in the place of the current regulatory approach could bring a halt to these efforts.

Finally, some officials pointed out that arguments in favor of incentives have not carried sufficient weight because the available evidence indicates that existing programs have been performing fairly adequately.[19] Although goals have not been entirely achieved, some progress has been made. In addition, reputable studies have demonstrated that the economic burden of making pollution reductions has not been excessive.[20]

These were the general comments officials made about the introduction of market and incentive schemes in place of the existing regulatory approach. Officials held, however, that most of the specific reform initiatives that EPA was trying were compatible with the existing system. They were mechanisms designed to deal with the deficiencies and immediate problems of these programs. The problems included promoting technological change above and beyond existing standards (the nitrogen-oxide charge); sustaining economic growth in clean air in nonattainment regions (the market schemes); maximizing the economic efficiency of pollution reduction (the bubbles mechanisms); and insuring the enforcement of pollution-control statutes (the stationary source and heavy-duty-engine noncompliance penalties).

Incompatibility with existing programs played a small role in the rejection of the solid-waste charge and the rejection of the operation-and-maintenance noncompliance penalty. The solid-waste program did not have a single base in the bureaucracy and therefore no ongoing program with which it could be joined and made compatible. The operation-and-maintenance program was at present a second-order priority, a problem that bureaucrats expected to become more troublesome in the future as more pollution sources were brought into compliance and the agency was left with the task of monitoring continued compliance.

Technical Problems

Technical problems associated with the use of markets and charges generally have been overlooked by economists. Those who write about the advantages of converting the notion to action tend to ignore this problem. However, other academics, particularly political scientists, have poked holes in the theory of the economists by revealing the implementation problems that would come into being if these schemes were adopted.[21]

Implementation problems cited in the literature and by EPA officials interviewed for this chapter include the following:

1. The persistent problem of monitoring: Although a pricing or market scheme abolishes the need to establish specific emission standards, it does not eliminate the need for monitoring emissions. The task of keeping track of the discharges from a multitude of factories and government operations is enormously complicated. Lettie McSpadden Wenner writes,

> Before we accept the notion that one advantage to the fee system over present methods of regulation is that it will be fairly automatic and will not require large administrative expenditures to keep it in operation, it is important to inquire into exactly how the method is expected to function. Will this method indeed be as automatic in administration as claimed? Once the individual waste discharger has been informed of the costs for discharging a given kind of waste, can he be trusted to inform the authorities of the amount and volume of waste he indeed discharges each day? . . . Monitoring devices placed at discharge points must be kept in constant operation to obtain any accurate record of the amounts of waste actually discharged.[22]

With direct regulation, exact monitoring of emissions may be less necessary. Either a firm complies with the regulation or it fails to comply. Even if it is on a compliance schedule, knowing exactly how much is emitted is less important because precise determinations of emissions will not determine monetary fines or charges.

2. The persistent problem of industrial influence: Industry, with its strong organization, focused interest, and close contact with authorities, would most likely continue to exert an important influence over administrative decisions, even if market or charge schemes were adopted. Giandomenico Majone argues that the reason for the lack of effective direct regulation is "its tendency to become 'a political process entailing bargaining between parties of unequal power.' "[23] The same tendency, he maintains, would affect incentive approaches.

According to J.C. Davies, the Ruhr Valley pollution-control authority, a West German authority responsible for the establishment of effluent charges, has been biased in industry's favor.[24] Bureaucratic favoritism, however, is not the only reason that industry can gain an advantage in fee-setting or permit-granting situations. Industry is better organized and more immediately affected by pollution-control decisions than the mass of individual citizens who might achieve some long-term health or recreation advantage. Industry, therefore, is more likely to keep track of the price-setting procedure and to use its right to due process if it is not satisfied.

3. The problem of assigning prices to pollution damage: If an administrative body was attempting to achieve economic efficiency under a pollution-charge proposal, it would have to determine the dollar value of all pollution harms. Assessing these harms is extremely difficult, if not impossible. Although air pollution has been directly associated with few diseases except bronchitis

and emphyszema, almost all medical researchers agree that it leads to gradual degeneration and decline in general cellular well-being.[25] With scientific information this imprecise, it is not possible to establish a credible damage function. Therefore economic efficiency cannot be the goal of a pollution-charge proposal. A politically determined environmental-quality standard has to replace the unknown-damage function.

4. The problem of achieving quality goals: In the case of pollution-control markets, if the fees are determined not as a means of internalizing precisely calculated damages but rather as a means of achieving a fixed standard, pricing schemes may suffer from another problem. Theoretically the schedule of fees can be adjusted upward or downward to achieve any level of quality, but the connection between fees and the achievement of a specific quality level is uncertain. If the technology is not available at a reasonable cost, industry has little choice but to pay the fees and pass costs on to the consumers. The federal administrator, who is trying to achieve a certain level of environmental quality, cannot predict with certainty how much higher prices will inhibit consumer demand and decrease both production and pollution. A trial-and-error approach would have to be used to work out the adjustments necessary for achieving environmental-quality goals.

5. The problem of equivalent trades between sources of pollution: EPA officials considered working out trades between equivalent sources of pollution to be a major technical problem with the bubbles scheme.[26] There were hundreds of air pollutants, and the harm they caused varied significantly. Sulfur-dioxide emissions could be exchanged only for sulfur-dioxide emissions, not for hydrocarbons or particulate matter. Hazardous pollutants could not offset reductions in nonhazardous pollutants. The basic criterion for governing trades between pollutants was that overall emissions could not increase and that air-quality effects had to remain the same. The bubbles schemes had to be qualified by safeguards that insured the equivalence of what was being traded.

Noncompliance penalties also had technical problems. For example, an issue raised in regard to the heavy-duty-engine noncompliance penalty was whether the penalty should be based on the actual sum a company saved by not complying or should it be based on a typical sum a company saved by not complying. Basing it on the typical sum was a simpler procedure, but it might give companies an advantage in continuing not to comply, if the typical sum was set lower than the actual sum. For the operation-and-maintenance scheme, a major technical problem was determining if improper operation and maintenance of pollution-control equipment actually was occurring. If occurring, how extensive was the problem?

Lack of Political Support

Given compatibility and technical problems, it is not surprising that the idea of using charges and markets received lukewarm support from the relevant political actors. The business community, for example, was ambivalent about the idea of using a different method of pollution control. The more liberal Committee on Economic Development, along with Weyerhaeuser and the American Paper Institute, announced that they accepted the incentives notion, but the National Association of Manufacturers and the steel industry opposed the idea.

Frederick Anderson et al. argue that under a pricing system,

> a firm is almost certain to have to pay the charge, or spend money to abate in order to reduce its charge payments. Under direct regulation, however, an industry might conclude that because the enforcement mechanism is so cumbersome and inefffective, it either will not have to pay for the most expensive kinds of abatement techniques, or will be able to gain the monetary advantages of years of delay past the official deadlines.[27]

The reason for business ambivalence may be that, although corporations favor charges theoretically (because they promise lower costs and increased managerial discretion), in actuality, some firms have been served well by the current regulatory regime. Delays have permitted them to escape most compliance costs, whereas under a charge system they would likely bear at least some pollution-reduction costs.

Environmentalists, like business interests, have been ambivalent about supporting incentive measures. In the eyes of many environmentalists, putting a price on pollution is equivalent to giving businesses a "license to pollute." Environmentalists fear that changing a system of direct regulation, which incorporates many of their goals and values, for markets or charges might lead to less overall pollution reduction.

The crucial actors in Congress have not supported alternative methods. Senator Edmund Muskie (Democrat, Maine) and Representative Henry Waxman (Democrat, California), chairpersons of the Senate and House pollution-control subcommittees, may be concerned that the adoption of new schemes would be interpreted as a failure of programs they helped author. In addition, if new schemes were adopted, the government might not achieve pollution reductions that the current system mandates. Another interpretation of the legislators' motivation for opposing incentives is provided by Leonard Lee Lane. Lane comments: "A regulatory solution allows the legislator to satisfy his constituents by voting for a 'tough' law. At the same time he can feel assurance that however rigorous the legislation appears to be, the regulators are unlikely to impose anything 'unreasonable' on a politically powerful industry."[28] Legislators therefore will not bear the burden of imposing costs on important economic interests. If the ambitious goals they set have not been achieved, they can blame the enforcement agency.

EPA officials offered the following information about the politics of some of the other reform initiatives. Industry vigorously opposed the noncompliance penalty for operation and maintenance, because it would add another burden and contribute to already high pollution-control costs. In the case of the heavy-duty-engine noncompliance penalty, on the other hand, the heavy-duty-engine manufacturers sought the introduction of a noncompliance penalty. Their reasoning was that the penalty would remove any advantage a company could gain from not complying. Without the penalty, a company that met national standards might lose competitive advantage to companies that could not meet the standards. Companies that could not meet the standards also favored the penalty, because without it these companies might be put out of business by the government if they failed to comply with the law. With the penalty they had the option of paying the penalty and delaying indefinitely. A noncompliance penalty therefore was favored by the heavy-duty-engine manufacturers to stabilize the competitive situation. The business request for a noncompliance penalty, however, was opposed by environmentalists. They felt that, since the technology existed to meet national standards, there was no reason that companies should be granted the option of paying a fine rather than complying.

Environmentalists also were concerned that permitting bubbles would lead to less pollution reduction. To mitigate the environmentalists' concern, the proponents of bubble schemes built in safeguards to assure that offsets would be substitutable and would not lead to an overall reduction in air quality. The burden of proof was placed on industry to come up with trade-offs that would actually save money while reducing pollution. The announced policy required a company to prove in advance that its system would work, and the EPA reserved the right of preemptive veto.

Conclusion

The idea of using economic incentives to control pollution, however theoretically compelling, is being converted only partially to action. Ideas, penned and authored by economists, have suffered setbacks. Markets and charges generally have been rejected, because they are difficult from a technical standpoint to implement. Compatibility and political considerations also have influenced the decision to reject them.

Theoretical notions of economists have been subject to conditions of divisibility and reversibility. The ideas have been divided into numerous units, and scaled-down versions are being tested and evaluated. Fragmented and reduced versions of the idea that are not able to prove compatibility, technical superiority, and political feasibility, will be rejected.

Policy innovation rests not only on good ideas. It requires that these ideas be plotted through to action. Abstract notions of economists have to be joined with practical suggestions of policy analysts. In 1975, Giandomenico Majone wrote that "feasibility should replace "rationality as the primary criterion of policy choice. "The most important task of policy analysis," he held, "consists of submitting plans and objectives to the most stringent tests of feasibility."[29]

Notes

1. See for instance, Larry E. Ruff, "The Economic Common Sense of Pollution," *The Public Interest* (Spring 1970): 69–85; Robert M. Solow, "The Economist's Approach to Pollution and Its Control," *Science* 173 6 August 1971): 498–503; Lawrence J. White, "Effluent Charges as a Faster Means of Achieving Pollution Abatement," *Public Policy* 25 (Winter 1976): 645–659; A. Myrick Freeman III, Robert H. Haveman, and Allen V. Kneese, *The Economics of Environmental Policy* (Santa Barbara, Calif.: John Wiley, 1973); and Allen V. Kneese and Charles L. Schultze, *Pollution, Prices, and Public Policy* (Washington, D.C.: Brookings Institution, 1975).

2. U.S. Environmental Protection Agency, *Regulatory Reform Initiatives,* quarterly progress report (Washington, D.C., December 1978), p. 1.

3. Ibid.

4. See Peter Nulty, "A Brave Experiment in Pollution Control," *Fortune,* 12 February 1979, p. 120.

5. See Charles L. Schultze, "The Public Use of Private Interest," *Regulation* 1 (September/October 1977): 10. Also see the book by Schultze, *The Public Use of Private Interest* (Washington, D.C.: Brookings Institution, 1977).

6. J.H. Dales, *Pollution, Property, and Prices* (Toronto: University of Toronto Press, 1968).

7. Giandomenico Majone, "Choice among Policy Instruments for Pollution Control," *Policy Analysis* 2 (Fall 1976):597.

8. See Peter Nulty, "Brave Experiment"; also see Bruce Yandle, The Emerging Market in Air Pollution Rights," *Regulation* 2 (July/August 1978): 21–29.

9. See David W. Tunderman, "Economic Enforcement Tools for Pollution Control: The Connecticut Plan," reprinted in Environment and Natural Resources Policy Division, Congressional Research Service, *Pollution Taxes, Effluent Charges, and Other Alternatives for Pollution Control* (Washington, D.C., May 1977), pp. 835–357. Also see William Drayton, "Comments" in *Approaches for Controlling Air Pollution,* ed. Ann F. Friedlaender (Cambridge, Mass.: MIT Press 1978), pp. 231–239.

10. See Friedlaender, *Controlling Air Pollution,* p. 8.

11. U.S. Environmental Protection Agency, *Regulatory Reform Initiatives.*

12. See Bradley I. Rapple, "Prevention of Significant Deterioration under the Clean Air Act—A Comprehensive Review," *Environmental Reporter* 10 (4 May 1979): 1–44; Environmental Research and Technology, Inc., *ERT Handbook on Industrial Expansion and the Clean Air Act Amendments* Concord, Mass. (June 1978): and Yandle; "Emerging Market."

13. See Douglas Martin, "EPA Ponders Letting Concerns Buy and Sell the 'Right' to Pollute Air," *Wall Street Journal*, 15 December 1978; "Agency Proposes More Flexible Pollution Rules," *Wall Street Journal*, 14 December 1978; Steven Rattner, Environmental Agency Softens Rules in Bid to Be More Moderate and Efficient," *The New York Times*, 19 January 1979; Nulty, "Brave Experiment"; and EPA, "Report of the Bubble Concept Task Force," Office of Policy Analysis, Washington, D.C., 1979.

14. See Robert L. Hayes and Stephen A. Besse, "Nonconformance Penalties for Heavy Duty Engines," prepared for Economic Analysis Division, U.S. Environmental Protection Agency, (5 April 1978); and "EPA 1983 and Later Model Year Heavy-Duty Engines," *Federal Register* 44 (13 February 1979).

15. Interview with EPA employee.

16. Interview with EPA employee.

17. See Gerald Zaltman and Robert Duncan, *Strategies for Planned Change* (New York: John Wiley, 1977), p. 14; also see Jack Rothman, *Planning and Organizing for Social Change* (New York: Columbia University Press, 1974), p. 446.

18. See Zaltman and Duncan, *Strategies for Planned Change*, p. 14.

19. See Alfred A. Marcus, *Promise and Performance: Choosing and Implementing an Environmental Policy* (Westport, Conn.: Greenwood Press, 1980).

20. See Council on Environmental Quality, *Environmental Quality: The Sixth Annual Report* (Washington, D.C.: U.S. Government Printing Office, 1975); and Chase Econometric Associates, Inc., "The Macroeconomic Impacts of Federal Pollution Control Programs: 1976 Assessment" (Washington, D.C.: Council on Environmental Quality, 1976).

21. See Alfred A. Marcus, "Recent Proposals to Improve Environmental Policy Making," *Harvard Environmental Law Review*, 1 (1976): 632-645.

22. Lettie McSpadden Wenner, *One Environment under Law* (Santa Barbara, Calif.: Goodyear, 1976), p. 152.

23. Majone, "Choice among Policy Instruments," p. 592.

24. See J. Clarence Davies and Barbara S. Davies, *The Politics of Pollution*, 2d ed. (Indianapolis: Bobbs-Merrill, 1975), p. 202.

25. See Rene Dubos, *Man Adapting*, 8th ed., (New Haven, Conn.: Yale University Press, 1972); and Walsh McDermott, "Air Pollution and Public Health," in Paul Ehrlich, John Holdren, and P. Holm, *Man and the Ecosphere* (San Francisco: W.H. Freeman, 1971), pp. 137-147.

26. See Nulty, "Brave Experiment."

27. Frederic R. Anderson, et al. *Environmental Improvement through Economic Incentives* (Baltimore: Johns Hopkins, 1977), p. 158.

28. Leonard Lee Lane, "The Politics of Pollution Taxes: New Opportunities," reprinted in Environment and Natural Resources Policy Division, *Alternatives for Pollution Control*, p. 683.

29. Giandomenico Majone, "The Feasibility of Social Policies," *Policy Sciences* 7 (1975): 50.

12 Response Options for Evaluating the Consequences of Pollution Charges

Jack A. Goldstone

Our experience with pollution charges is modest; thus evaluations of the consequences of proposed pollution charges must rely heavily on models of projected industry responses. Economic theory can demonstrate that, in a competitive market, properly set pollution charges will lead firms and consumers to make the most efficient trade-off between the costs and benefits of a cleaner environment. Even in a less than fully competitive market, and allowing for uncertainty about the expense of pollution control, economic models suggest that pollution charges will often be a less costly means of attaining a desired level of environmental quality than setting and enforcing uniform standards for emissions.[1] Yet the outcome that most interests economists—maximum efficiency in the use of environmental resources for the society as a whole—is only one item for the policymaker to consider. Policymakers must also be aware of how responses to pollution charges will affect the distribution of goods and services by firms and of how charges may affect consumers.

Evaluation of these consequences requires us to examine in detail the range of options open to firms and consumers when firms are faced with the choice of cleaning up or paying a charge, or fee, on their emissions. The freedom of firms to respond to pollution charges in the most cost-effective manner is often touted as a virtue of charge proposals. Yet such flexibility is a double-edged sword; it can also lead to unexpected problems unless the full range of response options is clearly considered. In particular, we must go beyond the short-term responses of individual firms and consider the responses of market structures, and consumers, and their interaction, to evaluate outcomes.

This chapter presents a conceptual run-through of possible industry and consumer responses to a simple pollution charge or effluent fee assessed against polluting firms and an indication of the various consequences that may result.[2] The conceptual model employed is a simple feedback model: once pollution charges are in place, individual firms respond with one or more of several options. The industry responses have consequences for the industry's market structure, the industry's distribution of goods and capital, and the buying habits of consumers. The changes in market structure, distribution, and

An earlier version of this chapter was presented to a study group at Harvard University, supported by U.S. Environmental Protection Agency grant R805–446–01–2.

consumer habits give rise to feedback responses by firms, which may change or reinforce their original responses to the charges.

The model is illustrated in figure 12-1. The remainder of this chapter is an explication of the model.[3]

Industry Response

The response of individual firms to pollution charges depends in part on how the charge is levied—as a charge on emissions (for example, a sulfur-emissions tax), an excise charge on final products (for example, an auto-emissions charge), or in some other form.[4] However, the range of response options is the same regardless of how the charge is applied.

First, the firm can simply pass the charges on to the consumer. However, even here a number of suboptions are available. The firms can pass on charges to all consumers equally or selectively. For example, a utility may pass on sulfur-emissions charges by an across-the-board rate increase for all consumers or by a selective rate increase for some subset of consumers, for example, industrial users. The consequences of the pass-on strategy obviously depend on the method of pass-on utilized, and the consumer groups available for selective pass-on. Moreover, a firm may transfer the pass-on of charges from one part of its production to another. For example, copper smelters put out high levels of sulfur dioxides and thus would incur substantial costs if sulfur-emissions charges were levied. Copper wire is already in a tight competitive struggle with aluminum wire for electrical-conductors markets; however, the demand for high-grade copper piping and for flat-rolled copper products is strong. Thus copper companies, if faced with sulfur-emissions charges, may pass on the emissions charges in higher prices on pipe and flat-rolled products while keeping wire prices competitive with aluminum, rather than raise prices proportionately on all copper products. Where opportunities for such transfer pass-ons exist, pollution charges may give rise to inefficient market adjustments.[5]

Second, the firm may absorb the higher operating costs or excise payments incurred in paying the charges. This cost absorption can be carried out in a variety of ways. Dividends may be reduced, borrowing increased, or new investment reduced. The particular option chosen, and its consequences, depends on the firm's stock policies, investment opportunities, assets, and cash-flow situation.

Finally, a firm may seek to avoid payment of charges by investing in pollution control. The level of control investment, as frequently pointed out, depends in part on the costs of control, the level of the charges incurred, and the availability of capital for investment. However, the level of control investment also depends on the availability of opportunities for pass-on or absorption of the charges.

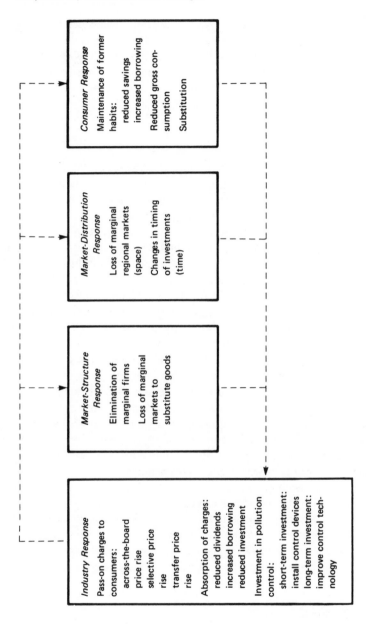

Figure 12-1. Response Options for Evaluating the Consequences of Pollution Charges

The option or options exercised by any given firm will depend both on the firm's specific objectives-that is, rapid growth, dividend maintenance, profit maximization—and on its financial situation and marketing opportunities. Thus the response to a given pollution charge—for example a sulfur-emissions tax— may vary significantly from industry to industry and from firm to firm.[6]

Market-Structure Response

Pollution charges may impose severe burdens on some firms in a given industry. A firm that is small and/or highly specialized and that is only marginally profit- able and without major assets may be unable to pass on costs, unable to absorb charges, and unable to raise sufficient capital to invest in pollution control. Such marginal firms may simply go under. The elimination of such marginal firms may have important effects on the industry's market structure, which in turn may have feedback effects on the responses of individual firms to the pollution charges.

For example, the loss of marginal firms in a moderately oligopolistic indus- try may leave the remaining firms with considerable oligopoly power. The remaining firms may thus gain opportunities for the pass-on of pollution charges that did not exist in the previously more competitive situation. Thus, if an industry's competitive-market structure is fragile, the impact of pollution charges on market structure may affect the industry's long-term response.

As marginal firms may be pressured by pollution charges, so may marginal- product markets. For example, sulfur-emissions charges may cause the loss of marginal copper-products markets to aluminum products; solid waste-disposal charges—which, if based on weight, compactability, and ease of recycling, would weigh more heavily on steel cans than on aluminum—may cause the loss of marginal steel-canning operations to aluminum canning.

There is nothing alarming per se in such market adjustments; shifts to substi- tute goods occur constantly with technical and marketing changes. However, the elimination of marginal markets for certain products may leave suppliers of substitute products in monopolistic or oligopolistic positions; thus oppor- tunities for pass-on or transfer of pollution charges would arise. Where such opportunities are created, firms may respond by increasing pass-on practices.

Market-Distribution Response

Distributional responses may occur in both distribution over space—that is, changes in regional-distribution patterns of goods—and in distribution over time—primarily in the form of changes in the timing of investment decisions.

For certain firms or products, specific regional markets—for example, distant or rural markets—may be marginally profitable. Pollution charges may initially put burdens on distribution to such marginal areas and lead to the elimination of distribution outlets for certain firms. As the elimination of some markets for one firm will be the gain of that market by others, whether direct competitors or suppliers of substitute goods, product shortages are not to be feared. However, the shuffling of distribution patterns may result in regional changes in product costs, in new opportunities for cost pass-ons, or new investment opportunities. Thus, such distributional changes could have long-term effects on the choice of response options of individual firms.

In addition, the choice of cost pass-on, absorption, or investment in control will affect the distribution of capital investments. Marginal investments may be put off while pollution charge costs are absorbed. Long-term investment in product development may be postponed in favor of short-term investment in pollution control. Or, investments in control-technology development may replace short-term investments in expanding existing plant capacity. For example, sulfur-emissions charges may lead to greater investment in pollution control, or pollution-control-technology development, by the utility industry and to less investment in capacity expansion or transmission technology. Whether such changes in investment timing are to society's benefit or not depends on the overall availability of capital, the opportunities for investment, and the value society places on present-day investments—such as solid-waste-disposal refinements and pollution controls—whose returns accrue largely to later generations.[7]

Consumer Response

It is likely that any pollution charges will give rise to changes in consumer prices, although the exact changes will depend on the response options and market-distribution consequences incurred by individual firms. Falling prices are not likely to be common. Instead, whether through pass-ons, falling dividends, or defraying firms' investments in pollution control, real consumer prices are likely to rise. There are a number of possible options for consumer response to such price increases.

First, consumers may simply maintain their former habits. If prices rise, savings may be reduced and borrowing increased to allow maintenance of consumption levels. Second, gross consumption may be reduced. Consumers may buy the same things they bought before but in smaller quantities. Third, consumers may substitute for some items in their consumption schedule and abandon others. However, the opportunities for substitution depend on the distributional effects of the pollution charges, the extent to which substitute goods exist, and the budget flexibility of the consumer. Low-income families, with little budget flexibility, are likely to be forced to simply reduce gross consumption in the face of rising real prices. Middle-income families are likely to have a greater range of budget alternatives—trading in the family car on newer, less polluting models, reducing consumption of disposable items, reducing electricity consumption, and so on. Thus middle-income families may be less burdened by the impacts of pollution charges. However, certain highly specific pollution charges—for example, on plastics, on disposable convenience goods, on industrial electric consumption—may be more burdensome to middle-income families and corporations than to low-income families. The impact of charges on consumer response, and hence on the regressive or progressive nature of charges, is thus fairly specific to the type of charge assessed and to the opportunities for substitution for the products involved.

Consumer response, in turn, will have a significant effect on industry responses to charges. If cost pass-ons result in consumer switches to substitute goods, investment in control or absorption of charges will be encouraged; if consumers reduce their rate of saving to maintain their former spending habits, pass-ons will be encouraged and investment opportunities will be reduced. The net impact of pollution charges thus will depend on a complex interplay between consumers and firms.

The preceding points have been made not to disparage the application of pollution charges but to point out some of their complexities. Most important, the problem of pass-ons, and their interaction with market structures, must be seriously considered. If a pollution charge is simply passed on to consumers by firms with substantial market power, or if pass-ons are concentrated on goods for which there are few close substitutes, a worst possible outcome may occur—no progress toward a cleaner environment, while consumers of certain goods and customers of oligopolistic industries subsidize the environmental costs incurred by all consumers. These complexities are not reasons for rejecting pollution charges. Certain taxes that are taken for granted today— liquor taxes, even the income tax—seemed no less complex when introduced and are no less complex in their consequences today. With proper attention to the problems of market structure and the possibilities for pass-ons, policymakers can frame charge proposals that will make a useful contribution to strategies for pollution control.

In most cases, a firm-by-firm analysis of industries liable to be affected by a pollution charge, as may appear necessary for prediction of its consequences, would be wasteful. However, the points made do imply that market structure, investment and pass-on opportunities, and surveys of consumer responses should receive preliminary attention in the development of any pollution-charges system if that system is to achieve its design goals.

Notes

1. Robert Dorfman and Nancy Dorfman, eds., *Economics of the Environment*, 2d ed. (New York: W.W. Norton, 1977); Frederick Anderson et al., *Environmental Improvement through Economic Incentives* (Baltimore, Md.: Resources for the Future/John Hopkins University Press, 1977).

2. In addition to effluent fees, various hybrids of standards and pollution charges have been proposed. Much of the discussion in this chapter also applies to such hybrid schemes. Spence and Weitzman provide a brief but solid discussion of the relative merits of standards, pollution charges, and hybrids, in A. Michael Spence and Martin L. Weitzman, "Regulatory Strategies for Pollution Control" in *Approaches to Controlling Air Pollution*, ed. Ann F. Friedlander (Cambridge, Mass.: MIT Press, 1978), pp. 207-212.

3. Of course considerable uncertainties arise to bedevil models of market and consumer responses. Both pollution charges and standards pose problems of uncertainty, but they are distinct problems: In levying a pollution standard, the costs of meeting that standard are uncertain and infinitely varied among firms. Thus predictions of market responses and associated effects are highly uncertain. In levying pollution charges, the degree of cleanup that will eventually result is uncertain, but the marginal costs to all firms are precisely known, as the marginal cost of polluting simply equals the levied charge. Thus for charges, the effects on markets, market structure, and consumer responses are more readily estimated.

The problem of uncertainty in pollution control is a rich one, and touches on problems of technical innovation and rationality far beyond the scope of this chapter. An interesting discussion of some of these issues is given by Lloyd D. Orr, "Social Costs, Incentives Structures, and Environmental Policies," *Western Political Quarterly* 32 (September 1979): 286-297, and by Starhl Edmunds, "Environmental Policy: Bounded Rationality Applied to Unbounded Ecological Problems," in *Environmental Policy Formation*, ed. Dean E. Mann (Lexington, Mass.: Lexington Books, D.C. Heath, 1981), pp. 191-201.

4. For a complete listing of ways in which pollution charges can be levied, see Blair Bower, Charles Ehler, and Allen Kneese, "Incentives for Managing the Environment," *Environmental Science and Technology* 11 (March 1977): 250-254.

5. This possibility may be compared with the more severe conclusion drawn by Hartman, Bozdogan, and Nadkarni in their discussion of a simple model for the effect of pollution control on investment in the copper-refining industry. They demonstrate that strict air-quality standards may drastically curtail capacity expansion, leading to increased prices, increased copper imports, and increased substitution of scrap and substitute materials for primary refined products. However, their analysis is based on the assumption of strict standards; it does not allow for the flexibility of industry responses and investment decisions described here as possible responses to pollution charges. R. Hartman, K. Bozdogan, and R. Nadkarni, "The Economic Impacts of Environmental Regulation on the U.S. Copper Industry," *Bell Journal of Economics* 10 (Autumn 1979): 587-618.

6. For information on how industry responds to current income, excise, and other taxes, see Joseph A. Pechman and Benjamin A. Okner, *Who Bears the Tax Burden*; (Washington, D.C.: Brookings Institution, 1974).

7. The investment-timing problem is particularly germane to the production of long-lived products. For example, if solid-waste-disposal charges are levied on structural aluminum products (such as prefabricated paneling/siding, and so forth), with lifetime use periods of about thirty years, disposal investment that would arise thirty years after production are shifted to disposal charges paid at the time of product sale. Similarly, if fees are assessed on utilities to cover the costs of decommissioning power plants, decommissioning costs will appear in the rates of present consumers rather than in the costs to consumers thirty to fifty years after initial operation, when decommissiong occurs.

13 An Examination of Population-Growth-Managing Communities

David E. Dowall

Until the early 1970s community planning was concerned with accommodating new development. Most planners designed plans that would absorb considerable new residential and commercial development. Although attitudes toward growth ranged from Chamber of Commerce boosterism to half-hearted resignation, few communities attempted overtly to control or limit development.

Since the 1970s, upheavals in environmental policy and planning, increased skepticism toward development, and the growing city-as-a-profit-making-enterprise mentality of local government officials and planners have predisposed many communities to develop and implement a variety of land-use and development controls that limit the rate of residential development.[1] In 1972, a report on local growth control identified 8 pioneer communities attempting to control growth.[2] (These communities were the focus of considerable attention. Close scrutiny of the more glamorous growth-management plans have been annual rituals at national planning conferences.) Between 1975 and 1980 the use of growth controls became widespread, particularly in rapid-growth metropolitan areas. For example, in the 1974 annual survey of local planning agencies in California, 340 communities indicated that, in addition to using traditional police powers, they were using a variety of planning tools to control population growth.[3] A more recent survey of Bay Area planning agencies indicates that eight agencies have adopted and seven are considering the adoption of formal growth-management programs that limit the number of building permits awarded annually, 40 communities have imposed moratoria during the past five years, and 33 downzoned significant portions of land.[4] Interest in growth management is increasing as more communities begin to question the benefits of continued growth. If present trends continue, severe constraints to residential development may emerge in many urban areas across the country.

In recent years, the inflationary effects of restrictive growth management and land-use controls have gained tremendous attention and generated considerable concern. By 1978, the inflationary impact of restrictive development controls was the topic of two federal government studies.[5] The Department of Housing and Urban Development (HUD) Task Force Report, while stopping short of recommending federal standards for land-use control, did indicate that overregulation of residential development was widespread and added significant costs to housing construction. Despite numerous studies of the effects of local development controls, little research has attempted to identify the underlying pressures that lead communities to adopt growth-control strategies. Without a clear understanding of which communities are attempting to control growth and why, prospects for identifying less inflationary but equally effective development controls appear to be limited.

This chapter reports on an empirical analysis of the fiscal, social, and environmental characteristics of growth-management communities and the pressures that they face. This type of cross-sectional empirical research provides useful information about the types of communities engaged in growth control and, to the extent the empirical evidence can be used to predict when other communities will opt for growth management, enables policy analysts to antici-pate future trends in local growth management. Furthermore, by understanding the specific pressures of growth-impacted communities, policymakers will be better able to develop alternative strategies for growth-impact mitigation that do not generate market dislocations as significant as those associated with the growth-rationing systems of Petaluma and Boulder.

Why Communities Want to Limit Population Growth

Population-growth limitation is aimed at stopping or slowing the flow of new migrants into the community. Additional residents mean more housing, increased demand for public services, congestion, diminished environmental quality, and the gradual loss of the small-town character of the community. Although the loss of small-town character appears to be a major motivation for adopting growth controls in small cities, there is evidence that larger urban places, such as Toronto and San Francisco, also view growth controls as an effective mechanism for maintaining their urban character. Depending on the rate of population growth, the availability of public services, and the environ-mental quality of the town, the range and severity of growth impacts can be considerable. For example, fiscal impacts of increased public-service demands, the disorienting and anxiety-provoking social and psychological effects of rapid immigration, and environmental impacts such as traffic congestion, extensive conversion of open lands, and increased air and water pollution can be enormous.[6]

Adverse effects of population growth can be attributed either to bottleneck or to size impacts. Bottleneck effects develop when communities are swamped with extremely rapid growth. The rate of increase is so great that the existing institutions of the town cannot cope. The quality of public services falls precipi-tously, and tax rates soar as needed capital facilities are quickly provided. Continued rapid growth outstrips the capacity of capital facilities and often leads communities to implement development controls that limit growth to a rate that can be accommodated by public services.

Size effects are, in the economists' jargon, diseconomies of scale—at some point the size of the town becomes too big. Optimum city size is a complex and controversial topic among economists, planners, and policymakers.[7] The best size depends on what aspects of the city are being considered. For example, the optimum city size with respect to theater, opera, and the arts is very large: New York, London, Paris. The best-sized city for efficient police protection may be small: 5,000 to 10,000 people. There are different economies of scale for each activity. The adding up of these activities to determine the overall optimum city size is very difficult and politically contentious. Each person has different preferences about what activities are important for considering optimum size. Theater lovers prefer big cities because only with size can the arts be diverse and of high quality. Environmentalists may vote for small towns that are less obtrusive environmentally. Despite significant differences of opinion, citizens frequently vote to limit the size of their cities.

The prelude to growth control is the concern that communities are growing too fast or that they are becoming too big. The costs of rapid growth or larger size are usually framed around several dimensions: fiscal impacts, environmental impacts, and changes in the social and economic structure of the community. Elsewhere I have argued that these impacts are the primary factors that cause communities to adopt growth controls.[8] In an effort to validate this proposition, and to increase our understanding of the type of communities engaged in growth management, an empirical analysis was conducted of 228 communities attempting to control population growth. The next section explains the method of analysis and presents the results.

Empirical Analysis

The analysis seeks to determine the unique characteristics and growth pressures faced by communities attempting to control their population growth. To the extent that these communities share similar fiscal categories, socioeconomic composition, environmental characteristics, and similar growth pressures, the empirical examination may validate the hypothesis that growth-controlling communities are responding to forces that threaten similar fiscal, environmental, and socioeconomic characteristics. Furthermore, since communities may implement growth controls for all or any one of these reasons, the empirical analysis should be able to identify different groupings of communities according to the types of pressures confronted.

The universe of communities examined was obtained from the International City Managers Association (ICMA) survey of its members' environmental policy.[9] A listing was obtained of all communities responding "yes" to question 16c: "Has your community adopted policies to limit the growth of its population?" The survey did not attempt to determine the strategy for growth limitation.

The affirmatively responding list includes communities that have downzoned land for residential development, instituted moratoria, and made general plan changes as well as places that have implemented the more glamorous growth-control rationing systems. In addition, respondents answering affirmatively to a similar California-survey question about growth limitations were merged with the ICMA survey.[10] The initial sample contained 253 cities and counties covered by the ICMA survey and 340 jurisdictions from the California survey. After adjusting for double-counting, the pool of local governments was 567.

Building on the theory that growth management is a response to adverse fiscal, socioeconomic, and environmental impacts of rapid growth, the next step was to select variables for inclusion in the empirical analysis. Lack of resources precluded the collection of data from each individual community. Published sources of secondary data compiled by the U.S. Department of the Census were examined. The initial reconnaissance of data generated fifty variables for inclusion in the analysis.[11] Data reflecting the fiscal, social, economic, ethnic, and environmental characteristics and recent growth experience of the cities and counties contained in the sample were selected. After assembling the data, and eliminating communities and variables for which no data were available, the list of communities was reduced to 228 jurisdictions and forty-three variables. Table 13-1 presents the variables included in the analysis and means and standard deviations for each. Note that these means and standard deviations are for a select group of communities. The average growth rate during the 1960s is over 30 percent. Also, the percentage of houses built in the 1960s and the percent changes of house values are significantly greater than the national norms. The first eleven variables measure the fiscal characteristics of the communities; variables included per-capita tax rates for the years 1962, 1967, and 1972, and the percent change between years. The tax rates are computed by dividing the constant-dollar per-capita tax by constant-dollar per-capita income. The next set of fiscal variables cover per-capita utility revenues, general revenues, educational expenditures per capita, and school-debt per capita.

The next twelve variables tap the social status, income, and ethnic composition of communities; 1960 and 1970 median school years completed, percentage of families with incomes below $3,000 and over $10,000 in 1960; percentage below poverty level and over $15,000 in 1970; and percentage minority population in 1960 and 1970. The last four variables compare the racial composition of cities or counties to other comparable cities or counties in the state in which the observation is located and a comparison of the racial composition of the city or county to that of the surrounding region. The twenty-fourth through twenty-sixth variables measure population and change for 1960 and 1970; the twenty-seventh and twenty-eighth variables are dummy variables indicating whether the observation is a city or a jurisdiction located in a SMSA. The twenty-ninth variable measures population density.

Table 13-1
Variables Included in the Analysis and Their Means and Standard Deviations

Variable Name	Mean	Standard Deviation
1962 per-capita local tax rate	.32	4.51
1962-1972 tax-rate-percent change	5.91	65.34
1967 per-capita local tax rate	.02	.01
1967-1972 tax-rate-percent change	10.76	33.21
1972 per-capita local tax rate	.02	.02
1972 per-capita utility revenue	.76	13.02
1972 per-capita general revenue	1.19	26.31
1972 per-capita educational capital expenditures	14.51	9.20
1972 per-capita sewer-system capital indebtedness	3.08	6.32
1972 per-capita long-term debt	124.27	180.12
1972 per-capita long-term school debt	88.34	45.76
1960 median school-years completed	11.39	1.17
1970 median school-years completed	12.20	.88
1960 percent families with income below $3,000	15.80	8.71
1960 percent families with income over $10,000	19.37	11.72
1970 percent families with income below poverty level	8.35	4.68
1970 percent families with income over $15,000	24.36	13.42
1960 percent of minority population	6.42	8.95
1970 percent of minority population	8.25	10.53
1970 percent minority = percent minority of comparable places	− 1.39	6.79
1970 percent minority = percent minority of comparable places	1.36	8.90
1960 percent minority = percent minority of surrounding places	0.14	6.02
1970 percent minority = percent minority of surrounding places	1.16	8.74
1970 population	96,623	186,572
1960 population	78,557	155,121
Percent population change 1960-1970	31.58	52.25
City dummy		
SMSA dummy		
1970 population density per square mile	3,566	3,040
Percent of houses built during the 1950s for 1960	36.02	21.49
Percent of houses built during the 1960s for 1970	26.73	14.60
Percent change in the number of houses built in 1950s v. 1960s	20.90	65.00
Percent change in the percent of houses built 1950s v. 1960s	− 16.14	39.98
1960 median house value	13,942	5,167
1970 median house value	20,080	8,655
Percent change in median house value 1960-1970	44.22	24.26
1969 county acres farmed	362.54	518.48
Percent change in county acres farmed 1959-1969	− 16.95	27.37
Percent of total county land in farms, 1959	47.46	28.28
Percent of total county land in farms, 1969	39.82	27.04
1959 value of farm output, $/Acre	109.08	108.73
1969 value of farm output, $/Acre	150.83	140.22
Percent change in value of output 1959-1969	52.55	52.43

Variables 30 and 31 measure the percentage of houses built in the 1950s and 1960s. Variable 32 measures the percent change in the number of houses built in the 1960s relative to the 1950s. Variable 33 measures the rate of increase in the percentage of houses built over the 1950s and 1960s. The next three variables report median house values and percent change.

The last seven variables cover agricultural acreages, percentage of county land in agriculture (all data are for counties; in the case of city observations the data are for the county in which the city is located), and the value of agricultural output and the change between 1959 and 1969. These variables are used as proxies to measure environmental decline and urbanization pressures.

Cluster analysis, developed by Tyron and Bailey, was used to identify the degree to which the forty-three variables "tapped" important dimensions of the character and growth pressures represented by the 228 communities.[12] The clustering analysis generated eight unique dimensions. Together, these eight dimensions accounted for 92 percent of the variance of the original data. Table 13-2 presents these dimensions, member variables, and the cumulative explained variance.

The standardized (means of 50 and standard deviations of 10) cluster scores of each city and county were used to generate groupings of cities and counties. The grouping procedure operates to minimize the euclidean distance of within-group scores and maximizes between group differences. The grouping algorithm developed by Tryon and Bailey generated eleven distinct community types. Mean scores for the eleven types of communities across the eight cluster dimensions are presented in table 13-3. The typing procedure was able to group 210 of the 228 cases, accounting for 92 percent of the communities. Table 13-4 presents the eleven types and their members. The 18 untyped cases are extremely unique and do not fit into the dimensions tapped by the variables analyzed. A list of the eleven community types follows.

1. Rural Places. This group is the largest, containing thirty-seven cities and counties, and accounts for 16 percent of the sample. This grouping is marked by its low population density, high proportion of farmland, and low income and growth. Many of these communities, such as Greeley, Colorado, and Tracy, California, have been faced with population-growth pressures since 1970.

2. Small Average-Income Growing Cities. Most of these communities have grown at a rate of over 30 percent between 1960 and 1970. This group contains twenty-seven cities, accounting for 12 percent of the sample.

3. Rapid-Growth Suburban or Rural Cities. This group's average growth rate is over one standard deviation larger than the sample. Many communities in this group experienced rapid conversion of farmland to urban use during the 1960s. This group contains twenty-seven cities, comprising 12 percent of the sample.

4. Moderate-Sized Cities with below-Average Growth. This cluster is perplexing. The growth impacts of the 1960s appear to be minimal, as do taxes

Table 13-2
Cluster Dimensions, Member Variables, and Cumulative Explained Variance

	Cumulative Explained Variance
1. High income and wealth	
1960 percent families with income over $10,000 1960 median house value 1970 percent families with income over $15,000 1970 median house value	.52
2. Tax rate	
1967 per-capita local tax rate 1962 per-capita local tax rate 1972 per-capita local tax rate	.61
3. Population size	
1970 population 1960 population Reflection of the city-dummy variable	.64
4. Housing-stock change	
Percent change in the number of houses built in 1950s vs. 1960s Percent change in the median house value 1960–1970 Change in the percent of houses built 1950s vs. 1960s.	.69
5. Minority composition of the community	
1970 percent minority population 1960 percent minority = percent minority of comparable places 1960 percent minority population 1970 percent minority = percent minority of comparable places 1970 percent minority = percent minority of surrounding places 1960 percent minority = percent minority of surrounding places	.83
6. Importance of farming and population density	
Percent of total county land in farms, 1969 Percent of total county land in farms, 1959 Reflection of population density 1970	.87
7. Rate of housing and population change	
Percent houses built in the 1960s for 1970 Percent houses built in the 1950s for 1960 Percent population change 1960–1970 SMSA dummy variable	.91
8. Agricultural production	
1959 value of farm output, $/Acre 1969 value of farm output, $/Acre	.92

Table 13-3
Cluster Means of Eleven Community Types

Type	Cluster Dimension							
	1	2	3	4	5	6	7	8
1	42.1	47.3	48.2	45.9	51.3	62.4	42.7	43.9
2	50.7	48.2	46.5	43.4	48.0	44.6	52.8	48.1
3	49.9	47.6	46.7	53.2	45.3	54.5	63.4	48.7
4	42.5	48.4	46.1	49.5	47.4	48.3	40.0	44.8
5	49.9	49.4	66.1	50.7	48.1	55.7	51.9	47.7
6	50.0	59.6	47.6	54.2	49.1	43.1	43.5	57.9
7	53.9	48.8	47.5	44.0	42.1	37.4	50.3	64.3
8	45.1	48.1	47.3	47.1	72.1	52.9	47.7	46.8
9	80.7	47.1	45.8	47.2	47.4	41.6	47.6	55.9
10	69.3	47.9	46.0	50.8	44.1	49.0	60.9	53.3
11	50.1	48.0	46.1	78.2	48.4	56.1	57.8	44.9

Note: Means are standardized to a score of 50, standard deviation of 10; see table 13-2 for definition of cluster dimensions.

Table 13-4
Community-type Membership

Type 1

Greeley, CO
Brandenton, FL
Lakeland, FL
Pocatello, ID
Jacksonville, IL
Mt. Vernon, IL
Marion, IN
Richmond, IN
Fort Mason, IA
Pittsburg, KS
Bowling Green, KY
Monroe, MI
Cleveland, MS
Moberly, MS
Fostoria, OH
Newark, OH
Springfield, OH
Duncan, OK
Durant, OK
El Reno, OK
Muskogee, OK
Shawnee, OK
Athens, TN
McKinney, TX
Odessa, TX

Synder, TX
White Settlement, TX
Spokane, WA
Pinal Cty, AZ
Lake Cty, FL
Houston Cty, GA
Douglas Cty, KS
Washington Cty, MN
Ward Cty, ND
Tracy, CA
Yuba City, CA
Sacramento, CA

Type 2

St. Petersburg, FL
Sarasota, FL
Forest Park, GA
Northlake, IL
Kenner, LA
Harper Woods, MI
Oak Park, MI
Wyoming, MI
Hopkins, MN
Richfield, MN
West Orange, NJ
Kenmore, NY

Lackawanna, NY
Chevoit, OH
Eugene, OR
Red Banks, TN
Greenfield, WI
Banning, CA
Chula Vista, CA
La Mesa, CA
National City, CA
Redlands, CA
San Anselmo, CA
San Leandro, CA
Fresno, CA
Redwood City, CA
San Bernardino, CA

Type 3

Aurora, CO
Boulder, CO
Hollywood, FL
Pinellas Park, FL
Bettendorf, IA
Coon Rapids, MI
Bethany, OK
Midwest City, OK
Garland, TX

Table 13-4 Continued

Bountiful, UT	Muskegon Cty, MI	Glendale, CA
Costa Mesa, CA	Cumberland Cty, NJ	Long Beach, CA
Pacifica, CA	Bernalillo Cty, NM	
Santa Ana, CA	Dutchess Cty, NY	*Type 8*
Upland, CA	Orange Cty, NY	
Antioch, CA	San Diego, CA	Forrest City, AK
Fairfield, CA	Butte Cty, CA	Daytona Beach, FL
Livermore, CA	Contra Costa Cty, CA	Del Ray Beach, FL
Lompoc, CA	El Dorado Cty, CA	Leesburg, FL
Modesto, CA	Fresno Cty, CA	Albany, GA
Monterey, CA	Marin Cty, CA	Decatur, GA
Napa, CA	Napa Cty, CA	Greensboro, NC
Novato, CA	San Luis Obispo Cty, CA	Aliquippa, PA
Oxnard, CA	Solano Cty, CA	Coatsville, PA
San Jose, CA	Sonoma, Cty, CA	Florence, SC
Santa Barbara, CA	Tulare, Cty, CA	Greenwood, SC
Santa Monica, CA		Cumberland Cty, NC
Vacaville, CA	*Type 6*	Delano, CA
		Menlo Park, CA
Type 4	Ansonia, CN	Richmond, CA
	Fairfield, CN	
New Albany, IN	Meridan, CN	*Type 9*
Brunswick, ME	Middletown, CN	
Cumberland, MD	Milford, CN	Evanston, IL
Escanaba, MI	New Haven, CN	Lake Forest, IL
Marquette, MI	Waterbury, CN	Winnetka, IL
Claremont, NH	Greenfield, MA	Clayton, MO
Cohoes, NY	Leomister, MA	Mamaroneck Town, NY
Troy, NY	Maldin, MA	Rye, NY
Utica, NY	Middleborough, MA	Arcadia, CA
Asheville, NC	Quincy, MA	Beverly Hills, CA
Lexington, NC	North Plainfield, NJ	San Marino, CA
Niles, OH	Cranston, RI	
Bend, OR	Santa Cruz, CA	*Type 10*
Salem, OR	Watsonville, CA	
Carlisle, PA	Santa Cruz Cty, CA	Lombard, IL
Lancaster, PA		Northbrook, IL
Waynesboro, PA	*Type 7*	Fairfax, VA
Elizabethton, TN		Belmont, CA
Logan, UT	Coral Gables, FL	Fullerton, CA
Longview, WA	North Miami, FL	Newport Beach, CA
Hungtington, WV	Audubon, NJ	San Carlos, CA
Martinsburg, WV	Clifton, NJ	Palo Alto, CA
Parkersburg, WV	Highland Park, NJ	Saratoga, CA
Sheboygan, WI	Wickliffe, OH	
Chico, CA	Dormont, PA	*Type 11*
	Bellflower, CA	
Type 5	Culver City, CA	Tempe, AZ
	Downey, CA	Lexington, KY
Pinellas Cty, FL	Huntington Park, CA	Troy, MI
Du Page Cty, IL	Lynwood, CA	Athens, OH
Polk Cty, IA	Santa Fe Springs, CA	Pullman, WA
Anne Arundel Cty, MD	Torrance, CA	Petaluma, CA
Montgomery Cty, MD		San Rafael, CA

and agricultural-land conversions. Perhaps growth pressures have developed since 1970. This group contains twenty-five cities, comprising 11 percent of the sample.

5. Growing Urban Counties with Substantial Agricultural Land Use. With the exception of San Diego, this sample contains all counties. High scores on clusters 3 and 5 suggest that growth pressures to convert agricultural land are great. This group contains twenty-one places, representing 9 percent of the sample.

6. High Taxes and Accelerating Growth. With the exception of Santa Cruz County, California, this grouping contains all cities. Per-capita taxes are very high, and growth pressures appear to be increasing. Fiscal pressures are likely to be influential in deciding for slow growth. This group contains seventeen communities, comprising 7 percent of the sample.

7. Moderately High Wealth, Growing Metropolitan Cities. Most of these communities are growing enclaves located in SMSAs. These places may be attempting to avoid congestion by downzoning vacant segments of land in the community. This type contains sixteen members, accounting for 7 percent of the sample.

8. Ethnic Cities. This group of fifteen cities is distinguished by its high score on cluster 5 (72.1). Growth pressures and the rate of development over the 1950–1970 period are about average. This group represents nearly 7 percent of the sample.

9. High-Wealth Islands. This group is made up of extremely wealthy cities. These cities are likely to restrict development to maintain their exclusive character. This group contains nine cities, representing 4 percent of the sample.

10. Wealthy High-Growth Towns. This group is also made up of wealthy towns, but they differ from type 9 in that they have experienced substantial growth during the 1960s. This group has nine cities, accounting for 4 percent of the sample.

11. Accelerating High-Growth Cities. This final grouping is composed of towns that have experienced an increase in the rate of housing growth over the 1950s and 1960s and a high rate of population growth in the 1960s. This group includes seven cities and accounts for 3 percent of the sample.

Conclusion

The results of the empirical analysis appear to support the proposition that communities tend to control growth to avoid adverse fiscal and environmental impacts and maintain the social and economic character of the community. The overall means and standard deviations of the variables indicates that the 228 communities tend to be faster growing, wealthier, whiter, and of a higher social status than national norms. The typing results, with the exception of types 4 and 8, confirm the notion that communities attempt to control growth to avoid adverse environmental, social, economic, and fiscal changes. Types 1, 2, 3, 5, and 11 appear to have been confronted with excessive growth that has placed considerable pressure on farmlands and housing markets. Type 6 illustrates the fiscal impacts of rapid growth and appears to be composed of communities that wish to avoid tax increases generated by continued growth. Types 7, 9, and 10 appear to be less concerned with the environmental impacts of continued growth than with the disruption of the current social and economic composition of the community. All score low on the minority cluster dimension and high on income and wealth. The categorizing of types 1, 2, 3, 5, and 11 as environmentally induced growth control, type 6 as fiscally motivated, and types 7, 9, and 10 as socially and economically motivated control tends to conform with notions of why communities act to limit growth. The poor showing of the fiscal motivations is disappointing, but also may be considered as part of the rationale for controlling growth of types 7, 9, and 10.

A replication of the analysis for California communities found fiscal considerations to be extremely important in explaining growth-control behavior. Fiscal variables show up in several of the cluster dimensions. Three of the nine California types are characterized by their high tax rates and per-capita debt. These three types account for 27 percent of the California sample, suggesting that, at least in California, fiscal considerations may be important in predisposing communities to control their growth.

The results of the empirical analysis suggest that adverse fiscal, environmental, social, and economic impacts play important roles in motivating communities to control growth. But because the data used in the empirical analysis are dated, and because they fail to tap more complex historical, political, and institutional factors, the results are very tentative. A thorough confirmation of the results awaits the findings of more detailed case studies of growth-management communities.

Despite the tentative nature of the results, several implications for the reform of local land-use control are suggested. As pointed out in the introduction, much concern over the inflationary effects of local growth management has surfaced recently. If policymakers are to check the growing use of growth-management controls, they must identify and promote the use of less inflationary but equally efficient land-use-control measures. The empirical evidence gives some insight about which avenues of reform are most promising. First, although not overwhelming and universal, fiscal impacts appear to play a major role in encouraging local communities to limit growth. Federal, state, and regional governments may want to consider alternative approaches to local-government finance so that the adverse fiscal impacts of growth can be offset.

The results also suggest that fiscal impacts are not the sole motivating factor behind growth control. The cluster dimensions suggest that environmental, social, and economic impacts are also important motivations for growth control. Here, the prospects for effective land-use reform are not as clear-cut.

If growth control is the result of perceived environmental degradation, efforts to improve the ability of land-use planning to maintain environmental quality are urgently needed. Better methods for controlling air pollution, traffic congestion, and the conversion of prime agricultural land are clear alternatives to growth control. Emphasis needs to be placed on controlling the location and character of new development, not on stopping development. On the other hand, if growth control is the result of exclusionary social and economic motivations, efforts to check racial and economic discrimination must be taken.

Because of the multiplicity of growth-control motivations, the design and implementation of alternative land-use-control mechanisms will be difficult. The results of the empirical analysis suggest that communities control growth for a variety of reasons; therefore, efforts to check the spread of growth control present a major challenge to land-use-policy reformers.

Notes

1. William K. Reilly, ed., *The Use of Land: A Citizens' Policy Guide to Urban Growth* (New York: Thomas Y. Crowell, 1973); William Alonso, "Urban Zero Population Growth" in *The No-Growth Society*, ed. M. Olson and H.H. Landsberg (New York: W.W. Norton, 1973); and Robert W. Burchell and David Listokin, *The Fiscal Impact Handbook* (Rutgers, N.J.: Center for Urban Policy Research, 1978).

2. American Society of Planning Officials, *Non Growth as a Planning Alternative*, P.A.S. Report no. 283 (Chicago, 1972).

3. Office of Planning and Research, *Local Government Planning Survey* (Sacramento, Calif.: State of California, 1976).

4. Local survey conducted by author, March to June 1979.

5. U.S. General Accounting Office, *Why Are New Housing Prices So High, How Are They Influenced by Government Regulation and Can Prices be Reduced?* (Washington, D.C., 1978); U.S. Department of Housing and Urban Development, *Final Report of the Task Force on Housing Costs* (Washington, D.C., 1978).

6. Richard P. Appelbaum, "City Size and Urban Life: A Preliminary Inquiry into Some Consequences of Growth in American Cities," *Urban Affairs Quarterly* (December 1976).

7. For a good review see P. Baum, *Issues in Optimal City Size* (Los Angeles: University of California Graduate School of Management, 1970).

8. David E. Dowall, "Fiscal Impact Rationale for Growth Management," *Annals of Regional Science* 12 (July 1978): 83–94.

9. International City Managers Association, "Managing the Environment at the Local Level," *Urban Data Service Report 2/74* (Washington, D.C., 1974).

10. Office of Planning and Research, *Local Government Planning Survey.*

11. Data came from U.S. Bureau of the Census, *Census of Local Governments*, City and County Data, *Census of Agriculture* (Washington, D.C., 1959, 1962, 1967, 1969, 1972).

12. R.C. Tryon and D.E. Bailey, *Cluster Analysis* (New York: McGraw-Hill, 1970).

14 The Politics of Local Growth Control

Robert A. Johnston

American cities have seldom exercised land use controls to further the general public welfare. Created by the states and empowered to promote the welfare of the general public, cities have most often regulated land development to promote the interests of those controlling city government.[1] Where those interests have sought rapid growth as a means of enhancing their property values, persons seeking to reside in those cities have been welcome. But low- and moderate-income persons have been segregated into apartment areas or working-class owner-occupied neighborhoods. Low-income persons have often been excluded entirely from new suburban communities by zoning and building-code requirements effectively prohibiting inexpensive housing. They have been able to afford only used rental housing in older neighborhoods, generally in central cities. This spatial segregation of the poor from the middle class and the rich by government action is nearly uniquely an American invention and serves to keep low-income families in low-quality environments and to separate them from the major new employment areas in the suburbs.[2]

This chapter will identify three types of growth-control mechanisms and review the literature to determine what motives have been attributed to the communities that have adopted these controls. Four case studies will be briefly presented, two involving growth-rate controls and two concerned with growth-phasing programs. Our conclusions will be compared to the earlier findings to better understand the reasons why growth controls are adopted. These conclusions lead to certain tentative prescriptions for policymakers interested in housing provision and local growth control.

Types of Growth Controls

With the rapid increase in incomes and mobility of the 1950s, suburban growth overtook small towns across the United States. The newcomers had a narrow and self-interested concept of zoning in many of these suburban municipalities.

The author wishes to thank the Institute of Governmental Affairs and the Kellogg Program of the University of California, Davis, for their support of this research, as well as the Water Resources Center and the California Policy Seminar of the University of California. Furthermore, the author appreciates the reviews of early drafts by Seymour I. Schwartz, Geoffrey Wandesforde-Smith, and Thomas Dietz of the Division of Environmental Studies, University of California, Davis, and Dean J. Misczynski of the California Office of Planning and Research.

These residents saw their communities as places of retreat and stability. Property values were protected through exclusion of low- and moderate-income persons via large-lot zoning, floor-area minimums, and prohibition of apartments.[3] In 1967, for example, 25 percent of metropolitan-area cities in the United States with 5,000 population or more had 0.5-acre-minimum-lot sizes, effectively excluding low- and moderate-income families. In the New York metropolitan area, 99.2 percent of all undeveloped residentially zoned land was zoned for single-family dwellings.[4] The federal courts have not held these exclusionary controls unconstitutional or in violation of federal civil-rights statutes unless intent to discriminate racially can be shown and concrete harms proven, nearly impossible tests.[5] On the other hand, state supreme courts in New Jersey and Pennsylvania have declared that these forms of de facto economic and racial exclusion, such as found in Mt. Laurel, New Jersey, do not serve the general welfare, and these courts have invalidated them.[6]

In the last fifteen years, a second type of growth control has emerged. Anxious about service costs (especially for federally mandated waste-treatment systems and for schools), many cities, such as Ramapo, New York, have adopted growth-phasing programs. These programs, which limit growth to areas that are contiguous to existing development and services, do not cause housing prices to increase as long as building permits are not restricted below market demand. These programs are not exclusionary per se, in intent or outcome.

Taxation and spending-limitation statutes recently adopted in many states have created widespread doubts among local governments as to whether more growth, of any kind, is fiscally wise. These worries, combined with concerns over environmental "carrying capacity" have given rise to the third and ultimate type of growth control, absolute population limits, as attempted in Boca Raton, Florida. A method with similar adverse effects on housing prices is growth-rate control, as exercised in Petaluma, California.

To analyze the politics of local growth control we must begin by defining these three types of growth regulation: (1) exclusionary controls affecting the economic composition of development (lot size, floor area, and so on); (2) growth-phasing programs regulating the location of development to minimize service costs (service areas, phased zoning); and (3) controls that reduce or stop population growth (building-permit allocation). In reality, most control systems will involve elements of two or three of these types. Clarifying the effects of these pure cases and the reasons for their adoption will allow us to analyze the hybrid systems more intelligently.

An inquiry into why cities and counties have adopted these three types of growth controls in the past will permit us to better estimate future events in local land-use management, and an analysis of the motives behind these local government actions will help state decision-makers and courts appreciate the problems perceived by local legislatures and take remedial action. Also, state and federal courts are increasingly taking judicial notice of deliberate economic and racial exclusion in local land-use controls. As housing and employment become harder to find in the future, pressures for equal access to suburban areas will grow, creating more problems for land-use management.

Motives for Growth Limitation: Malevolent or Benign?

"The earliest examples of zoning [in the U.S.] are those introduced in California toward the end of the nineteenth century as a means of discriminating against Chinese immigrants"—San Francisco generally prohibited laundries, effectively keeping Chinese workers out of most neighborhoods.[7] In the 1910s, Bassett drew up the first comprehensive zoning ordinance for New York City. In the 1920s, the U.S. Department of Commerce drew up a model state zoning statute, which was widely adopted by the states to enable local zoning. Both of the zoning systems were oriented toward the protection of private-property rights. Whereas it is very difficult to identify cases of racial exclusion, instances of economic exclusion with racial overtones are rather easy to identify. Richard Babcock and David Callies cite, for example, statements from the 1972 *Nucleus of Chicago Homeowners Association* v. *Lynn* (NO–CHA) case in Illinois. Property-owner groups attempted to block public housing "on scattered sites" in the southwestern areas of Chicago by asserting that the low-income families in the public housing would "possess certain social class characteristics which will be and have been inimical and harmful to the legitimate interests of the plaintiffs," including "a higher propensity toward criminal behavior," "a disregard for physical and aesthetic maintenance of real and personal property," and "a lower commitment to hard work for future-oriented goals."[8]

New Jersey and Connecticut communities, faced with the threat of minorities from New York City and relying heavily on property taxes for their revenues, exhibit economic exclusion in its purest form. In 1967, over half of the vacant residentially zoned land in Connecticut required 1-acre or larger lots. In 1970, four northeastern New Jersey counties, comprising the majority of suburbanizing lands to the west of New York City, zoned only 0.5 percent of their vacant lands for multifamily development, and most of these parcels could not have apartments with more than one bedroom. Mobile homes were excluded in all but three municipalities. Single-family houses had to be 1,200 square feet or larger on 77 percent of residentially zoned lands. Only 1 percent of these lands were zoned to permit lots of 7,500 square feet or less.[9]

It is probably accurate to say that the first type of growth control—regulations prohibiting moderate-cost and low-cost housing—is promulgated to support property values, keep taxes down, and to promote social (economic and racial) homogeneity. In addition, such controls promote neighborhood amenity, primarily open space, and low-traffic volumes. "Many people would like to live in an attractive neighborhood where the taxes are low and the neighbors congenial."[10]

The second type of growth control, phasing of development, and the third, slowing or stopping growth, appear to be motivated less by desires for social homogeneity than by ambitions to reduce taxes. Recently, natural-environmental-quality objectives appear to have become important in both these types of growth control. Babcock and Callies describe this conflict between ecology and housing in several brief case studies. Their description of events suggests that environmental goals are genuine and are not cover for economic exclusion motives: the environmentalists do not want anyone let in![11] In his review of San Francisco Bay Area land-use politics, Bernard Frieden disagrees with this analysis. He asserts that the environmental issues involved are trivial to the state or region and are often rather farfetched even as local issues, acting as cover for other beliefs. He found that only local environmental organizations, in concert with property groups, attacked projects. He is careful to note that the effect of this opposition is higher housing costs, since environmentalists generally seek lower densities or project denial. Frieden believes that environmentalists and homeowners are appropriating private (open-space) lands for their scenic enjoyment and are emotionally and abstractly against growth per se. He states that middle-class homeowners reject other members of the middle-class from entering their communities for three reasons: (1) fear of tax increases, (2) fear of school crowding, and (3) threatened loss of scenic qualities. In summation, Frieden says that "Public regulation is achieving mainly private purposes . . . the defense of privilege."[12]

Mary Brooks agrees with Frieden in saying that many communities and citizens groups are knowingly engaging in economic discrimination under the cover of pursuing environmental policies.[13] Robert Ellickson agrees with this view but emphasizes the importance of property-value increases in the logic of slowing or stopping growth.[14] He notes that dampening the demand for housing increases the property values of existing homeowners in suburbia. High development charges and excessive standards for floor area and lot sizes also serve both to limit the rate of development, creating a shortage of housing and consequent price rise, as well as to exclude undesirables outright. As owners of raw land get rich in rapidly growing cities, owners of homes gain wealth in slow-growth suburbs. In fact, Ellickson argues, large suburbs go through prodevelopment and antidevelopment phases, because when housing prices get very high from no growth, developers offer larger and larger sums to city-council candidates and eventually succeed in overturning the no-growth ordinances, at least for a while.[15]

Michelle White believes that slow-growth and no-growth communities are motivated by concerns for environmental quality, as well as the traditional objective of holding taxes down. She emphasizes the importance of high and rising interest rates for municipal bonds in pushing school construction costs up, resulting in opposition to growth.[16]

In a recent article, Nelson Rosenbaum reviewed the politics of the adoption of growth controls in Boulder, Petaluma, and Boca Raton, the first three major growth-slowing attempts in the United States.[17] He concluded that high growth rates created shock in the minds of the new suburban residents who were escaping from larger cities. Their examination of growth projections for their suburban jurisdictions led to popular and direct support for growth limitations: initiatives and referenda were used in all three cases. Closely related was a strong desire to preserve small-town character in these medium-sized free-standing communities. All three possessed visible identity and feared being overtaken by their metropoli (Denver, San Francisco, and Miami). The third primary reason was service deficiencies and fiscal strain (schools and waste-treatment facilities). In Boca Raton the fear of social-class change in the form of a rapid influx of apartment dwellers was another causal factor.

Voting in the three cities followed an expectable pattern of economic self-interest. Core-area residents and homeowners voted more heavily for the measures. Rosenbaum concludes by noting that there were 154 communities in the United States with growth rates averaging over 8 percent per year from 1960 to 1970. By examining their other characteristics such as size, economic independence, tax rates, and service shortages, he concludes that "the prospects for the diffusion of population controls are best in California" where many of the rapid-growth communities have high taxes and service problems and are freestanding small towns with identity.[18]

It is apparent from this interpretation of the literature that traditional exclusionary controls are motivated by: (1) protection of property values, (2) economic (and racial) exclusion, (3) tax minimization, (4) protection of social status and congeniality, and (5) maintenance of environmental quality (open space and low traffic volumes). It is difficult to rank these motives in order of importance, but items 1, 2, and 3 are interrelated and seem to be dominant. A more recent type of growth control, growth phasing, appears to be motivated primarily by desires for: (1) tax minimization, and (2) maintenance of environmental quality, in that order. The most recent and severe type of control, slowing or stopping growth, appears to be caused by desires for: (1) service quality (schools, sewers), (2) tax minimization, (3) environmental quality (scenic views, low traffic volumes), and (4) property-value increases (due to rationing), in order of importance. Citizens appear to have been initially shaken by continued rapid growth and the fear of service problems in these cities.

This brief comparison of motives (deduced by researchers) yields some interesting tentative findings. First, social (class) exclusion does not often appear to be a factor in the adoption of phasing or rate controls. Second, environmental protection is a motivating force in all three control situations, with traffic congestion and scenic open space being the most important factors in all three cases. Environmental quality is often called "small-town character" when referring to low traffic volumes, small size, and nearby open space. Third, tax minimization is also a cause of all three types of growth control, although for somewhat different reasons. Cities that control composition do so in an effort to get assessed value per capita up and to prevent property deterioration.

Location-control communities are attempting to minimize service-distance inefficiencies. Growth-rate-control jurisdictions seek to avoid high debt loads commonly assumed to accompany rapid growth.[19] Fourth, many suburbanites may perceive that slowing growth will enhance their property values through supply restriction. This reason, when added to the others, could lead to the widespread adoption of growth-rate controls. The author's home, Davis, and other cities and counties in northern California have recently adopted rate controls.

We will now examine the experiences of four northern California jurisdictions that adopted growth controls in the early 1970s.[20] Two are medium-size counties (300,000 to 650,000 populations) and two are small- to medium-size cities (25,000 to 80,000 population). Two cases are of locational controls, one using city sewer-trunk-line phasing (Modesto) and the other a county-services boundary and phased zoning (Sacramento County). The other two cases are of growth-rate controls, one a city rationing building permits (Petaluma) and the other a county not expanding its water-supply system (Marin County).

These four case studies were performed in 1974 and 1975 and involved interviewing all accessible public officials and many citizens-group representatives, agency people, and newspaper reporters. All available newspaper clips were utilized, as were many official public documents. The lengthy reports were reviewed by selected informants for accuracy. In our interviewing and in our reading of the records and newsclips, we paid special attention to the motives of the various actors and to the information they presented to bolster their arguments in the public arena. There is no way to know actual motives, of course.

Petaluma Building-Permit Allocation

Petaluma was a small farming community until suburban growth overtook it in the 1960s. Located 40 miles north of San Francisco on U.S. 101, Petaluma became an attractive, less expensive source of housing for Marin County and Bay Area commuters. The 1960 population of 14,035 grew to 24,570 in 1970.

The rapid growth of the 1960s occurred on the flat lands to the east of the 101 freeway. Shopping facilities and parks were inadequate on the east side, and road connections to the downtown and west-side parks and shops on the other side of the freeway were poor. The worst problem for the newcomers, however, was the crowding of schools, causing double sessions. Almost all the rapid growth was occurring on the east side, and the schools were not being built fast enough. City officials and residents were also disturbed that because of the rapid growth and higher standards adopted by the regional water-quality agency the municipal waste-treatment-plant expansion was needed earlier than had been planned.

East-side citizen groups forced the city planning department to perform a school study in the fall of 1970. This report projected a rapid worsening of the overcrowding and a rise in tax rates. In addition, the planning director recommended that the city adopt growth-rate and location controls and revise its general plan, using consultants backed by strong citizen involvement.

The consultants polled the city's residents by mail in early 1970. A majority of the 2,400 respondents favored a population cap of 40,000 or less. A two-day workshop was held with citizen representatives, the city council, planning commission, city staff, and county officials. This advisory group recommended the now-famous quota of "about 500" new housing units per year, tied to utility and school capacities, for a five-year period. Other recommendations were to promote an east-west balance in new development and to encourage multifamily units.

In 1972, the council adopted a new general plan that included the 500 quota. Whereas the 500 had just "come out" of the two-day workshop in 1971 (as a round number and about half of the current rate of construction), it was now backed by the rationale that there was only water and sewer capacity for 3,000 more residents. The 500 building permits per year for five years plus exempt (very small) developments would use up the excess capacity but would allow time for the sewer plant expansion and new aqueduct.

The council may have decided to adopt a building-permit quota, instead of limiting annexations and rezonings (as is often done), because the planning director wished to avoid driving up land prices. According to several decision makers, the strategy of limiting annexations would not have controlled actual residential buildout and also would have been more subject to political payoffs. There was no significant opposition to the stringent growth-control scheme. A referendum in 1973 showed that 82 percent of the voters supported the measure.

It appears that the shortage of schools and parks activated the east-side residents. Once growth control came onto the agenda, the city's officials added the problems of water and sewer capacity to the list. Subtly connecting those four issues was the threat of higher taxes needed to build the various facilities. (Rosenbaum shows property taxes in Petaluma rising from about 2 percent of market value in 1960 to about 3 percent in 1975. The same was true for Boulder.[21]) Protection of the aesthetics of small-town character also was a motive of many. The rapid east-side growth was monotonous and ugly to many of the commuters (on the elevated freeway) who had come to Petaluma to live near the green fields. Our research failed to disclose social-exclusion motives or any desire to raise property values through rationing. Petaluma, however, did turn down a low-income housing project in a 1977 referendum. The growth-rate controls appear to have increased new-house prices by about 10 percent, compared to nearby cities with about half of this difference because of the increase in size of the units.[22]

Marin County Water-Supply Restriction

Marin County, immediately north of San Francisco, is a stunningly beautiful region of wooded hills facing the Pacific to the west and San Francisco Bay to the east and south. The population was about 290,000 in 1970. The southern and eastern portions of the county are urbanized along the U.S. 101 corridor.

In 1971 the directors of the county's largest water agency, the Marin Municipal Water District (MMWD), sought legislation to permit them to commit $22 million to an intercounty aqueduct without a vote of the people. Citizen groups and the county supervisors strongly denounced this action, because the MMWD board had promised, one year earlier, to submit all aqueduct bonds to votes. The bill was withdrawn. Later that year, the MMWD board put a bond issue for $35 million to a vote, and it was defeated 31,708 to 3,732. Cost, $35 million plus interest, was one reason. Many people believed that the cost would be much higher. Second, the credibility of the district board was low. Third, opponents said that alternative means of supply should be examined, such as recycling, reclamation, and development of local watersheds. Fourth, the aqueduct would have allowed the MMWD population to grow from 166,000 to 355,000, since the area's growth was constrained by lack of water supplies. In the opinion of the district manager at the time, the growth issue was the most important.

In the following two years three conservationists were elected to the board on explicit growth-limitation campaigns. The year 1972 had been a dry year in Marin. The new board, fearing water shortages, placed a moratorium on new water-line extensions, effectively stopping all major new projects. The MMWD board was displeased by the lack of growth-rate controls in the county and decided to "put some teeth" into the county general plan. The county supervisors, after heated exchanges with the water board, requested that the MMWD build aqueduct facilities just sufficient for the 1990 population projected in the county general plan, in effect requesting a scaled-down intercounty aqueduct. The MMWD board majority felt that breaking the project into stages was not completely honest to the voters but placed a $7.5 million measure on the ballot, to be followed a few months later with another bond vote. The board also declared that this pipeline would be sized to carry the full supply of water turned down in 1971, subject to adding pumps to be voted on subsequently. To further tie the aqueduct bond vote to county growth-control in general, the board announced it would lift the hookup moratorium if the measure passed. Finally, the board refused to endorse its own bond proposal.

In an effort to stem the pro-growth-control vote, the county supervisors circulated a draft-growth-control ordinance, similar to Petaluma's, which would allocate building permits in the various portions of the county. The supervisors endorsed the bond measure, as did the building industry and real-estate interests. The proponent groups basically argued that the bond was needed to serve existing residents, to avoid rationing.

Opposition came from the many environmental organizations in Marin County, who argued that water must be limited until the county supervisors enforce the county general plan, which had been adopted in 1972 and supposedly limited growth to 2 percent per year. Opponents also maintained that the water board could go around the voters with rate increases and augment the water supply beyond that authorized by the bond after the full-sized aqueduct was built. Taxpayers groups also opposed the bond issue.

The 1973 bond issue lost 30,905 to 16,932, mainly because of the desires of the voters to protect open space and limit taxes. In Marin, there is a strong desire to protect the scenic hills from further development. Also, many feared that the water agency would increase supplies without referenda once the aqueduct was built. Exclusionary motives were not in evidence, nor did our research reveal any overt desires to increase property values through housing-supply restrictions.

Sacramento County Urban-Limit Line

Sacramento county lies in the heart of the Central Valley of California. With a population of 634,000 in 1970, the county consists of rich agricultural lands in the western half and rolling hills to the east. About half the population lives in the city of Sacramento, the capital of the state, with the rest of the population in adjacent unincorporated areas. The urbanizing area is surrounded by prime agricultural lands on the north and south.

During the 1950s the county's population grew at an average rate of 6 percent per year. In the 1960s the rate slowed to 2.5 percent. During this twenty-year period, much prime agricultural land was urbanized. The county permitted a large amount of noncontiguous development, and service problems from the low densities began to become severe in outlying areas in the late 1950s. In 1968, the first supervisor was elected on a growth-management/rational-planning platform.

In late 1970, the first U.S. census figures were released for Sacramento county. These numbers showed that recent population growth was considerably slower than had been expected. The county planning staff became convinced that sprawl would worsen, however, because of the now-perceived overcommitment of lands to development in the 1965 county general plan. In early 1971 the Council of Governments (COG) for the area adopted an advisory regional plan that showed a substantial reduction in the lands designated for development in the county. This plan was endorsed by the county supervisors. The regional plan also introduced, to promote service efficiency, the concepts of phased-land-use classifications to reserve agricultural lands and an urban limit line beyond which no services were to be provided.

The county planning staff decided to reformulate the county general plan using the basic idea of growth phasing. An urban area would be designated for

880,000 people, the 1990 population projected by the 1970 census. Urban reserve areas would be designated, to be kept in agricultural use until needed for urban growth. Finally, certain lands would be classified as agricultural preserve, for permanent agriculture. This scheme, the staff hoped, would lower farmers' taxes and make urban services more efficient. It was decided that the urban area would not have to be larger than the existing urbanized area, since over 50 percent of that land area was vacant. After designating the urban limit line and reserve land-use areas, the staff circulated the policies and map to the major environmental and building-industry groups for comment. The staff then recommended this plan to the county planning commission. The plan would redesignate from urban to nonurban classifications over 140,000 acres, or over 25 percent of the undeveloped land in the county. The urban limit line was included to facilitate an understanding of the policy distinction between the areas to be serviced and those not to be serviced. Also, subsequent plan amendments would be more difficult, since the conceptually important line would have to be moved.

In early 1972, the county planning commission held hearings on the proposed general plan. Over 1,000 persons came to one of the hearings. Representatives of dozens of major interest groups attended and presented their views. Opponents argued that land values in the urban area would rise, taxes would shift away from remote lands, and unemployment would rise. Environmentalists countered by saying that growth would not be slowed, only channeled (locationally), and that the high percentage of vacant land would prevent large land-value increases for many years. Three economic consultants verified this view at the hearings. The planning staff subsequently prepared an economic study showing that the phasing plan would lower service costs and not drive land values up significantly. Opponents also charged that those landowners whose lands would be redesignated from urban to nonurban uses would suffer losses in land values. The planning staff could not counter these claims and reasoned that protecting the agricultural economy required these losses. Lawsuits were filed by one developer and petitions to fire the planning director were circulated (neither effort was successful). The director dropped the limit line from the plan but retained the phasing policies. The planning commission voted not to adopt the plan.

There was now a conservationist majority on the board of supervisors, due to the 1970 and 1972 elections. The supervisors held their own hearings in the fall of 1972 and adopted the plan (without the urban limit line) in February of 1973. Basically, the supervisors agreed with the planning staff: too much land was designated for urban development, and growth had to be directed to serviceable lands. Significant factors explaining the adoption of the growth-phasing plan were: (1) the general environmental and growth-control sentiment in the county reflected in the supervisorial elections, (2) the aggressive and environmentally committed planning staff, (3) the dramatic downturn in population expectations, (4) the advisory regional plan of 1971, and (5) rising service costs. It appears that service efficiency (tax minimization) and agricultural protection (for economic and environmental reasons) were the chief motivations of the staff and the decision makers.

Modesto Sewer Phasing

Modesto is a thriving agricultural-service center lying 80 miles south of Sacramento in the Central Valley of California. Food processing, packing, and distribution are the dominant industries. The population of the city in 1974 was 84,000 and had doubled in fourteen years. In 1973, the Modesto area contained over half of the total population of Stanislaus County (210,000). Some decision makers became worried about the conversion of prime agricultural lands in the Modesto area during the late 1960s. Many farmers were worried that the area would become another "Santa Clara Valley," where San Jose and other cities had gobbled up prime orchard and crop lands in the 1940s and 1950s. In 1970, the Agricultural Extension director for the county held a workshop on soils and land-use planning. This conference stimulated thinking in Modesto and the county about agricultural-land conversion. In 1971 and 1972 similar conferences were held.

In 1972, the staff of the COG for the county prepared an advisory land-use plan that proposed guiding future urban development away from the prime agricultural lands. Specifically, the staff recommended that Modesto restrict growth to its existing phase-I (37-square-mile) sewer area. The COG board rejected the plan.

Meanwhile, an environmentalist newcomer proposed to the Modesto City Council that they adopt an advisory policy statement seeking to limit growth to the phase-I-sewer-service area. The Council treated this person rudely. Some long-time citizens were shocked at this and joined forces to place the policy statement on the 1973 ballot. The measure merely required written findings before any agency could approve development on prime agricultural lands. The council unanimously opposed the measure, as did the labor, building, and real-estate interests. The League of Women Voters supported the proposition. The initiative measure lost 7,165 to 5,046. Although the proposition failed, a strong supporter was elected to the council. The council was badly shaken.

The council declared a moratorium on sewer-trunk-line extensions until its capital-improvements committee could study land availability. This committee visited other cities having growth problems, held many public meetings, and toured Modesto to look at developable parcels. The committee's deliberations and reports changed the opinions of the council members and of most opponents. After meetings with the city planning commission, the city council adopted the 1974 urban-growth policy without substantial debate. This resolution directs urban growth to already serviced areas in a contiguous fashion. Any trunk extensions beyond the phase-I area require a general-plan amendment and hearings. The planning staff is directed to prepare an annual review of the effects of this policy on land availability and prices.

Also in 1974, the county replaced its 1-acre agricultural zoning with 10-acre zoning, discouraging hobby farms and protecting commercial agriculture. The county also decided to prohibit subdivisions on septic tanks and to not provide urban services anymore. These policies greatly enhanced the city's ability to prevent leapfrog development.

In Modesto, the motivation for growth phasing appears to have been the preservation of prime agricultural lands. The conservative Farm Bureau supported the city and county growth-phasing policies. The growth-control policies so violently opposed at first, were placidly accepted after they went through channels and were supported by political insiders. The city council rapidly accommodated to the new sentiments for agricultural-land protection.

Conclusions

Our case studies verify the earlier findings. Social (class) exclusion does not appear to be a motive in our two cases of locational controls or in the two cases of rate controls. Environmental quality, on the other hand, appears to have been a major reason in all four cases. In the rate-control communities, citizens wanted to avoid traffic congestion and to preserve scenic open space (without paying for it). These desires were often expressed as the need to preserve small-town character. In the two growth-phasing jurisdictions, protection of the agricultural industry was the chief aim, which is an economic issue more than a natural-environment one. However, protection of riparian lands, air quality, wildlife, and so forth were also stated as reasons.[23] Quality of services/tax minimization was a primary overt motivating factor in three of the four cases, and sewers, water, and schools were the specific services at issue.

There was no evidence that citizens in the two rate-control communities, when they adopted these schemes, were attempting to restrict the supply of new housing to increase existing property values, however. It remains to be seen whether this price effect enters into the politics of maintaining the rate controls in Marin County and Petaluma (and the other rate-control cities in the United States). The probability of price increase because of supply rationing is, of course, known intuitively to nearly all homeowners. Both Sacramento County and Modesto are well aware of the need to open up additional lands for development under their phasing programs before land values are pushed up by vacant-land scarcity.

The housing "crunch" of the late 1970s is making citizens and policymakers very sensitive to the adverse effects on housing prices of rate controls and other land-development regulations. One can not consider the exclusionary impacts of land-use policies in places like Marin County and Petaluma to be unintended, after the controls operate for two or three years, if these effects become evident in the housing market. If citizens become aware of the price effects of rationing, as well as the price increases because of high development fees, exactions, slow project reviews, large-lot requirements, and so on, then these exclusionary effects must be considered as intended in the perpetuation of the controls. Rate control, and locational controls if used too restrictively, can have the same kind of exclusionary effects as the more traditional compositional controls. Whereas exclusion does not appear to have been a motive in adopting the rate and location controls, it can be an effect, to some degree or another, especially of rate controls.

In the view of this author, decision makers interested in the general welfare of the citizens of their states, that is, state planning and housing officials, attorneys general, legislators, and judges, need to scruitinize all three types of growth controls to determine whether they serve the needs of all the citizenry in the region, such as for housing. The courts need to examine the effects of these ordinances on housing availability and price and not concern themselves with questions of intent.

Notes

1. Richard F. Babcock, *The Zoning Game: Municipal Practices and Policies* (Madison, Wis.: University of Wisconsin Press, 1966); John Delafons, *Land-Use Controls in the United States* (Cambridge, Mass.: M.I.T. Press, 1969); Anthony Downs, *Opening up the Suburbs* (New Haven, Conn.: Yale University Press, 1973); Richard F. Babcock and Fred P. Bosselman, *Exclusionary Zoning: Land Use Regulations and Housing in the 1970's* (New York: Praeger, 1973).

2. Downs, *Opening up the Suburbs*; William A. Steger, "Economic and Social Costs of Residential Segregation, in *Modernizing Urban Land Policy,* ed. Marion Clawson, (Baltimore: Johns Hopkins Press, 1973).

3. Babcock and Bosselman, *Exclusionary Zoning*; David Listokin, *Fair Share Housing Allocation* (New Brunswick, N.J.: Rutgers University Center for Urban Policy Research, 1976); James G. Coke and Charles S. Liebman, "Political Values and Population Density Control," *Land Economics* 38 (November 1961): 347–361; Norman Williams, Jr. and Thomas Norman, "Exclusionary Land-Use Controls: The Case of North-Eastern New Jersey, *Land-Use Controls Quarterly* 4 (1970): 1–26; Richard F. Babcock and David L. Callies, "Ecology and Housing: Virtues in Conflict," in Clawson, *Modernizing Urban Land Policy.*

4. Downs, *Opening up the Suburbs,* p. 49.

5. Village of Arlington Heights v. Metropolitan Housing Development Corporation, 97 Sup. Ct. 555 (1977), in which proof of intent was required to invalidate an ordinance; Warth v. Seldin, 422 U.S. 490 (1975), in which proof of concrete harms was required to invalidate an ordinance.

6. National Land and Investment Company v. Kohn, 419 Pa. 504, 215 A. 2d 597 (1965); In re Appeal of Girsh, 437 Pa. 237, 263 A. 2d 395 (1970), may not entirely prohibit multifamily dwellings; Molino v. Borough of Glassboro, 116 N.J. 195, 281 A. 2d 401 (1971); Oakwood at Madison v. Madison, 117 N.J. Super. 11, 283 A. 2d 353 (1971); Southern Burlington County NAACP v. Township of Mount Laurel, 67 N.J. 151, 336 A. 2d 713 (1975). The township's zoning prohibited multifamily dwellings and mobile homes, required minimum lot size and floor area, and placed restrictions on the number of children allowed in a dwelling.

7. Delafons, *Land-Use Controls*, p. 19.

8. Babcock and Callies, "Ecology and Housing," pp. 219–220.

9. Williams and Norman, "Exclusionary Land-Use Controls," pp. 11–15.

10. Coke and Liebman, "Political Values," p. 349. Listokin, *Fair Share Housing Allocation*, basically agrees (pp. 12–13). Downs agrees in *Opening up the Suburbs*, but emphasizes social concerns over the quality of schools, crime, and status (p. 52 and pp. 68–83). Molatch and Logan seem to believe that fiscal concerns are much more important than racial, or even class exclusion: Harvey Molotch, "The City as a Growth Machine," *American Journal of Sociology* 82 (1976): 309–332; John R. Logan, "Industrialization and the Stratification of Cities in Suburban Regions," *American Journal of Sociology* 82 (1976): 333–352.

11. Babcock and Callies, "Ecology and Housing."

12. Bernard J. Frieden, *The Environmental Protection Hustle* (Cambridge, Mass.: M.I.T. Press, (1979), p. 178 and all.

13. Mary E. Brooks, *Housing Equity and Environmental Protection: The Needless Conflict* (Washington, D.C.: American Institute of Planners, 1976), pp. 2–10.

14. Robert C. Ellickson, "Suburban Growth Controls: An Economic and Legal Analysis," *Yale Law Journal* 86 (January 1977): 385–511, at pp. 388–410.

15. Ibid., p. 409.

16. Michelle J. White, "Self-Interest in the Suburbs: The Trend toward No-Growth Zoning," *Policy Analysis* 4 (Spring 1978): 185–203, at pp. 194–195.

17. Nelson Rosenbaum, "Growth and Its Discontents: Origins of Local Population Controls," in *The Policy Cycle*, ed. Judith May and Aaron Wildavsky, Sage Yearbooks in Politics and Public Policy, vol. 5 (Beverly Hills, Calif.: 1978), pp. 43–61.

18. Ibid., p. 59.

19. White, "Self-Interest in Suburbs," maintains that apartment uses may not be so fiscally disadvantageous (p. 196). Coke and Liebman "Political Values," asserted (in 1961) that large-lot developments were not so fiscally beneficial as was commonly believed (p. 361). Frieden, *Environmental Protection Hustle,* claims (p. 170) that tax rates are not higher in high-growth-rate cities, citing Franklin J. James, Jr. with Oliver Duane Windsor, "Fiscal Zoning, Fiscal Reform, and Exclusionary Land Use Controls," *Journal of the American Institute of Planners* 42 (April 1976): 130–141.

20. These descriptions come from: Robert A. Johnston and Janet Gladfelter, "The Petaluma Plan," 63 pp.; Robert A. Johnston and John McNeece, "Water Supply in Marin County," 31 pp.; Robert A. Johnston and John McNeece, "The Sacramento County Urban Limit Line," 53 pp.; and Robert A. Johnston and Janet Gladfelter, "The Modesto Sewer Phasing Plan," 35 pp.; unpublished reports, Division of Environmental Studies, University of California, Davis, (August 1975).

21. Rosenbaum, "Growth and Its Discontents," p. 55.

22. Seymour I. Schwartz et al., "The Effect of Growth Management on New Housing Prices: Petaluma, California," Institute of Governmental Affairs, University of California, Davis, (July 1979).

23. The author believes that the protection of scenic views is often a hidden environmental motive; Frieden agrees, *Environmental Protection Hustle*, pp. 135, 167.

15 Equity Implications of Local Growth Management

Seymour I. Schwartz

Introduction

During the period 1975–1980, the cost of home ownership increased much faster than personal income. Consequently, a smaller proportion of American households can now afford to purchase a house. Potential first-time buyers have been most severely affected.[1] The diminished opportunity for home ownership caused by rapidly increasing house prices and mortgage-interest rates threatens attainment of the "American dream" for many families and holds the potential for serious social conflict.

During this period of rapidly increasing house prices, a movement to control population growth by restricting housing supply or land supply or imposing other requirements on development has become widespread in California and other parts of the nation. This coincidence of restrictive growth management and house-price increases is not entirely accidental. Several studies have attributed major housing-cost increases to various forms of growth control.[2]

The major concern of this chapter is the social impacts, especially the equity effects, of rising housing costs in general and growth control in particular. The chapter first examines the role of the environmental movement and environmental-quality concerns in motivating growth-control programs; the next section briefly surveys the evidence on house-price inflation and identifies major determinants of that inflation. The third section examines the effect of growth control on housing prices, and the next section discusses the equity impacts and related social consequences of rising housing costs and of growth control. The fifth section presents an illustrative calculation that compares the accumulation of financial assets between owners and renters, and the final section examines the existing and potential political responses to the problem of rising housing costs and the implications of these responses for public policy.

The Environmental Movement and Local Growth Control

Environmentalists strongly believe that population growth and economic growth must be sharply reduced, or preferably stopped, because of resource scarcity and

I thank Thomas M. Dietz, David E. Hansen, Robert A. Johnston, and Angus A. MacIntyre for very helpful comments and suggestions on earlier drafts. I am also grateful to the Kellogg Public Service Program, University of California, Davis, and the California Policy Seminar for financial support of research that motivated this paper.

the limited capacity of the environment to absorb pollution.[3] The most influential works of the environmental movement have stressed the importance of natural limits and the cataclysmic consequences that will result from continued population and economic growth.[4] These attitudes have fostered organizations advocating antinatalist policies (zero population growth) and have influenced efforts to control the population growth of cities. Environmentalists' belief in self-reliance within small communities is also a factor in growth-control activities. In the planning realm, the ecological concept of "carrying capacity" has been applied by Ian McHarg and Howard Odum in efforts to determine the appropriate size of human population in a region.[5] Several states have been influenced by Odum's work to consider ceilings on population and to regulate the timing and pattern of regional growth.[6] Thus environmentalism has provided a strong intellectual basis for growth control and has mobilized political action toward that objective.

The suburban migration after World War II can be seen as a return to nature or at least to a healthier small-town environment with parks, open space, cleaner air, and less noise than in the cities.[7] In the 1960s and 1970s, the quest for higher environmental quality in residential environments became more intense as perceptions of environmental-quality deterioration in cities increased. However, motives for growth control are more complex than simply protecting good-quality environments that were being threatened by rapid growth. Environmental quality, to most affluent suburbanites, meant more than physical factors such as air pollution and noise. It also includes parks and open spaces (farmland) nearby, a pleasant-looking neighborhood, little traffic congestion, a pleasant small-town atmosphere and life-style, and high-quality public services at a reasonable price (in property taxes).

Studies of the politics of growth control confirm that growth-control efforts are motivated by the entire set of amenity, environmental-quality, and public-service variables.[8] Preserving the small-town character of a community, although hard to define, has been prominent in debates over growth control, which is not surprising in view of the stated preference of most people to live in a community that is slightly smaller than the one in which they now live. In general, it appears that political efforts to control growth are a response to the perceived threat of continued growth to a set of amenities for which many people moved to desirable communities.[9]

Expectations for growth control include reduced air pollution, traffic congestion, noise, damage to ecologically sensitive areas, and reduced conversion of agricultural lands. At the local level it is likely that growth control will achieve most of these objectives, to some extent. However, at the regional level the net result of uncoordinated growth-limiting actions could be negative. If growth control shifts development further from an urban center, longer commuting trips will result in more energy use and more air pollution.[10] Similarly, shifting development to communities that allow lower densities of development than the growth-controlling cities could result in the conversion of more agricultural land. Growth control is likely to be effective in preventing damage to ecologically sensitive areas. Thus, whether environmental-quality benefits from growth control exceed the costs of environmental degradation to those who are harmed will depend on regional coordination of programs to avoid undesirable shifting of damages.

Housing-Cost Inflation[11]

The Affordability Problem

According to the traditional criterion that annual housing expense be no more than 25 percent of gross income, 40.5 percent of U.S. households were able to afford the median price new house in 1965, whereas by 1978 that proportion had dropped to 25 percent. At the time of peak interest rates in early 1980 it was estimated that fewer than 10 percent of U.S. households could afford the median-priced house.[12] From 1973 through 1980, the average price of a single-family house (nationwide) increased by 117 percent (an annual rate of 12 percent per year, compounded). Personal income increased by about 8 percent per year during this period.

In California the average price of a single-family house increased by 172 percent (15.4 percent average annual rate) in both the San Francisco region and the Los Angeles region between 1973 and 1980. Existing houses increased at about the same rates as new houses. During this period, total housing expense of California homebuyers rose by about 18 percent per year for a newly purchased average-priced house, whereas household income increased at an average rate of 10 percent per year.[13] The large difference between the rate of increase of housing expense and income accounts for the affordability problem that has been widely discussed.

Factors Accounting for the Increase in House Prices
and Housing Expense

House price is an important determinant of the annual housing expense, but there are others as well. These factors will be considered in turn.

House Price Increases. The very strong demand for housing (until early 1980), despite the rapid rise in prices, is attributable to demographic and economic factors. The high rate of household formations during this period was primarily a result of postwar baby-boom children entering the twenty-five to thirty-four year age group.[14] The liberalization of home-financing practices, which allowed unmarried women to qualify for home loans, created a new and large group of potential buyers. In addition, the earnings of working wives were counted more fully, so that many couples were able to qualify for a loan based on their combined incomes, where a husband's income had previously been inadequate.

Inflation, in general, has accelerated housing demand by changing attitudes about home ownership among young families and single people. Owning a home is widely seen as the best hedge against inflation available to a person of modest means, a view that is supported by more thorough analysis (this will be discussed further later). Because of inflation, people are willing to pay a much higher price for a house, in the expectation that it will be worth much more in the future. That is, an investment-value component has been added to the shelter value of the house, a result that is economically rational. Inflation has also stimulated a high level of speculation in single-family houses as rental property.

Consumer demand for higher housing quality is also partly responsible for the rapid price increase; quality changes accounted for more than half the real rate of increase in price between 1972 and 1976.[15] Part of the reason for this rise in quality was that many consumers bought much larger, more expensive houses (than they lived in before or thought they needed) as investments because of inflationary expectations.[16]

Some of the component costs of building a house have risen rapidly while others have not. Land and improvement costs have risen much more rapidly than total price, as have builder financing costs and profits. Increases in land costs can be partly attributed to land-use and environmental controls, which limit the supply of developable land, and partly to inflation-induced demand. Improvement costs are dependent on environmental regulations and local subdivision ordinances. (A fuller discussion of the effects of growth controls and other regulations follows later in the chapter.) However, from 1972 to 1980 the cost of labor and materials (51 percent of the new-house cost) increased at a lower rate than the overall consumer price index (CPI). Thus, inflation in construction costs does not explain the more rapid rise of house prices.[17]

Housing Expense. Rising sales price accounts for a major part of the increase in total housing expense but the interest rate on mortgages has also been very important. For example, on a $50,000 loan the difference in monthly payment between a 10-percent and a 13-percent interest rate is $114. Increasing the loan amount by $10,000 at 10-percent interest would add $88 to the monthly payment. Rapidly increasing utility costs during the past few years constitute a serious problem for many moderate-income households in poorly insulated or very large houses, especially in severe climates. Property taxes have also risen sharply where they are based on actual market value (ad valorem) and have not been restricted, as by Proposition 13 in California.

Growth Controls and House Prices

Several detailed studies of land-use controls and related environmental regulations indicate that their impact on housing costs is potentially large and should be of concern to policymakers.

Land Cost

Several studies have found that zoning contributes to higher house prices by increasing land costs, sometimes by large amounts.[18] Large-lot zoning directly causes higher lot prices and also creates a multiplying effect by promoting construction of larger, higher-quality houses. Growth-rate controls, which restrict the amount and location of new development, generally identify preferred locations for development, which raises land values in those areas. Schwartz et al. found evidence of large increases in lot values in Petaluma after growth controls were instituted.[19] Environmental-impact review processes contribute to costs as they often result in requiring developers to decrease density and permit opponents of projects to delay or otherwise challenge projects in legal actions. Widespread downzoning of land from residential to agricultural categories, coupled with citizen blockage of projects, has reduced sharply the number of available subdivision lots in the San Francisco Bay area.[20]

Subdivision and House Quality

Subdivision regulations for amenities and design quality (site improvements) can add substantially to the cost of land and housing. In cities with stringent growth-rate controls (for example, Petaluma and Davis, California), where subdivision proposals are scored and ranked, developers are competing for a limited number of development permits. There is strong incentive for them to provide costly amenities to present a quality proposal. Some growth-control communities provide additional incentives for such amenities through explicit evaluation criteria used in the housing-allocation process. For example, Boulder, Colorado, awards 30 of 100 points for design amenities and subdivision quality; Petaluma awards more than half its points for such items.[21] In Petaluma the result has indeed been to eliminate lower-quality projects from consideration and leave only large, high-quality, and expensive housing to be constructed.[22] This has probably been the most important result of Petaluma's growth-control system from the point of view of meeting moderate-cost housing needs. In contrast, Davis has vigorously promoted the production of smaller, moderate-cost houses while requiring substantial subdivision improvements and design amenities.

Delays

Delays caused by environmental review and growth-control-program requirements can be costly, in terms of financing charges, overhead, and materials-price
increases. Measuring the component caused by excessive regulation is complicated by disagreement over what constitutes appropriate regulation. Several
studies have found substantial excess delays in the subdivision-development
process.[23] A detailed study of the development process in Davis found that
excessive delays added 3 percent to 4 percent to the cost of production of
a new house.[24]

Other Factors

Both growth-rate-control (quota) programs and more traditional environmental
reviews reduce the size of projects and create scale costs for the developer
(inability to achieve efficiencies of scale). In Davis, for example, where it is
difficult for a developer to receive permission to build more than thirty dwelling
units in any year, developers have complained about the loss of efficiency and
increased costs.[25] Under such a quota limit, it is rational for the developer to
build the largest, most expensive house that can be sold to maximize profit.

A growth-control program may aid the formation of a builder's monopoly
by creating additional risks and procedural requirements that discourage new
builders from entering the market. Builders' profits, hence house prices, will
increase more if a monopoly occurs and demand for housing in the growth-
control city is strong (and relatively inelastic). It is also possible that local
homeowners, acting through their city government, can use a housing-permit
system to advantage by levying large fees or exactions.[26] Personal observation
of the politics of development in Davis supports this behavioral hypothesis.
Bargaining and competition for development units (permits) forces developers
to provide a variety of amenities and moderate-cost units. In either case, the
result is higher house prices. At issue is whether the developer or existing homeowners capture the major share of the benefits.

Price Effects in Petaluma

A study of Petaluma's growth-control program, which compared changes in
new house prices before and after growth control to prices in two other cities,
found a significant increase relative to one of the cities (Santa Rosa).[27] The
same-standard-quality house, starting at the same price in 1971 (adjusted for
city differences), was 7 percent more expensive in 1975. However, the house
of average characteristics that was actually built in Petaluma was much more

expensive than in Santa Rosa (17 percent) because house size (floor area) increased much more in Petaluma. Part of this relative increase in quality was attributed to incentives provided by the growth-control program.[28] Another important finding was that the land component of house price increased by 247 percent (in constant-dollar terms) in Petaluma and by 118 percent and 154 percent in the two other cities (between 1971 and 1975). Petaluma's larger increase is evidence of a local growth-control effect, which can be expected to show up in the value of land, and the increases in the other two cities support Bernard Frieden's claim that regionwide restrictions on housing development are affecting land supply and land price, even in cities that do not have explicit growth-limitation programs.[29]

Although the price effects of growth management and environmental regulations are difficult to determine precisely because of the many interacting variables, both theory and an accumulating body of empirical research indicate that they are potentially large.[30] It is also important to note that growth management and environmental regulations are not simply affecting a few isolated affluent suburbs. Large reductions have been observed in the availability of developable lots throughout a metropolitan region (San Francisco) as a result of numerous growth-control actions by jurisdictions and citizen groups.[31]

Equity Impacts and Social Consequences: Who Wins, Who Loses, and How

Impacts of Rising House Prices

Homeowners. Existing property owners benefit from rising house prices, and renters lose, relative to owners. However, among owners benefits are not equally distributed. In a study of the equity effects of rising property values, Paul Huszar found that upper-income, white, suburban families residing in the "better neighborhoods" of San Jose, California, gained the most, and lower-income, minority, central-city homeowners in less desirable neighborhoods gained the least.[32] During the period of his study, accessibility to employment, shopping, and entertainment also decreased for central-city residents. However, in Davis, a small growth-control city that is perceived as being of high quality, lower-priced houses appreciated more rapidly than higher-priced houses.[33] Such a result is not surprising where the lower-priced houses are located in good neighborhoods and are able to capture external benefits of larger and more expensive nearby housing.

Renters. Renters who are prospective home buyers are the principal losers when housing costs rise faster than incomes. They will either be delayed in their purchase of homes because of the higher cost relative to income or they will be excluded entirely from home ownership. Renters with low and moderate incomes are most seriously affected. Specific groups with low average income and low home-ownership rates (compared to households headed by white males) include several racial or ethnic minorities, female heads of households, and young adults.[34] Young adults have typically rented and not sought home ownership in large numbers, so there is little reason for concern about their inability to buy at this early age. The important question is whether their incomes will increase rapidly enough to permit them to buy when they approach the age of family formation. Since real incomes are declining and real housing costs are increasing, the percentage of young people able to buy houses using their own resources is likely to continue declining.[35] Young prospective owners have responded to this growing affordability problem by borrowing from parents, having parents co-own, buying with other people who are employed, or sacrificing important consumption items and accepting a decline in standard of living to obtain the benefits of ownership. These responses notwithstanding, the proportion of young families forced to rent in the future is likely to increase.

Evidence suggests that ". . . the rental market is increasingly becoming the refuge of lower income households.[36] In the 1970–1976 period, married households showed a net increase in home ownership of 5.3 million units and a decline in number of rental units occupied. On the other hand, households headed by single females had a far higher rate of growth in rental units than in owner units. During this period, the average income of renters increased by only 28.5 percent while that of owners increased by 48.5 percent.[37]

How Renters Lose. At this point, it is appropriate to explore the reasons why renters, especially those in low- and moderate-income groups, are at a disadvantage and identify the kinds of harms that exist. One major disadvantage is that renters' choice of desirable suburban communities is restricted. Many affluent suburbs limit the construction of multifamily units by not zoning land for such use.[38] Opposition to subsidized rental housing in the suburbs is often strong. In desirable city neighborhoods, housing (including rentals) is usually much more expensive than in the suburbs because of the proximity to the central business district. The consequence of restricted residential choice is likely to be poorer education for one's children, poorer environmental quality, greater threat to personal safety, and fewer amenities.[39]

The structure of the economy of metropolitan areas has undergone a major change in the past twenty years, with large shifts in employment from central city to suburbs. Thus, a major advantage of being able to afford a suburban home is job mobility. Being unable to afford a suburban home not only restricts locational choice but it also either reduces prospects for finding a good job or increases the cost of commuting and thereby reduces real income. A major study of the economic effects of limited housing choice found that, on the average, central-city residents suffered a 5 percent loss of income because of excessive commuting.[40] Low job mobility is also economically inefficient—there is a net loss of production in the national economy because of the geographical mismatch between labor supply and employment.

Economically, renters are unable to obtain the very large benefits of asset accumulation produced by rising house prices.[41] The inflation in house prices has been the major source of increased personal wealth for middle-income Americans and has made many favorably situated homeowners wealthy.[42] Renters suffer further economic disadvantage as a result of income-tax laws because they cannot deduct the portion of their rent that goes to pay property taxes, whereas owners are able to deduct both property taxes and interest expenses on their mortgage loan. These deductions reduce tax liability more as one's income and marginal tax rate increase. Hence, higher-income households are able to buy much more expensive houses than they could otherwise afford because they may be able to reduce their monthly housing expense by almost two-thirds. The result is a highly inequitable distribution of the tax benefits of home ownership—lower-income renters and owners are subsidizing higher-income owners in very large amounts. Also, the tax incentive contributes to the bidding up of housing prices, which reduces the changes of a moderate-income household to buy at all.

Socially, the net result of reduced housing opportunities is likely to be a hardening of existing social stratification and increasing economic dependence of future generations on parental wealth. Children of the affluent will have a relatively much greater advantage in relying on parental wealth; moderate-income families often will not be able to draw on their home equity to help their children buy homes. As a result, home ownership and wealth are likely to become much more concentrated. Since educational performance and employment prospects are importantly related to socioeconomic status and school quality, reduced home-ownership opportunity can be an important factor in promoting increased inequality.

Equity Impacts of Growth Control

Local growth-control programs are designed to achieve a specific distributional objective: to provide benefits to members of the growth-control community. Within these communities, however, benefits and costs resulting from the program are unequally distributed. Although all residents may receive certain amenity, environmental-quality, and public-service benefits, it is existing homeowners who benefit most through resulting increases in property values. Those who buy homes in the community after growth control is adopted will pay higher prices for any benefits, perhaps more than the value of the benefits to them. Renters in the growth-control community will face higher rents than they would otherwise. Some may be unable to afford rent increases and be forced to move.[43]

Local growth-control programs are rarely concerned with the housing needs and welfare of the larger region. The costs imposed on would-be homeowners who might like to move to the community are not considered. In fact, a variety of traditional growth-control methods such as large-lot zoning, minimum-floor-area requirements, and restriction of land for multifamily residences have long been used to maintain a healthy fiscal position and shape the socioeconomic character of communities by excluding lower-income households.[44] Prospective buyers who cannot afford to live in a growth-control community will still suffer a loss of welfare if they buy elsewhere in the region. They may have to drive longer distances or receive lower-quality services in their second-choice community. Still, they will become homeowners. Some individuals, at the margin, may be unable to buy at all if there is no suitable substitute community available or if there is a spill over of price increases into other communities. This group is most seriously affected.

Owners of undeveloped land will suffer losses in land value if their development prospects are reduced by growth control, and favorably situated landowners will realize large gains. The size of the gains and losses will depend on the extent to which the growth-control city specifies areas to be developed in different time periods and the amount of land designated for development. The smaller the growth area and more specifically it is identified, the greater the disparity of losses and gains will be.

Developers' profits can be enhanced by growth control if they are able to achieve a monopoly situation. However, local government, if it bargains effectively, could use the growth-control program to capture much of the developers' excess profits.[45]

Growth-control programs create important distributional impacts among jurisdictions as well as among groups of individuals. In the short term, at least, regional growth will depend on the regional economy rather than the policies of local communities. Growth that does not take place in one community will be shifted to another. A shift in demand from growth-control city to a nearby city will cause price increases in the nearby city. Developers' costs are likely to be higher if they shift operations to a new community. The more important consequence is that higher public-service costs will be imposed on the neighboring cities by the shift of development activity. Thus, it is in the best interests of that nearby community to adopt growth-control measures itself. Where several communities in a region have adopted growth controls, others are more likely to follow suit. Indeed, there is evidence to suggest a chain reaction of growth-control adoptions in communities between San Francisco and Sacramento following several years after the pioneering programs of Petaluma and Davis.

The situation today is the reverse of that which prevailed in the 1950s and 1960s, when communities were competing for growth by means of low tax rates and special concessions to developers. Existing homeowners were subsidizing new owners and bearing a disproportionate share of the costs of growth. Local planners, officials, and environmentalists argue that growth control and high development fees are now simply rectifying the inequities of the past. The result of this reversal and the probable spread of growth control programs is that added pressure will be placed on central cities and the larger older suburbs to absorb a larger share of growth. Much of this pressure will be placed on rental units, which are already in critically short supply in many cities.

The direct effect of suburban growth controls will probably fall most heavily on moderate- rather than low-income households, since owner housing is out of the reach of low-income people as first-time buyers. However, growth control could also affect low-income people as renters, both by increasing rents in the community in which they live and by restricting the supply of rental units in more desirable communities.

In addition to these disporportionate impacts of growth control on renters, it is important to emphasize the extent to which renters are already generally disadvantaged relative to owners—especially during periods of rapid inflation in house prices. Growth controls are one additional, albeit potentially significant, source of inequity for renters.

Economic Comparison of Renting and Ownership

Previously, I stated that the major economic advantage of ownership is the accumulation of wealth (assets) as a result of rising house prices. This section presents an economic comparison between renters and owners of housing to illustrate quantitatively the extent of the advantage of ownership and the possible contribution of growth controls to an already regressive situation. We address the following questions: What key variables affect the accumulation of assets? How do renters fare compared to owners in terms of accumulating assets? How do their relative positions change over time? Are renters in danger of missing out on home ownership?

To illustrate the equity implications of renting versus owning housing, two fundamentally different situations are examined. Case 1 assumes that renter and owner start at the same point—that is, equal income, assets, and income-tax bracket. It is the same as comparing renting and owning for a particular family. Case 2 compares unequal situations—lower-wealth and income families who must rent are compared to higher-wealth and income homeowners. Comparing unequal situations is more realistic inasmuch as it describes the situation of would-be owners who cannot buy because of inadequate assets for a down payment or inadequate income to qualify for a loan.

Case 1: Equivalent Initial Situations

The assumptions of Case 1 are:

1. Owner and renter households start with the same amount of savings—enough for a 20-percent down payment on a house.

2. The renter invests these savings in a mutual fund (common stock), which increases in asset value at 15 percent per year.

3. The renter pays no capital-gain taxes on the increase in value of the investment until the end of the time period of the analysis.

4. The renter also invests the difference between rent payments and the net annual housing expense he would have incurred if he bought a house instead of renting. If the rent is higher than the housing expense of the owner, the difference is withdrawn from the mutual fund.

5. The net annual housing expense includes principal and interest on the mortgage loan, property taxes, insurance, and maintenance and repair expenses. The income-tax benefit on the mortgage interest and property tax is subtracted from the housing expense (credited as a benefit). Utilities and other living expenses are assumed to be the same for owner and renter and are not included.

6. Owner and renter have the same marginal income-tax rate, which is assumed to remain constant through the period of the analysis. This implicitly assumes that tax rates will be indexed and that real incomes stay constant.

7. Net assets of the owner are calculated at the end of the period of analysis as if the home were sold at that time and capital-gains taxes paid. Selling costs (realtor commissions and closing costs) are assumed to be 8 percent of the total house value.[46]

Baseline Assumption for Case 1. The approach to the quantitative comparison is to define a baseline set of numerical values for the parameters of the model and then vary these systematically, in the form of a sensitivity analysis. Annual household income is $20,000, and the baseline parameter values are:

1. initial assets of renter and owner = $10,000
2. initial value of house (purchase price) = $50,000
3. down payment on house = $10,000
4. mortgage-loan interest rate = 12 percent
5. loan period = thirty years
6. rate of increase in house value = 12 percent per year (compounded)
7. initial monthly rent = $300
8. rate of increase in rent = 5 percent per year (compounded)
9. renter's rate of earnings on investment = 15 percent per year
10. income-tax rate of renter and owner = 29 percent (federal and state)

These parameters assume a household of about median income buying a very modest first home (well below the present median price of $70,000). The assumed rate of increase in house value is below the average of the past eight years. The initial monthly rent is slightly lower than the amount that would be obtained for the $50,000 house. The rate of increase in rent is somewhat below the average of the past eight years.[47] A 15-percent compounded annual return on investment is optimistic, having been achieved by only a few mutual funds over the past six years. My strategy is to make assumptions that consistently understate the benefits of ownership (that is, favor the renter). In this way, we know the direction of any error in the results and can place higher confidence in them if ownership is superior.

Results: Case 1. Using this baseline set of parameter values, the owner's assets are 1.9 times those of the renter after ten years and 2 times as great after twenty years. The size of the difference in dollar assets increases from $45,789 after ten years to $188,212 after twenty years (see table 15-1). It should be remembered that the assumptions and parameter values strongly favor the renter. With a more realistic value for the rate of rent increase at 7 percent per year and a rate of earnings on investment (renter) of 8 percent per year, the owner's assets are 4.3 times as large after ten years ($73,077 difference in amount) and 128.5 times as large after twenty years ($367,120 difference in amount). The striking thing about the renter's assets in this situation is that they actually decrease. Both the higher rate of rent increase, which causes the renter to pay more for housing than the owner within six years, and the lower rate of earnings on savings are responsible. In the second situation, the renter's assets are only $2,879 after twenty years compared to assets of $181,787 after twenty years in the first (baseline) situation. The owner's assets after twenty years are $369,999. These numbers illustrate both the potentially enormous differences in wealth between owner and renter—because of their housing situation—and the very large effect that a change in the rate of rent increase and the investment-earnings rate of the renter can have. It is the lower rate of earnings that accounts for the major share of this difference. If the rate of general inflation is higher than assumed here, the rate of increase in house value and in rental prices will also be higher. The result is an even greater advantage for ownership.

Case 2: Nonequivalent Situations

The major difference between this model and that of case 1 is that now the renter household is assumed to have lower income and less wealth, initially, than the owner household. Renters are assumed to rely on savings banks for investing their assets, which limits their earnings to 7 percent (before taxes) on average.[48] Otherwise the assumptions are as stated for case 1.

The baseline parameter values for this case are: owner's initial assets = $10,000; renter's initial assets = $2,000; renter's rate of earnings on investment = 7 percent per year; renter's income-tax rate (federal and state) = 25 percent; and rate on increase in rent = 5 percent per year. All other values are the same as the baseline set for case 1.

Table 15-1
Economic Comparison of Asset Accumulation by Renters and Owners during Specified Periods

Conditions Assumed[a,b]	Length of Period (years)	Owner's Assets at End of Period (dollars)	Renter's Assets at End of Period (dollars)
Case 1 (baseline set)			
Initial assets (owner and renter) = $10,000	5	$ 38,517	$ 24,328
Rate of rent increase = 5 percent/year	10	95,005	49,216
Rate of return on savings = 15 percent/year	20	369,999	181,787
Income-tax rate = 29 percent (owner and/renter)			
Case 1 (Set 2)			
Initial assets (owner and renter) = $10,000	5	38,517	17,522
Rate of rent increase = 7 percent/year	10	95,005	21,928
Rate of return on savings = 8 percent/year	20	369,999	2,879
Income-tax rate = 29 percent (owner and renter)			
Case 2 (Set 1)			
Initial assets of owner = $10,000	5	38,517	8,113
Initial Assets of renter = $2,000	10	95,005	12,136
Rate of rent increase = 5 percent/year	20	369,999	12,250
Rate of return on savings = 7 percent/year			
Renter income-tax rate = 25 percent			
Owner income tax rate = 29 percent			
Case 2 (set 2)			
Initial assets of owner = $10,000	5	38,517	6,870
Initial assets of renter = $2,000	10	95,005	5,938
Rate of rent increase = 7 percent/year	20	369,999	-31,598.
Rate of return on savings = 7 percent/year			
Renter income-tax rate = 25 percent			
Owner income-tax rate = 29 percent			

Case 2 (Set 3)

Initial assets of owner = $10,000		
Initial assets of renter = $5,000	5	10,657
Rate of rent increase = 7 percent/year	10	11,249
Rate of return on savings = 7 percent/year	20	-21,150
Renter income-tax rate = 25 percent		
Owner income-tax rate = 29 percent		

	38,517
	95,005
	369,999

[a]The parameter values (assumptions) not included in the table under "conditions assumed" are the same for all runs. Their values are: purchase price of house = $50,000; down payment = $10,000; loan interest rate = 12 percent (30 year loan period); rate of increase of house value = 12 percent per year; initial rent paid by renter = $300 per month.

[b]The numerical values of owner's assets and renter's assets are calculated for each of three time periods of the analysis (5 years, 10 years, or 20 years) and the set of assumptions specified in the "conditions assumed" column and in footnote[a].

Results: Case 2

For the baseline situation, the ratio of the owner's assets to the renter's assets increased from the initial value of 5.0 to 7.8 after ten years and to 30.2 after twenty years. If rents are assumed to increase by 7 percent per year instead of 5 percent, as in the baseline situation, the renter's situation becomes much worse, as he must dip into savings or current income to pay the difference between the rental-housing expense and the owner's costs. Thus, after ten years the renter's assets are only $5,938, and by fifteen years they are negative (after the investment fund is wiped out additional current income is used). If the renter starts with $5,000 in initial assets, the results are much the same, except that assets disappear at a later date.

The analysis shows that under realistic assumptions, a renter will be paying more for comparable housing than an owner within a relatively few years and will not accumulate the large amount of assets that owners derive from rising house prices. The protection that a fixed-rate mortgage gives the owner is an important and widely recognized benefit of home ownership in inflationary times. Renters have no such protection. In a similar analysis, Kain and Quigley found that preventing home ownership (in their situation, by racial discrimination) will raise the cost of housing by as much as 50 percent in a rising market.[49]

If the renter's rate of return on investment is lower than the rate of house-price appreciation, it will be difficult for the renter to accumulate enough assets to afford a down payment, unless he is able to invest a substantial amount of current income. On the other hand, if the renter is able to earn a higher rate than the rate of increase in house value, he will be able to accumulate a larger-percentage down payment than he had initially (sometime within the first ten years). However, because of the leveraged nature of home ownership, the renter is likely to end up far behind in total wealth (as shown in the baseline case). Furthermore, the probability of earning as much as 15 percent per year in any investment other than real estate is very small for the person of modest means.

Political and Policy Implications

Summary of Distributional Impacts and Social Issues
of Growth Controls

Before examining the political implications of rising housing costs and growth management and the policy instruments for addressing the problem, we summarize the major distributional impacts and social issues of growth control.

1. Despite the high level of home buying until early 1980, the rapid rise of housing expenses relative to income has created a severe problem for households seeking to buy a first home. This situation is likely to become worse.

2. The most seriously affected groups are minorities (blacks and Hispanics, who have a much lower rate of home ownership than whites), female heads of households, and young households, because of their lower than average incomes. Any household of moderate income or lower is increasingly likely to find the purchase of a first home difficult.

3. The inability to buy a house reduces a family's chances for obtaining a good-quality education for their children, for obtaining a good job, and for living in a physically and socially desirable environment. The result is likely to be less upward mobility and loss of income, especially for urban minorities.

4. Growth control can cause large increases in the price of new and existing houses both in the community that controls growth and, to a lesser extent, in neighboring communities. Within a metropolis, growth-control effects are not limited to the affluent suburbs that adopt them but can be widespread throughout the region.

5. Existing homeowners are the primary beneficiaries of growth control by way of increased house values. All residents of the growth-control community receive amenity and public-service benefits. Developers and favorably situated landowners are also likely to benefit substantially.

6. Renters in the growth-control city and in nearby cities are the principal losers because of increased rents and reduced opportunities to buy a house as prices rise.

7. Owners of land whose development prospects are reduced by growth control will suffer losses in market value, possibly of major proportions.

8. Growth control will place added pressure on central-city rentals and impose higher public-service costs on nearby cities. An already serious rental-housing shortage in many cities is likely to be exacerbated by widespread growth-control efforts.

9. Growth control in particular, and rising house prices in general, both provide higher-income groups with benefits while they harm lower-income groups the most. Inflation in house values is the major source of asset accumulation for most Americans, a source of wealth from which renters are excluded.

10. The net results of reduced opportunities for home ownership are likely to be: reduced upward mobility, greater concentration of wealth in the society, increased socioeconomic class divisions, and a greater potential for social conflict.

The housing affordability problem and its social consequences are only partly the result of growth controls. Demand factors and high interest rates have probably played a more important role to date. However, as growth-control actions become more widespread, their potential for exacerbating the problem is large.

Sources of Political Conflict

Growth-control programs pursue legitimate social objectives: improving the efficiency of land development with respect to resource use and the provision of public services and protecting environmental quality. However, in pursuing these objectives, growth-control programs conflict with equity objectives by producing regressive distributional consequences. We briefly will describe the sources of conflict and interest groups involved.

If new housing does not pay its own way, it must be subsidized by existing residents either through higher property taxes or a decline in services.[50] In states where restrictions have been imposed on property-tax rates or assessments, as Proposition 13 has done in California, it is questionable whether even very large development fees on new construction will cover the cost of services. Thus, a reduction of service quality is likely unless growth is controlled; existing homeowners' interests are in conflict with prospective owners. By creating spillover effects on both renters and owners in other jurisdictions, growth control can create conflict between affluent suburbs (which control growth) and cities that do not control growth. If the percentage of households unable to buy a house increases as a result of growth control (and inflation in general), the additional demand for rental housing and the short supply will cause higher rents and increased militancy among renters for rent control.[51] If successful, the rate of construction of new rental units will drop, more apartments will be converted to condominiums, and a crisis in rental housing could result. One of the consequences of such a crisis could be an attack on growth-control programs and other forms of regulation.

Already disadvantaged minority groups, single women who head households, and the young will be affected most seriously by growth control and rising housing costs. All these groups have much lower average income and ownership rates than the overall U.S. average. Minority groups in several large cities are being further affected by the revitalization movement, which has resulted in dilapidated housing being renovated by middle-class professionals, thus displacing many poor households and raising property values in those neighborhoods. High suburban-housing prices are undoubtedly a major factor in this return to the city. This displacement of lower-income people holds considerable potential not only for political conflict but for racial violence.[52]

Many young middle-class Americans now seriously doubt that they will ever be able to afford a house, a sharp reversal in expectations from those of the previous thirty years. If the present doubts are realized to a large extent, the general sense of disillusionment and deprivation among the young can be a source of intergenerational conflict, possibly resulting in attacks on social security and other programs for the aged as well as on programs that benefit affluent suburbanites.

Policy Alternatives

To reduce the conflict between the legitimate social purposes of growth control and equity goals, public intervention in land-use management and housing production seems necessary. There exist several alternatives for ameliorating the negative impacts of growth control and other alternatives for dealing with the larger issue of housing affordability.

Measures for Growth-Control Jurisdictions. Growth-control jurisdictions can take direct action to insure that a portion of the dwellings built there are initially affordable by low- or moderate-income households and that they remain affordable. Alternatives range from mandating a specified percentage of moderate-cost units as a condition of permission to build to incentives that rely on voluntary responses of builders. A mandatory requirement could also be accompanied by some quid pro quo—permission to build a higher than normal density (density bonus) for example. Incentives can take the form of preferential processing of development proposals or density bonuses in return for a certain percentage of moderate-cost units. Both of these methods are supported by builders who are facing the less appealing mandatory program with no compensation. Builders strongly support the removal of various requirements and regulations, such as environmental-impact assessment and minimum-lot sizes, which impose additional costs on the project. To insure that houses sold originally at moderate prices remain in the moderate price range requires controls on subsequent sales of the house. A quasi-public agency is needed to administer such a program, which restricts the rate of appreciation in house value a buyer can realize.

Ellickson proposes a judicial remedy for the inequities created by growth control. He recommends that suburban jurisdictions be allowed to pursue restrictive growth controls but that state courts should use the taking clause in their constitutions to entitle landowners and housing consumers to sue for damages. Ellickson's proposed rules would enable certain landowners to recover damages for land-value losses and consumers (in a class action) to recover damages they have suffered as a result of increased housing prices attributable to growth control. If the growth-control community can demonstrate that its program is both efficient and equitable to consumers of housing, it would not be subject to damages.[53] The result of this proposal is to shift the burden of proving that growth control is efficient and fair to the growth-control city. However, it could also place an impossible burden on the courts and on researchers to determine precise damage attributable to growth control.[54]

An alternative that is equally applicable to non-growth-control cities is the selling of local revenue bonds for the purpose of providing low-interest loans to moderate-income home buyers. The low interest rate is made possible by the tax-exempt status of municipal bonds.

Administrative procedures can be implemented to review local growth-control plans to insure that they address housing needs as well as environmental-quality and service-efficiency objectives. Growth-control jurisdictions can be required to include programs that provide a specified percentage of low- and moderate-cost housing (rentals as well as ownership units) and other methods that reduce the cost of producing housing or increase the ability of prospective buyers to qualify. Monitoring the performance of the program is essential to the success of administrative review.

Measures for Any Jurisdiction. Several possible measures for addressing the general problem of housing affordability are available; most require federal action. Already in place are loan-subsidy programs for buyers under the federal "245" program and local revenue-bond programs, as well as the section-8 program for renters (a rental-subsidy payment). Several tax-incentive or direct-grant options are available to the federal government. For example, a federal tax credit of, say, $3,000 can be given to first-time buyers. More appealing would be a direct payment to the buyer of a certain fraction of the down payment, up to a maximum amount (for example, a $1 federal payment for every $3 put up by the buyer, with a maximum $3,000 federal payment). Special bank accounts, which pay high interest rates and are not taxed, can be established for the specific purpose of buying a house.[55] Special tax credits can also be given to renters (as in California) or to home builders, providing they meet specific program requirements for low- and moderate-cost housing.

Political Responses to Policy Alternatives

Inflation has made people preoccupied with their personal financial well-being and unwilling to support programs that do not benefit them directly or growth that has a negative fiscal impact. The production of moderate-cost housing is fiscally unappealing to existing homeowners because it will not produce as much tax revenue as expensive housing and may result in service cutbacks because tax revenues are limited. Thus, we can expect suburban homeowners to oppose public efforts to require moderate-cost housing in their community. Prospective home buyers who earn more than needed to qualify for the moderate-cost housing will oppose programs in the belief that they will be subsidizing the moderate-cost units. Developers will be opposed for financial reasons, and free-market advocates will be opposed for philosophical reasons.

Tenants groups will become more militant as the rental-housing situation deteriorates and will fight to protect themselves against large rent increases. They will also favor rental-subsidy programs and programs for promoting the production of more rental units and moderate-cost housing that will aid them as prospective buyers. It is likely that rental-subsidy programs will be expanded as the rental-housing situation worsens, but subsidy programs will be in severe competition with other federal programs.[56] Incentives to the private sector to produce more moderate-cost units that do not require public funds can reduce pressure on the rental market and reduce conflict over the allocation of federal funds. Consequently, such programs as density bonuses or preferential processing to reduce delay costs should be undertaken, at least as an experiment.[57]

Housing advocacy organizations representing low-income and minority groups will oppose suburban growth-control efforts and fight for changes in statutes that make it more difficult for suburban communities to implement narrowly focused growth-control programs that do not deal with housing needs. One strategy is to shift the burden of proof to growth-control communities to show cause why growth control is needed. Housing advocates will also fight for more stringent federal and state enforcement of requirements that promote the provision of low- and moderate-income housing throughout a region. Regional councils of government (COGs) have not been notably successful in implementing fair-share programs.

Moderate-income people, such as blue-collar workers, do not generally identify with the poor or support social programs that benefit the poor. However, organizations to which they belong, especially labor unions, might join a coalition that advocates certain housing programs. (Labor groups have joined business and building-industry groups to oppose land-use and environmental-quality regulations in California.)

Young people, especially from middle-class backgrounds, generally will support growth control, because of their strong feeling for protecting environmental quality, without being aware of the potentially negative impacts of growth control on their housing status. It is also likely that many young people now in college see themselves as being quite affluent five or ten years from now and do not envision any problem in buying a house. Young people from affluent backgrounds may also be confident that the wealth accumulated by their parents through inflating house values will be available to help them buy a house. Young people from less affluent backgrounds are undoubtedly less optimistic and are likely to be more active in housing issues, probably through membership in organizations such as labor unions or tenants groups. Housing could heighten conflict along age lines and result in withdrawal of support for programs for the aged.

Environmentalists will, of course, strongly support growth-control programs as necessary for enhancing environmental quality and protecting agricultural lands. Whether they will support programs to meet the housing needs of low- and moderate-income people is uncertain, especially where there are conflicts between growth-control and housing objectives. There are environmentalists and housing advocates who believe that both environmental quality and housing goals can be achieved jointly and cooperatively.[58] However, this optimistic view is not yet justified by recent events. At a minimum, it seems necessary for growth-control communities to include substantial low- and moderate-cost housing in their programs and for their citizens to support other programs that would increase the supply of moderate-cost housing and the ability of moderate-income households to afford such housing. Otherwise, growth-control programs that provide high-quality environments primarily for the affluent will be difficult to justify.

Notes

1. See Seymour I. Schwartz and Robert A. Johnston, "Measures for Increasing the Supply of Moderate-Cost Housing in California" (Davis, Calif.: Institute of Governmental Affairs, University of California, 1980).

2. David E. Dowall, "The Effect of Land Use and Environmental Regulations on Housing Cost," *Policy Studies Journal*, Special Issue no. 1 (1979): 277-287; Seymour I. Schwartz et al., "The Effect of Growth Management on New Housing Prices: Petaluma, California" (Davis, Calif.: Institute of Governmental Affairs, University of California, 1979).

3. Ideological roots of the environmental movement are described in T. O'Riordan, *Environmentalism* (London: Pion Limited, 1976).

4. See Paul Ehrlich, *The Population Bomb* (New York: Ballantine Books, 1968); Garret Hardin, "The Tragedy of the Commons," *Science* 162 (13 December 1968): 1243-1248; and D.H. Meadows et al., *The Limits to Growth* (New York: Universe Books, 1972).

5. Ian L. McHarg, *Design with Nature* (New York: Natural History Press, 1969); Howard Odum, *Environment, Power and Society* (New York: John Wiley, 1971).

6. O'Riordan, *Environmentalism*, p. 7

7. See Lewis Mumford, *The City in History* (New York: Harcourt Brace Jovanovich, 1961), pp. 487-496 and O'Riordan, *Environmentalism*, pp. 127-129.

8. Michael Gleeson et al., *Urban Growth Management Systems: An Evaluation of Policy-Related Research* (Chicago: American Society of Planning Officials, 1975); Nelson Rosenbaum, "Growth and Its Discontents; Origins of Local Population Controls," in *The Policy Cycle*, ed. Judith V. May and Aaron B. Wildavsky (Beverly Hills, Calif.: Sage Publishers, 1978), pp. 43-64; Robert A. Johnston, "The Politics of Local Growth Control," *Policy Studies Journal*, Symposium Issue on Environmental Policy, December 1980.

9. O'Riordan, comments that many Americans are willing to pay a high price, in housing costs, for high amenity areas and that such areas have experienced exceptional increases in land and house value in recent years, *Environmentalism*, pp. 128-130.

10. Frieden believes this has occurred in the San Francisco region. Bernard J. Frieden, *The Environmental Protection Hustle* (Cambridge, Mass.: MIT Press, 1979).

11. The problem of rising house prices and housing expense has been much discussed in the press as well as in academic sources. Hence, I will present only a brief summary of the relevant data and the major causes of those increases. For a comprehensive treatment, see Leo Grebler and Frank G. Mittelbach, *The Inflation of House Prices* (Lexington, Mass.: Lexington Books, D.C. Heath, 1979).

12. Stephen R. Seidel, *Housing Costs and Government Regulations: Confronting the Regulatory Maze* (New Brunswick, N.J.: Center for Urban Policy

Research, Rutgers University, 1978) for 1965 estimate and *Christian Science Monitor*, 25 October 1978, p. 1 for 1978 estimate.

13. See Schwartz and Johnston, "Measures for Increasing Supply," pp. 3-6, for a detailed discussion.

14. Bernard J. Frieden and Arthur J. Solomon, *The Nation's Housing: 1975 to 1985* (Cambridge, Mass.: Joint Center for Urban Studies, Massachusetts Institute of Technology and Harvard University, 1977).

15. U.S. Department of Housing and Urban Development, "Final Report of the Task Force on Housing Costs" (Washington, D.C.: U.S. Government Printing Office, 1978) p. 3.

16. Grebler and Mittelbach, *Inflation of House Prices*, p. 83.

17. See U.S. Department of Housing and Urban Development " Final Report," p. 3; Evelle J. Younger, and C. Foster Knight, "Attorney General's Report on Low and Moderate Income Housing" (Sacramento, Calif., January 1976), pp. 3-4.

18. William J. Stull, "Community Environment, Zoning, and the Value of Single Family Homes," *Journal of Law and Economics* 18 (1975): 535-557; George E. Peterson, "Land Prices and Factor Substitution in the Metropolitan Housing Market" (Washington, D.C.: Urban Institute, 1974); Lynne B. Sagalyn and George Sternlieb, *Zoning and Housing Costs: The Impact of Land Use Controls on Housing Price* (New Brunswick, N.J.: Center for Urban Policy Research, Rutgers University, 1972).

19. Schwartz et al., "Effects of Growth Management."

20. Frieden, *Environmental Protection Hustle.*

21. Petaluma, California, Resolution no. 6990, 7 June 1975.

22. Schwartz, et al., "Effect of Growth Management, p. 55.

23. Seidel, *Housing Costs*; Rice Center for Community Design and Research, *The Delay Costs of Government Regulation in the Houston Housing Market* (Houston, Tex.: Rice University, 1978).

24. Robert A. Johnston, Seymour I. Schwartz, and William Hunt, "The Effect of Local Development Regulations on Single Family Housing Costs in Davis, California" (Davis, Calif.: Division of Environmental Studies, 1980) unpublished manuscript.

25. Ibid.

26. A city can capture part of the developer's profits by imposing large development fees or requiring the developer to pay for all utilities or dedicate land for use as parks, schools, or greenbelts. Present residents will benefit from the high development fees in the form of lower tax rates for public services and from the amenities that are part of the new development. See Robert C. Ellickson, "Suburban Growth Controls: An Economic and Legal Analysis," *Yale Law Review* 86 (January 1977): 389, for a more detailed treatment.

27. Schwartz "Effect of Growth Management," et al., pp. 43-49. The other comparison city, Rohnert Park, was much closer to Petaluma and was

influenced by its growth-control program. Therefore, it was not considered to be a suitable control.

28. The comparison for the standard house assumes a house of the same characteristics for each city and time period. The standard house is a statistical composite, which consists of the average value for each characteristic over the entire sample. In contrast, the actual-house analysis compares houses of average characteristics for the particular city and time period. Thus, the standard-house comparison is for a product of constant quality whereas the actual-house comparison is for a product of varying quality.

29. The results reported in this section are from Schwartz et al., "Effect of Growth Management," pp. 43-49.

30. Claude Gruen, "The Implications of the Current Trends in Local Planning Controls," *Proceedings of the Fourth Annual Lincoln Institute/U.S.C. Seminar on Land Policy* (Los Angeles: University of Southern California Law Center, forthcoming).

31. Frieden, *Environmental Protection Hustle*, Dowall, "Effect of Regulations."

32. Paul C. Huszar, "Equity and Urban Growth: Real Property Value Appreciation in San Jose, California," *American Journal of Economics and Sociology* 36 (July 1977): 251-261.

33. Robert A. Johnston et al., "The Effectiveness of the Moderate Cost Housing Program of Davis, California" (Davis, Calif.: Division of Environmental Studies, University of California, 1980), unpublished manuscript.

34. U.S. Department of Commerce, Bureau of the Census, *Current Housing Reports, Annual Housing Survey: 1977*, series H-150-77 (Washington, D.C.: U.S. Government Printing Office, September 1979).

35. Median household income peaked in 1973 and was 2.3 percent lower, in constant dollars, in 1978. U.S. Bureau of the Census, *Current Population Reports, Consumer Income*, series P-60, no. 121 (Washington, D.C.: U.S. Government Printing Office, February 1980). Hourly compensation rates for all nonfarm business employees was no higher in July 1980 than in early 1972. *Wall Street Journal*, 25 August 1980, p. 1, citing U.S. Department of Commerce, *Business Conditions Digest*.

36. George Sternlieb and James W. Hughes, "Changes in the Rental Market: The Uncertain Future of Rental Housing," *Policy Studies Journal*, Special Issue no. 1 (1979): 250.

37. Ibid.

38. See Anthony Downs, *Opening up the Suburbs*, (New Haven, Conn.: Yale University Press, 1973), pp. 1-13, for a superb analysis.

39. Ibid., pp. 13-46, 68-79.

40. Wilbur A. Steger, "Economic and Social Costs of Residential Segregation," in *Modernizing Urban Land Policy*, ed. Marion Clawson (Baltimore, Md.: Johns Hopkins Press, 1973), pp. 83-113.

41. See the fourth section of this chapter for a detailed quantitative analysis.

42. George Sternlieb and James W. Hughes, "Housing and Shelter Costs: The Schizoid Problem of the Central City, in *America's Housing: Prospects and Problems* (New Brunswick, N.J.: Rutgers University, Center for Urban Policy Research, 1980), pp. 122-123.

43. See Ellickson, "Suburban Growth Controls," for a discussion of distributional impacts.

44. Downs, *Opening up the Suburbs*, pp. 3-10, 48-53; for additional evidence also see Richard F. Babcock and Fred P. Bosselman, *Exclusionary Zoning: Land Use Regulation and Housing in the 1970s* (New York: Praeger Publishers, 1973).

45. Ellickson believes that a homeowner's monopoly (cartel), acting through its city government's growth-control program would capture developers' excess profits. The ability of suburban homeowners to exercise monopoly power is challenged empirically in William A. Fischel, "Zoning and the Exercise of Monopoly Power: A Reevaluation," *Journal of Urban Economics* (forthcoming).

46. In reality, most homeowners defer paying capital-gains tax at the time of sale by buying another house of greater value within eighteen months. This provides a large benefit to the homeowner, which is not accounted for in this calculation.

47. Sternlieb and Hughes, "Changes in Rental Market," p. 254, show an average annual increase of 7.5 percent from 1970 to 1976.

48. Even with higher rates available on money-market or long-term accounts, a 7 percent average rate seems reasonable.

49. John F. Kain and John M. Quigley, "Housing Market Discrimination, Homeownership, and Savings Behavior," *American Economic Review* (June 1972).

50. New housing "pays its way" if it contributes enough to the city coffers, through development fees and property-tax revenue, to pay the full cost of services required by the occupants.

51. The overwhelming defeat of Proposition 10 in California (June 1980) is evidence of the increasing political power of the tenants movement. The measure would have effectively prohibited local government from imposing rent controls.

52. Patrick Hare comments: ". . . increased demand for inner-city housing raises the possibility of urban racial terrorism in response to the displacement of poor minorities by affluent whites." Patrick Hare, "A Scary Scenario for Urban Pioneering," *Planning* 46 (January 1980): 6-7.

53. Ellickson, "Suburban Growth Controls," pp. 468-470.

54. See Schwartz et al., "Effect of Growth Management," for a discussion of methodological difficulties of such an effort.

55. See John Cunniff, "A Penny Saved . . . Is it Just a Penny Wasted?" *Sacramento Bee* 5 August 1980, p. C7, for a description of programs in various countries.

56. The House approved a program to provide rental subsidies to middle-income renters (those with incomes below 150 percent of the area's median income) and another program for mortgage subsidies to developers constructing new apartments. However, the effect of the programs will be small; only $61 million will be spent on rental subsidies. *Wall Street Journal*, 25 August 1980, p. 6.

57. Schwartz and Johnston, "Measures for Increasing Supply," for a discussion of alternatives.

58. See, for example, Mary Brooks, *Housing Equity and Environmental Protection: The Needless Conflict* (Washington, D.C.: American Institute of Planners, 1976).

Index of Names

Ackerman, Susan Rose, 155
Aldrich, Howard E., 105
Alexandre, A., 171
Alonso, William, 204
Altree, Lilian R., 170
Anagnoson, A. Theodore, 31, 32
Anderson, Frederick R., 33, 105, 181, 184, 190
Andrews, Richard N.L., 105, 107
Appelbaum, Richard P., 204
Aron, Joan B., 23, 33

Babcock, Richard F., 209, 210, 219, 220, 247
Backoff, Robert W., 154, 155, 156
Baden, John, 25, 33
Bailey, D.E., 198, 205
Bailey, R.G., 77
Ball, Bruce P., 110, 122
Banfield, Edward C., 64
Banks, Arthur S., 85, 93
Bardach, Eugene, 48, 107
Baucus, M., 75, 77
Baum, P., 204
Baumol, William J., 155, 170
Baxter, William F., 170
Baybrooke, D., 105
Berman, Paul, 4, 31
Bernard, Chester I., 156
Besse, Stephen A., 184
Beyle, T. L., 106, 107, 108
Bish, Robert L., 155
Black, B.J., 106
Borde, J.P., 171
Bosselman, Fred P., 219, 247
Bower, Blair, 191
Bowers, R.V., 106
Bozdogan, K., 191
Brobst, D.A., 76
Bromley, Daniel W., 106
Bronstein, Daniel, 49
Brooks, Mary E., 210, 220, 248
Buchell, Robert W., 204
Burke, Roy, 106

Cahn, Robert, 33
Call, Charles, 156
Calleo, David, 33
Callies, David L., 209, 210, 219, 220
Canter, Larry W., 106
Canute, King, 31
Carnes, Dam A., ix, 16, 35, 48, 49, 50
Carter, Pres., 9, 122

Cathcart, J.B., 76
Cell, Donald C., ix, 26, 157
Cell, Edward, 157
Clark, Gail, xi
Clark, Peter B., 156
Clawson, Marion, 75, 219, 246
Clotfelter, Charles T., 31
Coke, James G., 219, 220
Costle, Douglas, 41, 46, 48, 175
Cover, Steven, 156
Culliton, Barbara, 49
Cunniff, John, 247

Dahl, Robert, 154
Dales, J.H., 155, 174, 183
Daley, Herman E., 17, 32
Davies, Barbara S., 184
Davies, J. Clarence, 179, 184
Davis, Otto A., 154
DeAlisse, Louis, 156
Delafons, John, 219, 220
DeVille, William, 50
Dickerson, C. Robert, 94
Dietz, Thomas, 207, 223
Dolgin, Erica, 170
Dorfman, Nancy, 190
Dorfman, Robert, 190
Dowall, David E., x, 29, 193, 204, 244
Downs, Anthony, 101, 106, 108, 156, 219, 220, 246
Drayton, William, 183
Dubos, Rene, 184
Duncan, Robert, 184

Easton, David, 1, 31
Eckert, Ross D., 156
Edmunds, Stahrl, 107, 191
Ehler, Charles, 191
Ehrlich, Paul, 184, 244
Eisenbud, Merrill, 105
Elazar, Daniel J., 33
Elkin, Stephen, 154
Ellickson, Robert C., 210, 220, 241, 245, 247
Ewing, L.A., 95
Eyestone, Robert, ix, 24, 127

Fiorino, Daniel J., 155
Fischel, William A., 247
Fisher, Anthony C., 32
Fort, Rodney D., 33
Fox, Douglas M., 32
Freeman, A. Myrick III, 16, 21, 171, 183

Frieden, Bernard J., 33, 64, 210, 220, 221, 244, 245
Friedlaender, Ann F., 175, 183, 191
Fukui, Haruhiro, 20, 33

Gamble, John K., 86, 93, 94
Gendler, Michey, 107
Getz, Malcolm, ix, 51
Gledfelter, Janet, 221
Gleeson, Michael, 244
Goldberg, Victor P., 154
Goldfarb, William, 50
Goldstone, Jack A., ix, 28, 184
Gormley, William T. Jr., 156
Grebler, Leo, 224, 245
Gruen, Claude, 246
Guetzkow, Harold, 106
Guilbert, Thomas G.P., 170
Gulbrandsen, R.A., 76

Haas, Ernst B., 93
Haefele, Erwin T., 155
Hahn, John C., 31
Haigh, John A., 32
Hanf, Kenneth, 137
Hanrieder, Wolfram F., 33
Hansen, David E., 223
Hardin, Garret, 244
Hart, Daniel, 157
Hartman, R., 191
Haszar, Paul C., 246
Haveman, Robert H., 32, 154, 183
Haver, R.H., 106
Hayes, Robert L., 184
Healey, Martin R., 33
Heaney, James P., 106
Hendley, William, 157, 169
Holden, John, 184
Holdren, J.P., 13, 49
Hollick, Ann, 94
Holm, P., 184
House, Peter W., 49
Hughes, James W., 246, 247
Hunt, William, 245
Hunter, Lori, 156

Ikard, Frank N., 94
Ingram, Helen M., 6, 31, 32, 65, 107
Inhaber, Herbert, 43, 49

James, Frank J., 220
Johnston, Robert A., x, 29, 207, 221, 223, 244, 245
Jones, Charles O., 48, 110, 122

Kain, John F., 238, 247
Kamien, Morton I., 154

Kase, H.M., 106
Katzenstein, Peter J., 93
Kaufman, William, 49
Kelley, Donald L., 93
Keohane, Robert O., 93
Kirschten, J. Dickey, 122, 123, 124
Kneese, Allen V., 32, 33, 155, 183, 191
Knight, C. Foster, 245
Krier, James E., 8
Krutilla, John V., 32

Lake, William, 170
Landsberg, H.H., 204
Lane, Leonard Lee, 181, 184
Lester, James P., ix, 20, 79, 93, 94
Letey, John, 107
Lieber, Harvey, 123
Liebman, Charles S., 219, 220
Lindblom, C., 105
Lindbloom, Charles E., 100, 107, 154
Liroff, Richard A., 107
Listokin, David, 204, 219, 220
Logan, John R., 220
Lowi, Theodore J., 31, 33, 48
Luce, R.D., 77
Lund, Oscar, 127

McCormick, James M., 79
McDermott, Walsh, 184
M'Conigle, R. Michael, 93, 94
McGuire, John R., 71, 77
McHarg, Ian L., 244
MacIntyre, Angus A., 223
Mackay, D.I., 137
Mackay, G.A., 137
McKeen, Roland, 11, 32
McNeece, John, 221
Magnuson, Sen., 94
Majone, Giandomenico, 32, 33, 174, 179, 182, 183, 184
Mann, Dean E., ix, 1, 6, 31, 32, 65, 139, 157, 191
March, James G., 156
Marcus, Alfred A., ix, 10, 27, 32, 155, 173, 184
Margolis, J., 106, 155
Martin, Douglas, 184
May, Judith, 220, 244
Mazmanian, Daniel, 3, 13, 31, 32, 36, 41, 48
Meadows, D.H., 244
Meyerson, Martin, 64
Misczynski, Dean J., 207
Mitnick, Barry M., ix, 26, 33, 139, 154, 155, 156
Mitnick, Margery M., 156
Mitrany, David, 93

Mittelbach, Frank G., 244, 245
Molnar, Joseph J., ix, 21, 95, 107
Molotch, Harvey, 220
Montjoy, Robert S., 101, 107
Morrall, John, 169, 170
Mulford, C.L., 101, 106, 107
Mumford, Lewis, 244
Muskie, Sen. Edmund, 181

Nadkarni, R., 191
Nagel, Stuart S., xi, 155
Nash, R., 75
Nau, Henry R., 79, 93
Nelkin, Dorothy, 47
Nelson, Jon P., 170, 171
Nienaber, Jeanne, 13, 32
Nixon, Pres., 9
Noll, Robert G., 156
Norman, Thomas, 219, 220
Nulty, Peter, 183, 184
Nye, Joseph S., Jr., 93

Oates, Wallace R., 155, 170
Odum, Howard, 244
Ogle, Richard E., 106, 107
O'Hare, Michael, 64
Okner, Benjamin A., 191
Olson, Mancur, 63, 204
O'Riordan, Timothy, 106, 244
Orr, Lloyd D., 191
O'Toole, Laurence, 95, 101, 107

Paarlberg, Robert L., 81, 93
Park, Robert, 157
Park, T. Hardie, 157
Parker, F.H., 106, 107, 108
Partridge, Edward, 32
Pechman, Joseph A., 191
Peddicord, T.E., 106, 107, 108
Peterson, Frederick M., 32
Peterson, George E., 245
Petulla, Joseph M., 105
Pollak, Michael, 50
Pratt, W.P., 76
Pressman, Jeffrey, 6, 32, 48, 96, 105

Quigley, John M., 238, 247

Raiffa, H., 77
Rainey, Hal G., 148, 154, 155, 156
Rapple, Bradley I., 183
Rattner, Steven, 184
Regens, James L., ix, 18, 65, 75
Reich, C., 107
Reilly, William K., 204
Reitze, Arnold, 157
Roberts, Rebecca, 156

Rockman, Bert, 156
Rodinelli, Dennis A., 107, 108
Rogers, David L., ix, 21, 95, 101, 106,
   107
Rosenbaum, Nelson, 210, 220, 244
Ross, Stephen A., 154
Rothman, Jack, 184
Rowland, Benjamin, 33
Ruff, Larry E., 183
Ruggie, John G., 86, 94
Rundquist, Barry S., 124
Russell, Clifford S., 28, 32

Sabatier, Paul, 3, 14, 31, 36, 41, 48
Sagalyn, Lynne B., 245
Scharpf, Fritz W., 137
Schultze, Charles L., 33, 106, 155, 183
Schwartz, Seymour I., x, 30, 207, 221, 222,
   244, 245
Seidel, Stephen R., 244
Seidman, H., 107, 108
Shannon, R.E., 76
Sharp, Basil M., 106
Shields, Mark, 65
Simmons, Malcolm, 123
Simon, Herbert, 155, 156
Sjoberg, Lennart, 49
Skolnikoff, Eugene B., 93
Smith, Fred, 157
Smith, L., 77
Smith, V. Kerry, 32
Solomon, Arthur J., 245
Solow, Robert M., 183
Spence, A. Michael, 191
Sprout, Harold, 33
Sprout, Margaret, 33
Stam, Jerome, 106
Steger, William A., 219, 246
Sternlieb, George, 245, 246, 247
Stewart, Richard B., 48
Stiglitz, J.E., 17, 32
Stoil, Michael J., 79
Stone, Alan, 31
Stroup, Richard, 33
Stubbart, Charles, 156
Stull, William J., 245
Sylves, Richard T., ix, 23, 109

Textor, Robert B., 85, 93
Thomas, Robert D., 109, 122
Thompson, James F., 107
Toenniessen, Gary, xi
Tomassoni, Mark E., 171
Tryon, R.C., 198, 205
Tucker, Harvey J., 79
Tunderman, David W., 183
Turek, Edward F., 49

Ullery, Scott, 10, 32

Voelker, Alfred H., 65

Waldeck, Robert F., 124, 125
Walter, Benjamin, ix, 16, 51
Wandesforde-Smith, Geoffrey, 207
Warren, Roland L., 106
Watt, James, 7
Waxman, Rep. Henry, 181
Weiner, Sanford, 51, 62
Weiss, Charles, Jr., 156
Wenner, Lettie McSpadden, 21, 31, 33, 177, 184
Whettan, David, 106
White, I.L., 75
White, Lawrence J., 183

White, Michelle J., 210, 220
Wildavsky, Aaron, 6, 7, 31, 32, 48, 49, 51, 62, 96, 105, 220, 244
Williams, Norman, Jr., 219, 220
Williamson, Oliver, 155
Wilson, James Q., 156
Wilson, Jeffrey, 156
Windsor, Oliver Duane, 220
Worobee, Mary, 37, 48, 50
Wright, Quincy, 93

Yandle, 183
Younger, Evele J., 245

Zacher, Mark W., 93, 94
Zaltman, Gerald, 184
Zile, Ziguards L., 33

Index of Subjects

Aircraft noise: control of, 157–169; problem, 157–158
Analysis, implementation: environmental policy, 3–5
Army Corps of Engineers, RCRA and, 22

Boca Raton, Florida: population control, 208–210
Boulder, Colorado: growth control, 210
Britain, oil exploration, 127–137
Bureau of Land Management, 21
Bureau of Reclamation, 9, 18–24

California, 44, 223
Canada, 22
CEQ (Council on Environmental Quality), EPA and, 35
Chicago, growth limitation, 209
Chrysler Corporation, 9
Clean Air Act, RCRA and, 42
Clean Water Act of 1972, 23, 42
Clean Water Act of 1977, P.L. 95-217; CW and, 109–122
Coal strip mining, SMCRA and, 148–153
Community control: population growth, 223–244; analysis, empirical, 195–202
Community growth control, 193–204: Boca Raton, 208–211; Boulder, 210; California, 223; Chicago, 209; Davis, 232; Marin County, 214–215; Modesto, 217–218; Petaluma, 208–210, 212–213, 228–229, 232; Ramapo, 208; Sacramento, 215–217, 232; San Francisco, 194, 211, 232; San Jose, 229; Santa Rosa, 228; Toronto, 194
Community growth controls: housing-costs impact, 223–244; types of, 207–219
Community growth management, equity and, 223–244
Congress, water pollution policy, 109–122
Conservation Foundation, CW and, 119
Control, regulator: direct, 140–141; incentive, 140–141
Conventions, international: ocean pollution and, 79–83
Coordination, interorganizational: environmental protection, 95–104; definition, 96–97; and overload of, 99, and participation, 98, and process, 96–100
Council on Environmental Quality, 8, 10: environmental management and, 95–104
CW (Cleveland-Wright Amendment): decentralization, 109–122; EPA sewer-grant program, 110–122; implementation, 119; intent of, 11–112; origins of, 112–116; state environmental agencies, 116–119; state jurisdiction, 109–122

Decentralization, water-pollution policy, 109–122

EDA (Economic Development Administration), 7
EIS (Environmental Impact Statement), RARE I inventory and, 68
Energy needs, environmental quality and, 65–74
Energy policy, wilderness preservation, 65–74
England, Scottish Office, 24
Environmental Defense Fund, CW and, 119
Environmental laws, implementation, 14–30
Environmental local opposition, North Sea Oil, 133–138
Environmental management: interorganizational coordination, 95–104; objectives, 95–104; process, 95–104; strategy, 95–104
Environmental policies, Scotland, 127–137
Environmental policy: implementation, 1–31; research for, 9–10; resources, 9–10; scope, 9–10; variables, 9–10; wilderness preservation, 65–74
Environmental protection, interagency coordination: administrative objectives, 104–105, and alliances, 101–103, and corporate models, 103–104, and mutual adjustment, 101, and strategies, 100–104; interorganizational coordination, 95–104; statutes, RCRA and, 41–42
Environmental regulation: agents (regulators), 139–147; control, 139–147; stripmining and, 147–152; incentive system control, 148–153; systems in, 139–154
Environmental Response, Compensation and Liability Act, P.L. 96-510 (1980), 40
Environmental movement, local control, 223–225
EPA (Environmental Protection Agency, 4, 8, 9; authority, CW and, 109–122; control grant technique, state pollution control, 109–122; CW state certification and, 118; executive redirection, 41–42;

Federal project grants, 117; general Accounting Office and, 113; legislative oversight and, 41–42; Love Canal and, 40; municipal political influence and, 117; national objectives, state actions and, 109–118; OMB and, 41–42; pollution reduction: political support, 180–182, and reform initiaties, 176–177, and system existing, 177–178, and technical problems, 178–180; regulation, direct: incentive, economic, 173–175, and pollution reduction, 173–175; review function, CW municipal allocation, 109–122; rule making, waste, 36–48; sections, 3001-3005, 36–48

EPA, sections: 3005, 42; 3006, 42–43; sewer-grant authority, CW and, 110–122; state distrust of, 116; waste management: state implementation, 36–37, and statutory provisions, 36–37; waste regulations, implementation, 39–40; waste rule making: complexity, 37–38, and uncertainty, 37–38; water-pollution policy, 109–122

Equity: impacts, hosuing costs, 229–231; issues, wilderness preservation, 65–74; local growth management, 223–244; RARE II process and, 66–69

FAA (Federal Aviation Administration), aircraft-noise regulation, 159–161

Factors, implementation: environmental policy, 8–9

FAO (Food and Agriculture Organization), ocean pollution and, 85

Federal Fish and Wildlife Service, 22

Federal sewer-grant program: implementation, 109–122; state certification, 118

Forest service, wilderness preservation, 25

FWPCA (Federal Water Pollution Control Act), EPA and, 112–113

Grand Canyon, 17

Growth control: community, 193–204; equity impact, 229–233; housing costs, 225–226; jurisdiction, measure for, 241–243; local, politics of, 207–219; private property rights, 209–210; property value, 209–210; social consequences, 229–233; tax reduction, 210; types, 207–219

Growth controls, land cost, 227–228

Growth management, community: analysis, characteristics, 194–204; population, 193–204

Growth, population: community planning, 193–204

Hazardous-waste-management policy, 35–48

Hazardous-waste policy, implementation, 35–37

Housing costs, growth control: consequences of, 229–233; equity impact, 229–231

HUD (Housing and Urban Development), community growth and, 193

ICMA (International City Managers Association): survey, local environmental, 196–202

Illinois: EPA sewer-grant certification, 121; population control, 209

IMC (Intergovernmental Maritime Committee), ocean pollution, 85

IMCO (Intergovernmental Maritime, Consultative Organization, 83–93

Implementation, environmental policy: behavioral assumptions, 11–14; conditions, 5–14; factors, 9; history, 6–7; problem solving, 4

Implementation, environmental protection: central government and, 22; coherence of, 18–24; states role, 23

implementation: management policy, waste, 35–38

Implementation process, environmental laws, 14–30

Implementation, state waste program: RCRA and, 44–46

Implementation, waste policy: complexity, 35–38; EPA, 36–48; uncertainty, 35–48

Incentive system: regulation: hierarchical, 141–142, and social-choice process, 141–142; regulators, control, 147–152; regulatory means, 139

Incentive systems, environmental regulation, 139–154

Incentives, economic: direct regulation, 173–175; pollution control, affluent charges, 175; pollution reduction, 173–185

Indiana Solid Waste Management Program, 46

Industry response, pollution charges, 186–188

International ocean-pollution regulation: national interest and, 83–93; variables: dependent, 83–93, and independent, 83–93

IOC (Intergovernmental Oceanographic Commission), ocean pollution, 85

Kentucky, state pollution program, 40

LPA (Local Planning Authority), SO (Scottish Office) and, 132–137

Land costs, growth control and, 227–228

Landuse, local: North Sea oil, 133–138

Law of the sea, ocean pollution, 20

Laws, environmental: implementation, 14–30
League of Women Voters: CW and, 119; Modesto County, 217
Local growth control: Environmental movement, 223–225; Politics and, 239–240
Logan Airport, Boston, 160
London, 195
Louisiana, State pollution program, 40
Love Canal, New York, 11, 15, 16, 40–41, 43
Luxembourg, 23

Maine, state pollution program, 40
Management, environmental: policy sector, 95–104
Management, local growth: equity in, 223, 244
Management policy, hazardous waste, 35–37
Marin County, county growth control: water-supply restriction, 214–215
Marine environment protection: international cooperation, 79–93; ocean pollution, 79–93
Massachusetts, state pollution program, 40
MEPC (Marine Environmental Protection Committee), 83–93
Michigan, state pollution program, 40
Miami, Florida: growth control, 211
Modesto, California: community growth control, sewer service area, 217–219
Monaco, 23
Mt. Laurel, N.J., 208
MWD (Marine County Water District) county growth control, 214–215

NASA, 10
National Airport, Washington, 160
National Association of Counties, EPA and, 40–117
National Conference of State Legislatures, EPA and, 117
National Governors Conference, EPA and, 40, 117
National League of Cities, EPA and, 117
National Park Service, 11
Natural Environmental Policy Act, 7: environmental management and, 95–104; interagency cooperation, 95–104
Natural Resources Defense Council, CW and, 118
New Hampshire, EPA sewer-grants certification, 119, 120
New Jersey, waste-management authority, 44
New York, 195, 208–209: Love Canal, 40; zoning, 209
Niagara Falls, 40
Noise, aircraft: charges regulation, 157–

169; control, 157–159; regulation, 157–160
Noise charges, aircraft: cost-effectiveness, 159–168; regulation, 157–169
Noise charges: allocative efficiency, 165–168; EPNdB (Effective Perceived Noise), 162–165; NEF (Noise Exposure Forecast), 162–165; quiet value, 165–168; retrofitting, 162–168
Noise regulation, FAA and, 159–161
North Sea oil: environment, local, 128–129; local authority, 130–131; local land use, 133–138; national powers, 130; Scottish local authority, 127–137; venture capital, 129
NSF (National Science Foundation), 10, 20
NWPS (National Wilderness Preservation System), 66

Ocean pollution: international cooperation, 79–93; national structures, 79–93; regulation, 79–93; technologies, 79–93
Ohio, waste-management authority, 46
Oil exploration: Scotland, environmental policies, 127–137
OMB (Office of Management and Budget), EPA and, 41–42
OPEC (Organization of Petrole Exportation Countries), 2, 19
Options, compliance: pollution charges and, 185–190
OSO (Offshore Supplies Office), North Sea oil boom, 130

Paris, 195
Pennsylvania, waste-management authority, 44
Petaluma, California: community growth control, 208–210, 228–229, and building permit quota, 212–213
Pine Barrens, New Jersey, 15
Pine River, Michigan, 51
Policies, environmental: Scotland, 127–137
Policy analysis, implementation, 1–31
Policy consequences, SMCRA enforcement system, 153
Policy, environmental protection: public control, 25; regulation versus charges, 24–28
Policy, water-pollution grant, 109–122: decentralization, 109–122; state and, 109–122
Politics, local growth control, 207–219, 238–241
Pollution charges: consequences of, 185–190; evaluation options, 185–190; option consequences, 185–190; responses: consumer, 189–190, and industry, 186–188

Pollution control: EPA incentives, 173–175; policy, 16
Pollution, reduction: incentives, economic, 173–183
Population growth: community control, 194–204; community planning, 193–204
Public policy, environmental policy and, 1–31
Puerto Rico, 67

RARE II (Roadless Area Review and Evaluation), 18; wilderness preservation, 66–69
Ramapo, New York: growth control, 208
RCRA (Resource Conservation and Recovery Act), P.L. 94-580, 15, 16, 35; environmental protection statutes, 41–42; implementation, 41–42; permit program, EPA, 42–44; rulemaking, 43–44; state permits, section 3005, 42; subtitle C., 36–37: hazardous waste, 37–37, and state implementation, 44–46
Regulation, environmental: incentive systems for, 139–154
Regulation, public: stripmining, 139–154
Regulators and regulatees: control, interaction, 152–153
Regulators, control: strip mining, 147–152; incentives, environment, 147–152
Regulatory, control, EPA: dimensions, 142–147; enforcement, 142, 144; target levels, 142–143
Regulatory Agency Review Group, EPA and, 42
Responses, pollution charges: consumer, 189–190; industry, 186–189
Retrofitting, noise charges and, 162–169

Sacramento County: county growth control, urban line limitation, 215–217
Safe drinking water act, 42, RCRA and, 42
San Francisco, growth control, 194, 211
San Jose, California: growth control, 229
Santa Rosa, growth control, 228
Scotland, environmental policies: local decisions, 127–137; North Sea oil, 127–137
Scottish Office Authority, North Sea oil, 131–132
Sewer-grant program: CW and, 110–112; EPA and, 109–122
Sierra Club, 66
SMRC (Surface Mining Control and Reclamation Act, 1977): inspectors, 148–152; state implementation, 148–153; system: hierarchical, 153, and incentive, 148–153
Soap and Detergent Association, EPA and, 39

State certification, federal sewer program, 109–122
State guidelines, EPA section 2006, 42–43
State implementation, EPA waste management, 36–37; RCRA subtitle C., 44–46; SMCRA, 148–153
State jurisdiction, CW, 109–122
State pollution control: California, 44, 223; Illinois, 121, 209; Indiana, 46; Kentucky, 40; Louisiana, 40; Maine, 40; Massachusetts, 40; Michigan, 40; New Hampshire, 199, 120; New Jersey, 44; New York, 40, 195, 208, 209; Ohio, 46; Pennsylvania, 44; Tennessee, 40; Wisconsin, 116
State waste-management authority, 44, RCRA, 44–46
State water-pollution programs, EPA, 110
States, sewer programs, EPA, 119
States, water-pollution policy, 109–122
Statutes, environmental protection: RCRA, 41–42
Sullee, Arkansas, 15
Stripmining: environmental control, 147–152; public regulation, 139–154; reclamation inspectors, 148–152
Systems analysis, environmental policy, 1–31
Systems, incentive: environmental regulation, 139–154

Tennessee, state pollution program, 40
Texas: EPA sewer-grant certification, 119–121; waste-management authority, 44
Three Mile Island, state pollution program, 40
Topology, regulatory, 142–147
Toronto, population growth, 194
TSCA (Toxic Substances Control Act), 4, 16
Types, community: growth control, 207–219

UNEF (UN Environmental Program), ocean pollution, 85
United States, 2, 19, 20, 65, 67, 208, 211; ocean pollution, 79–93
Upper Mississippi River Basin Commission, 22
U.S. Fish and Wildlife Service, 9
USFS (U.S. Forest Service), wilderness preservation, 65–68

Valley of Drums, 15

Washington, D.C., 5
Waste, hazardous: legislation, 16, 35–48
Waste, management: policy, 35–48; RERA subtitle C., 36

Water resources council, 10
Wayerhouser Company, wilderness preservation, 25
WC (Whitehall Government), LPA versus, 133
WEO (Western European and Other States), ocean-pollution regulation, 83–93

Wilderness Act of 1964, P.L. 88-577, 67
Wilderness preservation: energy policy and, 65–74; environmental policy, 65–74; equity issues, 65–74
Wisconsin, CW, opposition to, 116
World Health Organization, ocean pollution and, 85

About the Contributors

Sam A. Carnes is a political scientist on the research staff of the Social Impacts Analysis Group of the Energy Division, Oak Ridge National Laboratory. His recent research activities have included policy analyses of hazardous- and radioactive-waste management and exploratory research in local planning for conservation and renewable-resource development.

Donald C. Cell, received the Ph.D. from Columbia University and is professor of economics and business at Cornell College in Mount Vernon, Iowa. His present research focuses on regulatory policy and law. Professor Cell's publications include "Policy Influence without Policy Choice," in the *Journal of Political Economy* and "A Theory of Voter Influence over Foreign Policy," published by the New York Academy of Sciences. He has authored reports on economic trends in higher education in the *AAUP Bulletin* and currently serves as secretary-treasurer of American Association of University Professors.

David E. Dowall is an assistant professor in the Department of City and Regional Planning at the University of California, Berkeley. He is also a researcher at the Institute for Urban and Regional Development and at the Center for Real Estate and Urban Economics at the University of California. His teaching and research interests are in land-use planning and land economics. He has recently completed a study of the effects of land-use and environmental regulations on land and housing markets in the San Francisco Bay area. He is a member of the Economic Development Advisory Committee of the Association of Bay Area Government, and the Steering Committee and Housing Task Force of the Bay Area Council.

Robert Eyestone received the Ph.D. in political science from Stanford University. At present he is an associate professor of political science at the University of Minnesota. His most recent book is *From Social Issues to Public Policy*.

Malcolm Getz is an associate professor of economics at Vanderbilt and senior research associate of the Vanderbilt Institute for Public Policy Studies. He is the author of *The Economics of the Urban Fire Department* (1979) and *Public Libraries: An Economic View* (1980) and coauthor of *Price Theory and Its Uses*, 5th ed. (1981). He received the Ph.D. from Yale University.

Jack A. Goldstone is a Ph.D. candidate in sociology at Harvard University. He has participated in studies of environmental policy and occupational safety and health policy at Harvard's John F. Kennedy School of Government, and his work has appeared in *The American Journal of Sociology, World Politics,* and other journals.

Robert A. Johnston teaches environmental-policy analysis and planning in the Division of Environmental Studies, University of California, Davis. His research involves the utilization of land-use controls for open-space protection, reducing housing costs, and improving transit-system ridership, as well as social-impact assessment and project-evaluation methods.

James P. Lester received the Ph.D. in political science from George Washington University in 1980, and teaches courses in science, technology, and public policy in the Department of Political Science at Texas A&M University. His chapter in this book is part of a larger study on *Technology, Politics, and World Order: Domestic Structure and International Technological Collaboration* (forthcoming). His articles have appeared in *World Affairs, Ocean Development and International Law, Environment and Behavior, Teaching Political Science,* and *Simulation and Games.*

Alfred A. Marcus, a policy analyst at the Battelle Science and Government Study Center in Seattle, has written about environmental policies, government regulation of business, and the politics of implementation. His book, *Promise and Performance: Choosing and Implementing an Environmental Policy,* was published in 1980. Dr. Marcus is currently working on organizational and management assessments of nuclear power plants.

Barry M. Mitnick is an associate professor in the Graduate School of Business at the University of Pittsburgh. His current research interests include the theory, design, and strategic use of regulation; incentive systems approaches to organizations; and the theory of agency. He is the author of *The Political Economy of Regulation: Creating, Designing, and Removing Regulatory Forms* (1980) and serves on the editorial board of the *American Journal of Political Science.*

Joseph J. Molnar is an assistant professor of rural sociology in the Department of Agricultural Economics and Rural Sociology at Auburn University, Auburn, Alabama. His research interests include institutional processes in environmental management, the functioning of networks of elites in rural communities, and the social impacts of industrialized agriculture. Recent publications have appeared in the *Administrative Science Quarterly, Rural Sociology,* and *Sociology and Social Research.* He received the Ph.D. in sociology from Iowa State University.

James L. Regens is an associate professor of political science and research Fellow in the Institute of Natural Resources at the University of Georgia. He has been a visiting research Fellow at Oak Ridge National Laboratory and is currently on leave to serve as the senior technical advisor to the deputy administrator of the U.S. Environmental Protection Agency. His primary research interests include policy analysis, with a particular emphasis on technology assessment, and energy-natural resource issues.

David L. Rogers is professor and chairman of the Department of Sociology at Colorado State University. He has published articles on interorganizational coordination and on the management of natural resources in *Administrative Science Quarterly, Journal of Soil and Water Conservation, Rural Sociology,* and *Sociology and Social Research.* Some of his work is also published in monographs on interagency management of natural resources. He is currently conducting research on intergovernmental relations among cities in western "boomtowns."

Seymour I. Schwartz is associate professor in the Division of Environmental Studies at the University of California, Davis. Dr. Schwartz teaches several policy-analysis courses and conducts research in land-use and housing policy. He has published more than a dozen articles and monographs from his work on the implementation, effectiveness, and equity impacts of agricultural-land preservation and land-use controls. Recent publications focus on the housing-price impacts of growth management and the implementation of measures for increasing the supply of moderate-cost housing. Dr. Schwartz is a member of the Housing Advisory Committee of the California Legislature's Joint Committee on the State's Economy.

Richard T. Sylves is an assistant professor of political science at the University of Delaware. He received the Ph.D. in political science from the University of Illinois (1978). He has been a staff researcher for the New York State Senate Finance Committee (1972) and an assistant professor at the University of Cincinnati (1976-1977). He has published articles and has pursued grant-supported research in the energy and environmental-policy areas.

Benjamin Walter is professor of political science at Vanderbilt University and senior research associate of the Vanderbilt Institute for Public Policy Studies. He is coauthor of *On the City's Rim* (1972) and author of articles on urban policy and policy analysis.

About the Editor

Dean E. Mann is professor of political science at the University of California, Santa Barbara. He has written extensively and continues to write on water policy in the West, and coauthored a study on policies of local governments toward earthquake-damage mitigation, on the climatic implications of increased carbon dioxide in the atmosphere, and on policy implications of weather modification.